Lecture Notes in Computer Science   10087

Commenced Publication in 1973
Founding and Former Series Editors:
Gerhard Goos, Juris Hartmanis, and Jan van Leeuwen

More information about this series at http://www.springer.com/series/7407

Katrin Amunts · Lucio Grandinetti
Thomas Lippert · Nicolai Petkov (Eds.)

Brain-Inspired Computing

Second International Workshop, BrainComp 2015
Cetraro, Italy, July 6–10, 2015
Revised Selected Papers

 Springer

Editors
Katrin Amunts
Forschungszentrum Jülich
Jülich
Germany

Lucio Grandinetti
University of Calabria
Rende
Italy

Thomas Lippert
Forschungszentrum Jülich
Jülich
Germany

Nicolai Petkov
University of Groningen
Groningen
The Netherlands

ISSN 0302-9743   ISSN 1611-3349   (electronic)
Lecture Notes in Computer Science
ISBN 978-3-319-50861-0   ISBN 978-3-319-50862-7   (eBook)
DOI 10.1007/978-3-319-50862-7

Library of Congress Control Number: 2016959636

LNCS Sublibrary: SL1 – Theoretical Computer Science and General Issues

Printed on acid-free paper

This Springer imprint is published by Springer Nature
The registered company is Springer International Publishing AG
The registered company address is: Gewerbestrasse 11, 6330 Cham, Switzerland

Preface

Brain-inspired computing is a fast-developing research topic. On one hand, it relates to fundamental neuroscience research that leads to insights in the information-processing function of the brain. On the other hand, it is aimed at utilizing these insights in new methods and technologies for information processing and might even initiate a paradigm change in this area. Brain-inspired computing creates opportunities for collaboration between scientists from various disciplines: neuroscience, computer science, engineering, natural sciences, and mathematics. The understanding of the importance of this area led to the initiation of the EU flagship "Human Brain Project" in the framework of the EU program for future and emerging technologies (FET). The current book includes contributions from renowned scientists who participated in the International Workshop on Brain-Inspired Computing in Cetraro, Italy, during July 6–10, 2015. It contains contributions that concern brain structure and function, computational models, and brain-inspired computing methods with practical applications, high-performance computing, and visualization for brain simulations.

July 2015

Katrin Amunts
Lucio Grandinetti
Thomas Lippert
Nicolai Petkov

Organization

BrainComp2015 was organized by the Department of Electronics, Informatics, and Systems, University of Calabria, Italy, Forschungszentrum Juelich GmbH, Germany, and Johann Bernoulli Institute of Mathematics and Computer Science, University of Groningen, The Netherlands.

Program Committee

Nicolai Petkov	University of Groningen, The Netherlands (co-chair)
Thomas Lippert	Forschungzentrum Jülich GmbH, Germany (co-chair)
Katrin Amunts	Forschungzentrum Jülich GmbH, Germany
Lucio Grandinetti	University of Calabria, Italy
Jack Dongarra	University of Tennessee and Oak Ridge National Laboratory, USA
Frank Baetke	Hewlett Packard Enterprise, Germany
Gerhard Joubert	Technical University of Clausthal, Germany
Deo Prakash Vidyarthi	Jawaharlal Nehru University, School of Computer and Systems Sciences, India
Francesco Pavone	University of Florence, Italy

Speakers

Katrin Amunts	Forschungszentrum Jülich GmbH, Germany
Markus Axer	Forschungszentrum Jülich GmbH, Germany
George Azzopardi	University of Malta and TNO, The Netherlands
Antonio Bandera Rubio	University of Malaga, Spain
Costas Bekas	Foundations of Cognitive Computing IBM Research, Zurich
Michael Biehl	University of Groningen, The Netherlands
Ganesh Dasika	ARM, USA
Michael Denker	Forschungszentrum Jülich GmbH, Germany
Alain Destexhe	Centre National de la Recherche Scientifique, France
Marcus Diesmann	Forschungszentrum Jülich GmbH, Germany
Bart ter Haar Romeny	Eindhoven University of Technology, The Netherlands
Wolfgang Halang	FernUniversität, Germany
Claus Hilgetag	University of Hamburg, Germany
Tianzi Jiang	The Chinese Academy of Sciences, China
Torsten Kuhlen	RWTH Aachen, Germany
Marcel Kunze	University of Heidelberg, Germany
Thomas Lippert	Forschungszentrum Jülich GmbH, Germany
Rebeca Marfil Rubio	University of Malaga, Spain
Miriam Menzel	Forschungszentrum Jülich GmbH, Germany

Abigail Morrison	Forschungszentrum Jülich GmbH, Germany
Heiko Neumann	University of Ulm, Germany
Luis Pastor	Universidad Rey Juan Carlos, Spain
Francesco Pavone	University of Florence, Italy
Alessandro Sarti	CNRS, France
Thomas Schulthess	Swiss National Supercomputing Centre, Switzerland
Felix Schuermann	Ecole Polytechnique Federale de Lausanne, Switzerland
Karl Solchenbach	Intel GmbH, Germany
Thomas Sterling	Indiana University, USA
Adrian Tate ·	Cray, Inc., USA
Thomas Villmann	University of Applied Sciences Mittweida, Germany
Deo Prakash Vidyarthi	Jawaharlal Nehru University, School of Computer and Systems Sciences, India

Sponsoring Institutions

Hewlett Packard
NVIDIA
Cray
IBM
ICAR CNR
Intel
ParTec Cluster Competence Center

Contents

Human Brainnetome Atlas and Its Potential Applications in Brain-Inspired Computing

Lingzhong Fan[1], Hai Li[1,2], Shan Yu[1,3], and Tianzi Jiang[1,2,3,4,5](✉)

[1] Brainnetome Center, Institute of Automation, Chinese Academy of Sciences,
Beijing 100190, China
jiangtz@nlpr.ia.ac.cn
[2] National Laboratory of Pattern Recognition, Institute of Automation,
Chinese Academy of Sciences, Beijing 100190, China
jiangtz@nlpr.ia.ac.cn
[3] CAS Center for Excellence in Brain Science and Intelligence Technology,
Institute of Automation, Chinese Academy of Sciences, Beijing 100190, China
[4] Key Laboratory for NeuroInformation of the Ministry of Education,
School of Life Science and Technology,
University of Electronic Science and Technology of China, Chengdu 625014, China
[5] The Queensland Brain Institute, University of Queensland, Brisbane, QLD 4072, Australia

Abstract. Brain atlases are considered to be the cornerstone of neuroscience, but most available brain atlases lack fine-grained parcellation results and do not provide information about functionally important connectivity. Recently, novel methodologies and computerized brain mapping techniques could be used to explore the structure, function, and spatio-temporal changes in the human brain. The human Brainnetome Atlas is an in vivo map that includes fine-grained functional brain subregions and detailed anatomical and functional connection patterns for each area. These features should enable researchers to describe the large scale architecture of the human brain more accurately. Using the human Brainnetome Atlas, researchers could simulate and model brain networks using informatics and simulation technologies to elucidate the basic organizing principles of the brain. Others could use this same atlas to design novel neuromorphic systems that are inspired by the architecture of the brain. Therefore, this cutting-edge human Brainnetome Atlas paves the way for constructing an even more fine-grained atlas of the human brain and offers the potential for applications in brain-inspired computing.

Keywords: Brainnetome Atlas · Connectivity · Diffusion tensor imaging · Brain-inspired computing

1 Introduction

Over more than a century, tremendous progress has been made in understanding the structure, function, and connection of the human brain at different spatial-temporal scales. However, because of the complexity of the brain, accurately defining the brain

© Springer International Publishing AG 2016
K. Amunts et al. (Eds.): BrainComp 2015, LNCS 10087, pp. 1–14, 2016.
DOI: 10.1007/978-3-319-50862-7_1

regions and mapping their functions and connections are extremely challenging, even on a large scale. Just as modern cartography helped us know planet Earth, the existing brain atlases, based on various mapping techniques, have served as navigators of the human brain and can be considered to be the cornerstone of basic and clinical neuroscience [1–6]. Thus, the long-term goal of mapping the human brain is to understand the organizing principles underlying the architecture of this most complex organ. This understanding will guide us in further exploring how the human brain is organized and how it gives rise to cognitive behaviors. Once we comprehend how the human brain is organized as a network and understand its structures, functions, and connections, computer scientists should be able to begin to mimic the brain as a mathematical network based on its biological substrates.

Currently, however, even on a large scale, no widely accepted criteria exist for partitioning the cortical and subcortical structures. Early parcellation efforts at defining regional boundaries, including the widely-used Brodmann's maps, only employed postmortem architecture using a limited number of samples [2, 6, 7]. Although the Brodmann's schematic drawings of the cerebral cortex are still widely used, the limitations of this map have become more and more obvious, increasing the importance of defining brain areas using new methodologies. To resolve the misfit of the Brodmann's and other earlier brain maps to the human brain, neuroanatomists have developed additional postmortem brain mapping techniques for brain atlas construction, e.g. combining quantitative cytoarchitectonics with in vitro receptor architectonic analyses of the brain [6]. Although this approach is currently the only technique which can actually map the brain directly, accurate border detection remains subject to unavoidable histological defects [8]. Moreover, systematic cytoarchitectonic mapping procedures are extremely time-consuming and labor-intensive. Although the atlases formed using these techniques have provided invaluable information, the microscale cytoarchitectonic measurements are still insufficient to completely represent brain organization [3, 9].

In addition, in the last two decades information gained using advancing neuroimaging technologies, especially magnetic resonance imaging (MRI), has been extensively used to solve brain parcellation problems. In the early stages, because of the large number of brain regions, a huge amount of inter-subject variation, the complex relationship between regional boundaries, and limits on the spatial resolution of all the neuroimaging methods, the brain atlases based on macro anatomical landmarks or coordinate systems were not valid indicators of regional specialization [5, 10]. Many issues still exist for these atlases, including their roughness, lack of correspondence, shortage of sub-regional information, and variability in the relationships between functional borders and macroscopic landmarks [5, 11]. Recently, exploring brain connectivity via imaging technologies such as diffusion MRI and functional MRI has offered new insights into the functional organization of the human brain and has supplied alternative ways of solving brain parcellation problems. Local areas that have different functions tend to be connected differently to other brain areas. In other words, disparate brain regions maintain their own connectivity profiles [12]. Therefore, the basic idea underlying connectivity-based parcellation is to suppose that all the structural elements belonging to a given brain area share similar connectivity patterns.

The Brainnetome project [4] was launched to investigate the hierarchy in the human brain from genetics to neuronal circuits to behaviors, conceptualizing two components (nodes and connections) as the basic research unit. One of the key elements of this project focuses on optimizing the framework for connectivity-based parcellation with the goal of producing a new human brain atlas, i.e. the human Brainnetome Atlas, which is based on connectional architecture. Moreover, like the detailed information about the long range corticocortical connections in the macaque monkey brain [13, 14], such a new human brain atlas should also represent the detailed structural and functional connections of the human brain at the macro scale. So far, we have employed the above-mentioned strategy to identify 246 regions in the brain and have integrated this data with connectivity analyses and functional characterizations to build the human Brainnetome Atlas. This new brain atlas has the following four features: (A) It establishes a fine-grained brain parcellation scheme for 210 cortical and 36 subcortical regions with a coherent pattern of anatomical connections. (B) It supplies a detailed map of anatomical and functional connections. (C) It decodes brain functions using a meta-analytical approach. And (D) it will be an open resource for researchers to use for analyzing whole brain parcellations, connections, and functions. The human Brainnetome Atlas can be expected to be a major breakthrough among human brain atlases and should provide the basis for new lines of inquiry about the brain organization and functions. It will enable the generation of future brain atlases that are more finely defined and that will advance from single anatomical descriptions to an integrated atlas that includes structure, function, and connectivity along with other potential sources of information. In this paper, we will focus on recent developments in building the human Brainnetome Atlas based on connectional architecture and provide an overview of its potential applications in brain-inspired computing.

2 Human Brainnetome Atlas Based on Connectional Architecture

2.1 The Framework of the Brainnetome Atlas Construction: Connectivity-Based Parcellation

The framework of the Brainnetome Atlas construction primarily consists of the following components (Fig. 1): First, using high resolution structural MRI data, a brain region of interest is defined and extracted from individual participant T1-weighted images. Second, using multimodal MRI data that include diffusion MRI and resting state fMRI data, the anatomical and functional connectivity information is acquired for each voxel in the brain region. Then, the connections between voxels in the brain region and all of the remaining voxels in the brain are estimated and stored. Next, based on the native connectivity matrix, a cross-correlation matrix is calculated to quantify the similarity/dissimilarity between the connectivity profiles of the seed voxels. After this, the cross-correlation matrix is processed using clustering algorithms and reordered a process which can group data on the basis of its similarity to other data. The more similar their connectivity profiles, the more likely it is that the voxels will be grouped together. We then acquire the connectivity-defined clusters and map them back onto the brain. Using this framework, our group is now working on collecting data from different groups of normal populations. We then parcellate the brain regions and finally generate the brain atlas. In the following material, we will further discuss several key methodological issues, including the clustering algorithms, in the framework and show how we determine the optimal number of subregions.

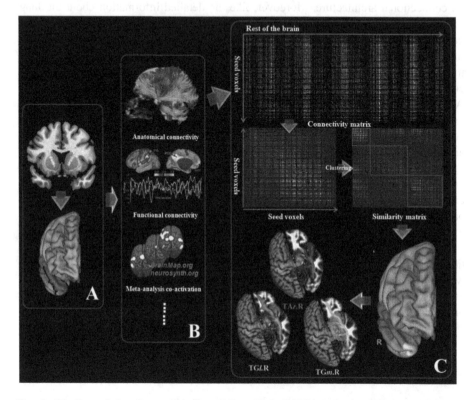

Fig. 1. Pipeline of the Connectivity-based Parcellation: Taking the parcellation of human temporal pole using diffusion tensor imaging as an example, A. Defining the boundary of the human temporal pole (TP). B. Mapping the connectional architecture using various MRI modalities, such as anatomical connectivity, resting state functional connectivity and meta-analysis-based co-activation. C. Calculating the similarity/dissimilarity between the connectivity profiles. The TP has been subdivided into sub-regions with distinguishing anatomical connectivity patterns.

First, for the diffusion-weighted imaging tractography-based parcellation studies, unsupervised clustering methods have been introduced to automatically identify different subregions in a specific brain area. Johansen-Berg H et al. (2004) first proposed identifying brain subareas by using a spectral reordering algorithm [15]. Subsequently, other research groups also introduced methods for determining different anatomical connectivity patterns for other brain areas [16]. Several clustering methods, including spectral reordering, K-means, spectral clustering, spectral clustering with edge-weighted centroidal voronoi tessellations, and independent component analysis, have been used to define subregions according to their distinct anatomical connections. Additionally, many clustering methods, such as k-means, spectral clustering, and hierarchical clustering, have been used in connectivity-based parcellations using resting state fMRI data. Of these, spectral clustering, including the normalized cut method [17], is one of the most commonly used clustering methods. Spectral clustering requires a similarity matrix as the input to build a similarity graph and calculates the spectral embedding of the data as a nonlinear dimensionality reduction process [18]. However, the definition of similarity has a huge impact on the final clustering results. One of the most commonly used similarity measures, the Gaussian weighted kernel function, has achieved satisfactory results in many applications, but the scaling parameter is difficult to choose, and it can limit the scalability of the method [19]. Many other similarity methods have been proposed for resting state fMRI-based brain parcellation [20–26]. However, each feature has properties which may bias the parcellation results in different ways. Specifically, cross-correlation calculates the synchronization in the fluctuation between two signals regardless of their magnitudes, but it requires some thresholds or transformations to deal with negative functional connections. A simple transformation of cross-correlation, the functional distance correlation, overcomes the effect of negative elements but puts a greater emphasis on negative than on positive functional connections. One of the most popular distance measures, Euclidean distance, calculates the sum of the square of the differences between two signals in Euclidean space but loses its detection capability for particular features of high dimensional data and is sensitive to scattered outliers. An extension of Euclidean distance, eta2, calculates the differences between two images that have been normalized by their total variances. This improves its sensitivity on particular features, but the user must still deal with the problem of dimensionality in that even small differences can be accumulated into a high level of variability in the boundary detection [16, 27].

Second, determining the appropriate number of subregions is still an open question in machine learning. In the case of connectivity-based parcellation, researchers have attempted to guide the choice of the appropriate number of subregions by estimating the homogeneity, accuracy, reproducibility, or stability of the brain areas [16]. Specifically, researchers performed the clustering analysis repeatedly with different pre-defined number of clusters and chose the appropriate number of subregions based on some indicator. In general, three types of indexes can be used. The first is obtained by using the objective function for the clustering analysis; in this case the number of subregions is automatically decided by optimizing the objective function [28–30]. But this method often provides local extrema rather than a single result and thus can return several parcellation results with similar objective values. In addition, this method is sensitive to the definition of the objective function and to the chosen features. For instance, different ways of calculating the connectivity or different scanning conditions can have a huge impact on the final parcellation results. Thus, the tradeoff between the sensitivity of choosing different cluster numbers and the robustness of the parcellation should be taken into consideration. As an illustration, spectral clustering which has been widely used in image clustering and segmentation, identifies subregions by clustering the eigenvectors of Laplacian matrices derived from the data [18]. Additionally, the number of subregions could also be inferred by the distribution of the eigenvalues [18, 31]. The second type of index is the stability index. Similar to the leave-one-out cross-validation (LOOCV) strategy, a bootstrap-sampling scheme is used to evaluate the consistency of the parcellation between random subgroups [27]. Specifically, the whole group of subjects is randomly split into two sub-groups and the parcellation results from these two subgroups are compared by calculating the similarity scores, including the dice index, normalized mutual information, Rand index, Jaccard similarity coefficient, Hamming distance, and the variation of information distance. This procedure is usually repeated 100 times to achieve a better estimate of the stability of the parcellation. There are also other types of indexes that can be used to calculate reproducibility. For instance, some researchers calculated the similarity index between the similarity graphs rather than calculating the distances between the clusters [25]. In addition, Yeo et al. (2011) trained a k-nearest neighbors (KNN) classifier on one subgroup and predicted the parcellation results on the other group [26]. The agreement between the predicted and actual parcellation results from the second sub-group was estimated as the stability of the clustering of these indexes. In fact, probably because it is easy to implement and independent of the chosen clustering algorithms, the stability index is the most commonly used index for predicting the suitable cluster number. In addition, the power of the clustering process can also be improved by repeatedly performing the clustering using random samples [32–36]. Thus, when forming the human Brainnetome Atlas, we chose this approach as the best method for estimating the most stable parcellation solutions.

2.2   Progress of the Construction of the Human Brainnetome Atlas and Its Main Characteristics

The unique anatomical connectivity of a brain area can not only determine the local function but also define the information processing hierarchies of the area and is, therefore, critical for understanding brain function [12, 37, 38]. Using data from the Human Connectome Project, which was obtained using cutting-edge noninvasive neuroimaging technologies, we employed a connectivity-based parcellation strategy to identify 246 regions in the brain and then integrated these using connectivity analyses to build the human Brainnetome Atlas [39]. To characterize the functional–anatomical organization of the brain, this new atlas addresses two major areas: (A) It establishes a fine-grained brain parcellation scheme (210 cortical regions and 36 subcortical regions maintain a coherent pattern of anatomical connections). (B) It supplies a map of the detailed anatomical and functional connections (Fig. 2).

in vivo neuroimaging studies have demonstrated the need for more fine-grained parcellations of large regions of the human brain. The Brainnetome Atlas, based on connectivity architecture, has not only confirmed some of the accepted structural differentiations from earlier cytoarchitectonic maps but has also revealed numerous anatomical subdivisions that had been missed previously. One example is the frontal and temporal polar cortexes, i.e. Brodmann areas 10 and 38, which are typically seen as cytoarchitectonically homogenous areas. However, increasing evidence supports roles in various high order cognitive functions, findings which indicate the potential for subregions in these areas. Using a connectivity-based parcellation based on diffusion

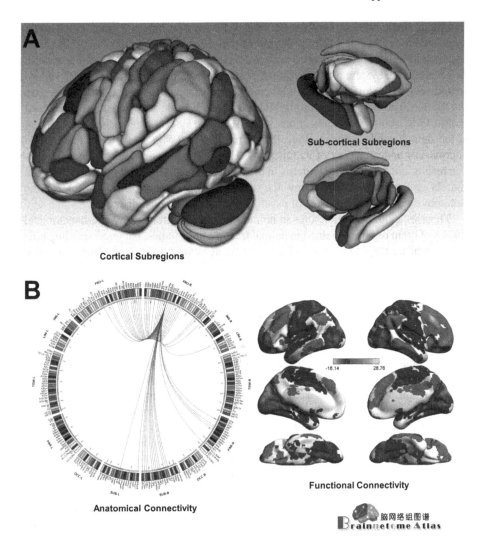

Fig. 2. The human Brainnetome Atlas: A. Parcellation scheme of the human brain in the Brainnetome Atlas. B. Example of the subregional connectogram and of the resting state functional connectivity for areas of the right middle frontal gyrus (MFG) subregion, i.e. A8vl (ventrolateral area 8).

MRI data, we found three subregions within the human temporal pole [32], a finding which seems to be consistent with 2 recently published histological works. Specifically, the TGm and TGl in our study correspond approximately to the temporopolar area TG described by Ding SL et al. (2009) [40] and the TPC (with medial and lateral subdivisions TPCm and TPCl) from the study by Blaizot X et al. (2010) [41]. Other examples are in a variety of other complex cytoarchitectonic areas. For example, the posteromedial cortex (PMC) has not yet been clearly mapped and is taken as a single structure in most in vivo neuroimaging studies. In another work from our group, Zhang Y et al. (2014)

identified 5 distinct subregions in the human PMC using probabilistic tractography with diffusion tensor imaging [42]. Furthermore, analyses of the anatomical and functional connectivity patterns demonstrated that the dorsal-anterior PMC primarily connects with the sensorimotor system while the dorsal-posterior PMC interacts strongly with vision-related areas. The dorsal-central PMC could be considered to be an association region and the dorsal portion of the ventral PMC may be a transition zone. In addition, the most ventral PMC shows rich connections with the limbic system, suggesting involvement in the default mode network. Parcellating the human PMC at a subtler level could improve our understanding of its functions. Therefore, the more fine-grained parcellation results and connectivity patterns in the next-generation brain atlas could lead to an entirely new understanding of how the brain works as well as shedding light on the pathophysiological mechanisms of psychiatric and neurological disorders.

Theories about brain functions in humans have been informed by neuroanatomical studies of brain regions obtained in animal tract-tracing studies, but understanding how these elucidate the connectivity of brain areas in humans is limited. This is a major function of the Brainnetome Atlas. Combining diffusion magnetic resonance imaging with tractography could enable researchers to reconstruct the major fiber bundles; while functional connectivity analysis of functional magnetic resonance images could also provide a noninvasive means of assessing in vivo the large-scale connectivity in the brain. Such approaches can relate connectivity data to a particular parcellation scheme, a relationship which can be useful for detailed investigations of a particular subsystem. Existing brain atlases were not intended to be connectivity maps, so this type of data has not previously been made available in a whole human brain atlas. Different connectivity fingerprints will be presented throughout the Brainnetome Atlas. Take the subregions of the human temporal pole as an example. Because little is known about the connectivity and function of the human TP, it has been referred to as "the enigmatic TP". Based on a connectivity-based parcellation using diffusion tensor imaging, three distinct subregions with characteristic fiber pathways, the dorsal (TAr), the medial (TGm), and lateral (TGl) subregions, which are located ventrally, were identified. The connectivity patterns showed a dorsal/ventral sensory segregation of auditory and visual processing and olfactory processing involvement in the medial TGm. By combining these results with a complementary resting-state functional connectivity analysis, we were able to observe connections of the TGm with the orbitofrontal cortex and other emotion-related areas, connections of the TGl with the medial prefrontal cortex and major default mode network regions, and connections of the TAr with the perisylvian language areas [32].

2.3 Potential Applications of the Brainnetome Atlas in Brain-Inspired Computing

The first goal of the Brainnetome project is to identify brain networks, from the finest scale to the most macroscopic one, and to explore the relationships between them using multimodal neuroimaging techniques. The Brainnetome Atlas will combine brain connectivity with cytoarchitecture and integrate other information. This will provide much more information than is available in existing brain atlases. Second, the project will study the dynamics and characteristics of brain networks throughout development, during aging, and in connection with evolutionary processes and investigate how the brain networks mediate human behavioral variability. With such a comprehensive understanding of the biological substrate of brain networks, on one hand, we should be able to create models to explore how brain networks are organized and how they give rise to behavior and cognition. On the other hand, we could design completely new hardware or algorithms for computing systems that are inspired by the brain's architecture. Because the current Brainnetome Atlas provides more complete information about the macroscale brain network by associating individual nodes with their distinct connectivity patterns and with their functional profiles, this new atlas could serve as a backbone for brain-based cognitive modeling and brain-inspired computer chips. In the following paragraphs we discuss in more detail how the Brainnetome Atlas can be used for these purposes.

From a computational point of view, the Brainnetome Atlas provides new insights into how the brain can be conceptualized as being constructed of a collection of interacting modules, with each of the modules having a specific and perhaps unique role in a complex sequence of information processing, with cognition and intelligent behavior emerging at the level of modular interaction. The advantage of building a complex system using modules has long been known by computer scientists [43]. First, a modular structure simplifies the design of a complex system by factoring any difficult task into a number of relatively easy sub-tasks; therefore each of the tasks can be accomplished within a less complex sub-system (module). Second, such a structure allows improvements to be made gradually. To endow the system with new functionality, one module can simply be modified or added while keeping the other parts unchanged. Accordingly, if a design error is spotted in the system, it can be isolated and fixed locally within its module, without the need to search for the solution across the entire system. Third, since different problems may contain the same sub-problems, a modular system can be compact because standard modules can be utilized to solve those sub-problems and can achieve versatility simply by dynamically organizing different modules for different tasks at hand.

In addition to those functional advantages, if we look from an evolutionary perspective, it is not difficult to understand why the brain is organized this way, as evolution can only improve the system a little bit at a time, and such improvement has to be built upon what has already been accomplished. In other words, any improvement has to be incremental, rather than dramatically changing the parts that have been working. Indeed, the modular nature has been suggested as the central designing principle of the human cognitive architecture [44]. Consequently, if we are interested in building artificial systems that are inspired by the brain, it is vital to learn how various cognitive tasks can be factored into small parts, with each one processed by a relatively simple part, and how the information is routed across all these parts, thereby "binding" the distributed processing into a coherent one. Simply put, this is what the Brainnetome Atlas can tell us. Its detailed parcellation can be used to identify the number of modules utilized by the brain, and the connection map between individual brain regions or sub-regions provides a parsimonious way to describe the information flow throughout the entire system. Arguably, what we can learn from this modular structure may be one of the most important inspirations that the brain can offer for designing an intelligent system, because it reflects the condensed knowledge accumulated during evolution about the structure of the world, as well as how one can exploit such a structure in order to survive.

A recent example of using a brain-like modular structure to achieve various interesting behaviors is a system named Spaun, produced by researchers at the University of Waterloo, Canada [45]. Spaun consists of 2.5 million artificial neurons, which are organized into various modules that mimic a number of cortical and subcortical structures. The input to the system is numbers and characters displayed on 28 by 28 images. Through a series of hierarchical visual processing stages that are similar to the ventral stream in primate brains, Spaun recognizes the symbols on the display and uses them to guide a robotic arm to write down its response. Depending on the content of the input, the proper responses range from simply copying what is on the input image to carrying out logistic reasoning. The choice of proper action is primarily controlled by a module similar to a subcortical structure- the thalamus. Additionally, Spaun's "cognition" is supported by a "working memory" function achieved in a module similar to the prefrontal cortex. Once the proper action is decided, the execution is carried out by first planning the appropriate sequence of movements of a robotic arm in a module similar to the premotor areas in the brain, followed by translating this planning into detailed movement commands in a module similar to the primary motor area. Finally, the commands are routed to the robotic arm to guide the behavior. With the aid of this brain-like modularity, Spaun is able to perform 8 different tasks, all with the same initial configuration, demonstrating the power of versatility by factoring different tasks into standard sub-tasks (e.g., vision, choice of action, working memory, motion, etc.) and preparing individual modules to deal with them separately.

Clearly, Spaun exploits a very rough structure reflecting the brain's modularity, with the entire system being parcellated into only a dozen or so modules. Now, with the Brainnetome Atlas, we can obtain a much more detailed view of this modularity, and we can reasonably expect that a much higher level of versatility can be achieved if this knowledge can be put into use in future system designs. Clearly, a notable piece of information that is currently missing is the functionality of individual sub-regions in the atlas. To add this will be necessary to fully harness the power of the brain's modularity structure for artificial intelligence (AI). This would be one of the primary goals in the further development of the Brainnetome Atlas. Ideally, the functionality can first be elucidated in a number of sub-systems that are most relevant for AI, such as memory processing [36], language processing [46], and decision making [47]. Identifying these essential sub-systems should lead to better ways of factoring difficult problems into sub-problems and enable deeper understanding and, eventually, better performance.

Furthermore, the Brainnetome Atlas will give us a reference framework to unite computer science and neuroscience and reveal potential applications that will help in designing and building the next generation of computing systems. Because cognitive modeling grows from hundreds of neurons, to the mouse brain scale, to the rat brain scale, and finally to the human brain scale, the same hierarchical organization of the brain could be used. Based on insights provided by the brain's architecture at difference scales, researchers can start to design neuromorphic chips that mimic the brain's connectivity. For example, TrueNorth is a neuromorphic chip produced by IBM [48]. The architectural design of TrueNorth was inspired by findings from neuroscience. For example, the neurosynaptic core was inspired by the canonical cortical microcircuit, the network of the neurosynaptic cores was inspired by the two-dimensional sheet of the cerebral cortex, and the multichip network was inspired by the white-matter graph in the macaque monkey brain [49]. To facilitate future investigations of the human brain and to fulfill the requirements of brain-inspired computing, the Brainnetome Atlas, accompanied by related software, will be made freely available for download via http:// atlas.brainnetome.org, along with the subregional structural and functional connections.

3 Conclusions

The quest for next generation information and communication technology requires new breakthroughs in brain-inspired computing, which involves a massive set of interconnections that include entirely new computing architectures, system designs, and programming paradigms [48, 50]. Brain-inspired design depends on possessing much more concrete information about the brain. Therefore, we need to understand a lot more about the brain, such as how it is organized and how the basic units in the human brain are structured, to mimic the brain as accurately as possible. The human brain is not only the probably most complex biological structure but also a highly topographically organized organ. Currently, many approaches parcellating the brain into areas with different criteria became available, but there is still no definitive map of the human brain [51, 52]. Therefore, the goal of the future brain map for the Brainnetome project, i.e. the Brainnetome Atlas, is to understand the organizing principles underlying the anatomy of the brain. At this stage, the Brainnetome Atlas utilizes in vivo data, has fine-grained subregions, and reveals detailed anatomical and functional connection patterns for each region. The next stage of the Brainnetome Atlas will be multimodal in rather than unimodal and dynamic rather than static by including other brain mapping information, such as genetic expression patterns and dynamic spatiotemporal changes during normal development and in the aging process or in different disease states. Furthermore, in order to complete such brain maps across different scales, collaborations between brain research institutes in different fields, such as laboratories that employ brain tissue clearing techniques [53] and micro-imaging methods [54] to map the nervous system at the micro scale, will be necessary for establishing the next generation Brainnetome Atlas.

Acknowledgements. We thank Yu Zhang, Yong Yang, Junjie Zhuo, and Jiaojian Wang for their help with manuscript preparation and Rhoda E. and Edmund F. Perozzi for editing assistance and discussions. This work was partially supported by the National Key Basic Research and Development Program (973) (Grant No. 2011CB707801 and 2012CB720702), the Strategic Priority Research Program of the Chinese Academy of Sciences (Grant No. XDB02030300), the Natural Science Foundation of China (Grant Nos. 91432302, 91132301, 31620103905, 81270020 and 81501179).

References

1. Sporns, O.: Cerebral cartography and connectomics. Philos. Trans. Roy. Soc. Lond. B Biol. Sci. **370** (2015). doi:10.1098/rstb.2014.0173
2. Amunts, K., Zilles, K.: Architectonic mapping of the human brain beyond brodmann. Neuron **88**, 1086–1107 (2015)
3. Van Essen, D.C.: Cartography and connectomes. Neuron **80**, 775–790 (2013)
4. Jiang, T.: Brainnetome: a new -ome to understand the brain and its disorders. Neuroimage **80**, 263–272 (2013)
5. Evans, A.C., Janke, A.L., Collins, D.L., Baillet, S.: Brain templates and atlases. Neuroimage **62**, 911–922 (2012)
6. Zilles, K., Amunts, K.: Centenary of Brodmann's map–conception and fate. Nat. Rev. Neurosci. **11**, 139–145 (2010)
7. Brodmann, K.: Vergleichende Lokalisationslehre der Großhirnrinde in ihren Prinzipien dargestellt auf Grund des Zellenbaues. Verlag von Johann Ambrosius Barth, Leipzig (Germany) (1909)
8. Amunts, K., Lepage, C., Borgeat, L., Mohlberg, H., Dickscheid, T., Rousseau, M.E., Bludau, S., Bazin, P.L., Lewis, L.B., Oros-Peusquens, A.M., Shah, N.J., Lippert, T., Zilles, K., Evans, A.C.: BigBrain: an ultrahigh-resolution 3D human brain model. Science **340**, 1472–1475 (2013)
9. Kaas, J.H.: The organization of neocortex in mammals: implications for theories of brain function. Annu. Rev. Psychol. **38**, 129–151 (1987)
10. Van Essen, D.C.: A Population-Average, Landmark- and Surface-based (PALS) atlas of human cerebral cortex. Neuroimage **28**, 635–662 (2005)
11. Bohland, J.W., Bokil, H., Allen, C.B., Mitra, P.P.: The brain atlas concordance problem: quantitative comparison of anatomical parcellations. PLoS ONE **4**, e7200 (2009)
12. Passingham, R.E., Stephan, K.E., Kotter, R.: The anatomical basis of functional localization in the cortex. Nat. Rev. Neurosci. **3**, 606–616 (2002)
13. Markov, N.T., Ercsey-Ravasz, M.M.: Ribeiro Gomes, A.R., Lamy, C., Magrou, L., Vezoli, J., Misery, P., Falchier, A., Quilodran, R., Gariel, M.A., Sallet, J., Gamanut, R., Huissoud, C., Clavagnier, S., Giroud, P., Sappey-Marinier, D., Barone, P., Dehay, C., Toroczkai, Z., Knoblauch, K., Van Essen, D.C., Kennedy, H.: A weighted and directed interareal connectivity matrix for macaque cerebral cortex. Cereb. Cortex **24**, 17–36 (2014)
14. Dyhrfjeld-Johnsen, J., Maier, J., Schubert, D., Staiger, J., Luhmann, H.J., Stephan, K.E., Kotter, R.: CoCoDat: a database system for organizing and selecting quantitative data on single neurons and neuronal microcircuitry. J. Neurosci. Methods **141**, 291–308 (2005)
15. Johansen-Berg, H., Behrens, T.E., Robson, M.D., Drobnjak, I., Rushworth, M.F., Brady, J.M., Smith, S.M., Higham, D.J., Matthews, P.M.: Changes in connectivity profiles define functionally distinct regions in human medial frontal cortex. Proc. Natl. Acad. Sci. USA **101**, 13335–13340 (2004)
16. Eickhoff, S.B., Thirion, B., Varoquaux, G., Bzdok, D.: Connectivity-based parcellation: critique and implications. Hum. Brain Mapp. **36**(12), 4771–4792 (2015)
17. Yu, S.X., Shi, J.: Multiclass spectral clustering. In: Ninth IEEE International Conference on Computer Vision, 2003. Proceedings, vol. 1, pp. 313–319 (2003)
18. von Luxburg, U.: A tutorial on spectral clustering. Stat. Comput. **17**, 395–416 (2007)
19. Perona, P., Zelnik-Manor, L.: Self-tuning spectral clustering. Adv. Neural Inf. Process. Syst. **17**, 1601–1608 (2004)

20. Cohen, A.L., Fair, D.A., Dosenbach, N.U., Miezin, F.M., Dierker, D., Van Essen, D.C., Schlaggar, B.L., Petersen, S.E.: Defining functional areas in individual human brains using resting functional connectivity MRI. Neuroimage **41**, 45–57 (2008)
21. Kelly, C., Toro, R., Di Martino, A., Cox, C.L., Bellec, P., Castellanos, F.X., Milham, M.P.: A convergent functional architecture of the insula emerges across imaging modalities. Neuroimage **61**, 1129–1142 (2012)
22. Chang, L.J., Yarkoni, T., Khaw, M.W., Sanfey, A.G.: Decoding the role of the insula in human cognition: functional parcellation and large-scale reverse inference. Cereb. Cortex **23**(2), 739–749 (2012)
23. Kim, J.H., Lee, J.M., Jo, H.J., Kim, S.H., Lee, J.H., Kim, S.T., Seo, S.W., Cox, R.W., Na, D.L., Kim, S.I., Saad, Z.S.: Defining functional SMA and pre-SMA subregions in human MFC using resting state fMRI: functional connectivity-based parcellation method. Neuroimage **49**, 2375–2386 (2010)
24. Nelson, S.M., Cohen, A.L., Power, J.D., Wig, G.S., Miezin, F.M., Wheeler, M.E., Velanova, K., Donaldson, D.I., Phillips, J.S., Schlaggar, B.L., Petersen, S.E.: A parcellation scheme for human left lateral parietal cortex. Neuron **67**, 156–170 (2010)
25. Craddock, R.C., James, G.A., Holtzheimer 3rd, P.E., Hu, X.P., Mayberg, H.S.: A whole brain fMRI atlas generated via spatially constrained spectral clustering. Hum. Brain Mapp. **33**, 1914–1928 (2012)
26. Yeo, B.T., Krienen, F.M., Sepulcre, J., Sabuncu, M.R., Lashkari, D., Hollinshead, M., Roffman, J.L., Smoller, J.W., Zollei, L., Polimeni, J.R., Fischl, B., Liu, H., Buckner, R.L.: The organization of the human cerebral cortex estimated by intrinsic functional connectivity. J. Neurophysiol. **106**, 1125–1165 (2011)
27. Zhang, Y., Caspers, S., Fan, L., Fan, Y., Song, M., Liu, C., Mo, Y., Roski, C., Eickhoff, S., Amunts, K., Jiang, T.: Robust brain parcellation using sparse representation on resting-state fMRI. Brain Struct. Funct. **220**, 3565–3579 (2015)
28. Mishra, A., Rogers, B.P., Chen, L.M., Gore, J.C.: Functional connectivity-based parcellation of amygdala using self-organized mapping: a data driven approach. Hum. Brain Mapp. **35**, 1247–1260 (2014)
29. Wig, G.S., Laumann, T.O., Cohen, A.L., Power, J.D., Nelson, S.M., Glasser, M.F., Miezin, F.M., Snyder, A.Z., Schlaggar, B.L., Petersen, S.E.: Parcellating an individual subject's cortical and subcortical brain structures using snowball sampling of resting-state correlations. Cereb. Cortex **24**, 2036–2054 (2014)
30. Ryali, S., Chen, T., Supekar, K., Menon, V.: A parcellation scheme based on von Mises-Fisher distributions and Markov random fields for segmenting brain regions using resting-state fMRI. Neuroimage **65**, 83–96 (2013)
31. Azran, A., Ghahramani, Z.: Spectral methods for automatic multiscale data clustering. In: Proceeding of 2006 IEEE Computer Society Conference on Computer Vision and Pattern Recognition, vol. 1, pp. 190–197 (2006)
32. Fan, L., Wang, J., Zhang, Y., Han, W., Yu, C., Jiang, T.: Connectivity-based parcellation of the human temporal pole using diffusion tensor imaging. Cereb. Cortex **24**, 3365–3378 (2014)
33. Liu, H., Qin, W., Li, W., Fan, L., Wang, J., Jiang, T., Yu, C.: Connectivity-based parcellation of the human frontal pole with diffusion tensor imaging. J. Neurosci. **33**, 6782–6790 (2013)
34. Beckmann, M., Johansen-Berg, H., Rushworth, M.F.: Connectivity-based parcellation of human cingulate cortex and its relation to functional specialization. J. Neurosci. **29**, 1175–1190 (2009)
35. Neubert, F.X., Mars, R.B., Thomas, A.G., Sallet, J., Rushworth, M.F.: Comparison of human ventral frontal cortex areas for cognitive control and language with areas in monkey frontal cortex. Neuron **81**, 700–713 (2014)

36. Zhuo, J., Fan, L., Liu, Y., Zhang, Y., Yu, C., Jiang, T.: Connectivity profiles reveal a transition subarea in the parahippocampal region that integrates the anterior temporal-posterior medial systems. J. Neurosci. **36**, 2782–2795 (2016)
37. Felleman, D.J., Van Essen, D.C.: Distributed hierarchical processing in the primate cerebral cortex. Cereb. Cortex **1**, 1–47 (1991)
38. Jbabdi, S., Sotiropoulos, S.N., Haber, S.N., Van Essen, D.C., Behrens, T.E.: Measuring macroscopic brain connections in vivo. Nat. Neurosci. **18**, 1546–1555 (2015)
39. Fan, L., Li, H., Zhuo, J., Zhang, Y., Wang, J., Chen, L., Yang, Z., Chu, C., Xie, S., Laird, A.R., Fox, P.T., Eickhoff, S.B., Yu, C., Jiang, T.: The human brainnetome atlas: a new brain atlas based on connectional architecture. Cereb. Cortex **26**, 3508–3526 (2016)
40. Ding, S.L., Van Hoesen, G.W., Cassell, M.D., Poremba, A.: Parcellation of human temporal polar cortex: a combined analysis of multiple cytoarchitectonic, chemoarchitectonic, and pathological markers. J. Comp. Neurol. **514**, 595–623 (2009)
41. Blaizot, X., Mansilla, F., Insausti, A.M., Constans, J.M., Salinas-Alaman, A., Pro-Sistiaga, P., Mohedano-Moriano, A., Insausti, R.: The human parahippocampal region: I. temporal pole cytoarchitectonic and MRI correlation. Cereb. Cortex **20**, 2198–2212 (2010)
42. Zhang, Y., Fan, L., Zhang, Y., Wang, J., Zhu, M., Zhang, Y., Yu, C., Jiang, T.: Connectivity-based parcellation of the human posteromedial cortex. Cereb. Cortex **24**, 719–727 (2014)
43. Baum, E.B.: What is Thought? MIT Press, Cambridge (2004)
44. Fodor, J.A.: The Modularity of Mind. MIT Press, Cambridge (1983)
45. Eliasmith, C., Stewart, T.C., Choo, X., Bekolay, T., DeWolf, T., Tang, Y., Rasmussen, D.: A large-scale model of the functioning brain. Science **338**, 1202–1205 (2012)
46. Wang, J., Fan, L., Wang, Y., Xu, W., Jiang, T., Fox, P.T., Eickhoff, S.B., Yu, C., Jiang, T.: Determination of the posterior boundary of Wernicke's area based on multimodal connectivity profiles. Hum. Brain Mapp. **36**, 1908–1924 (2015)
47. Liu, H., Qin, W., Qi, H., Jiang, T., Yu, C.: Parcellation of the human orbitofrontal cortex based on gray matter volume covariance. Hum. Brain Mapp. **36**, 538–548 (2015)
48. Merolla, P.A., Arthur, J.V., Alvarez-Icaza, R., Cassidy, A.S., Sawada, J., Akopyan, F., Jackson, B.L., Imam, N., Guo, C., Nakamura, Y., Brezzo, B., Vo, I., Esser, S.K., Appuswamy, R., Taba, B., Amir, A., Flickner, M.D., Risk, W.P., Manohar, R., Modha, D.S.: Artificial brains. A million spiking-neuron integrated circuit with a scalable communication network and interface. Science **345**, 668–673 (2014)
49. Modha, D.S., Singh, R.: Network architecture of the long-distance pathways in the macaque brain. Proc. Natl. Acad. Sci. USA **107**, 13485–13490 (2010)
50. Frackowiak, R., Markram, H.: The future of human cerebral cartography: a novel approach. Philos. Trans. Roy. Soc. Lond. B Biol. Sci. **370** (2015). doi:10.1098/rstb.2014.0171
51. Glasser, M.F., Coalson, T.S., Robinson, E.C., Hacker, C.D., Harwell, J., Yacoub, E., Ugurbil, K., Andersson, J., Beckmann, C.F., Jenkinson, M., Smith, S.M., Van Essen, D.C.: A multi-modal parcellation of human cerebral cortex. Nature **536**, 171–178 (2016)
52. Paxinos, G.: Human brainnetome atlas: a new chapter of brain cartography. Sci. China Life Sci. **59**(9), 965–967 (2016)
53. Richardson, D.S., Lichtman, J.W.: Clarifying tissue clearing. Cell **162**, 246–257 (2015)
54. Kasthuri, N., Hayworth, K.J., Berger, D.R., Schalek, R.L., Conchello, J.A., Knowles-Barley, S., Lee, D., Vazquez-Reina, A., Kaynig, V., Jones, T.R., Roberts, M., Morgan, J.L., Tapia, J.C., Seung, H.S., Roncal, W.G., Vogelstein, J.T., Burns, R., Sussman, D.L., Priebe, C.E., Pfister, H., Lichtman, J.W.: Saturated reconstruction of a volume of neocortex. Cell **162**, 648–661 (2015)

Workflows for Ultra-High Resolution 3D Models of the Human Brain on Massively Parallel Supercomputers

Hartmut Mohlberg[1]($\boxtimes$), Bastian Tweddell[2], Thomas Lippert[2], and Katrin Amunts[1,3]

[1] Institute of Neuroscience and Medicine (INM-1),
Research Centre Juelich and JARA-Brain, 52428 Jülich, Germany
{h.mohlberg,k.amunts}@fz-juelich.de
[2] Juelich Supercomputing Centre (JSC), IAS, and JARA-HPC,
Research Centre Juelich, 52428 Jülich, Germany
{b.tweddell,th.lippert}@fz-juelich.de
[3] C. and O. Vogt Institute of Brain Research,
Heinrich-Heine University, 40225 Düsseldorf, Germany
k.amunts@uni-duesseldorf.de

Abstract. Human brain atlases [1] are indispensable tools to achieve a better understanding of the multilevel organization of the brain through integrating and analyzing data from different brains, sources, and modalities while considering the functionally relevant topography of the brain [4]. The spatial resolution of most of these electronic atlases is in the range of millimeters, which does not allow the integration of the information at the level of cortical layers, columns, microcircuits or cells. Therefore, we introduced in 2013 the first BigBrain data set with a resolution of $20\,\mu$m isotropic. This data set allows to specify morphometric parameters of human brain organization, which serve as a "gold standard" for neuroimaging data obtained at a lower spatial resolution. It provides, in addition, an essential basis for realistic brain models concerning structural analysis and simulation [2]. For the generation of other, even higher-resolution data sets of the human brain, we developed an improved and more efficient data processing workflow employing high performance computing to 3D reconstruct histological data sets. To facilitate the analysis of intersubject variability on a microscopic level, the new processing framework was applied for reconstructing a second BigBrain data set with 7676 sections. Efficient data processing of a large amount of data sets with a complex nested reconstruction workflow using large number of compute nodes required optimized distributed processing workflows as well as parallel programming. A detailed documentation of the processing steps and the complex inter-dependencies of the data sets at each level of the multi-step reconstruction workflow was essential to enable transformations to images of the same histological sections obtained with even higher spatial resolution. We have addressed these challenges, and achieved efficient high throughput processing of thousands of images of histological sections in combination with sufficient flexibility, based on an effective, successive coarse-to-fine hierarchical processing.

© Springer International Publishing AG 2016
K. Amunts et al. (Eds.): BrainComp 2015, LNCS 10087, pp. 15–27, 2016.
DOI: 10.1007/978-3-319-50862-7_2

Keywords: Ultra-high resolution brain models · BigBrain · Cytoarchitecture · Microstructure · High performance computing · Workflows · Human Brain Atlas

1   Introduction

The cerebral cortex of the human brain is a highly heterogeneous structure. It is segregated into cortical areas, which differ between each other in their cellular architecture, but also in their molecular composition, connectivity, function, and other aspects of brain organization [1]. By analyzing Nissl-stained histological sections with a light microscope, Korbinian Brodmann has observed at the beginning of the last century that every cortical area showed a characteristic cellular architecture (cytoarchitecture) specified by the spatial distribution of neurons, the presence of particular cell types, the clustering of cell bodies, and the formation of cortical layers (thickness, density, etc.), which run in parallel to the cortical surface [5]. Based on these differences Brodmann published a map with 43 cortical cytoarchitectonic areas in humans (Fig. 1a). He was convinced that each cortical area subserves a certain function, although this had not been demonstrated for the majority of brain areas in these days.

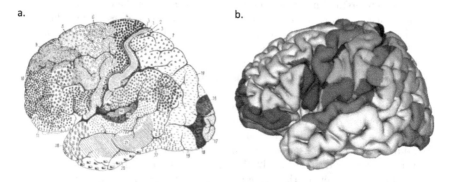

Fig. 1. (a) Brodmanns schematic map of the cerebral cortex of the human brain. Cortical areas are labeled with different patterns and numbers [5]. (b) Probabilistic JuBrain Atlas; areas are labeled by different gray values [17].

In contrast to the 2D map as drawn by Brodmann, the JuBrain atlas [17] represents a true 3D representation of cytoarchitectonic areas at a resolution of 1 mm isotropic, covers also areas buried in the depths of the sulci, and includes subcortical nuclei. In order to consider intersubject variability, each cytoarchitectonic area was mapped for 10 postmortem brains and has been 3D-reconstructed and normalized to the stereotaxic reference space of a single subject template provided by the Montreal Neurological Insitute MNI [8]. As a result, probability maps could be calculated (e.g., [6]). The parcellation shown in Fig. 1b associates a label to that area, which had the highest probability at this particular position in the atlas space (maximum probability map [7]). The combined analysis of modern in vivo neuroimaging studies and cytoarchitectonic probabilistic maps provides a deeper understanding of the role of cortical areas in complex brain functions including memory, language, abstraction, creativity, emotion and attention, and allows identifying networks of brain areas, which are involved in specific brain functions.

Such type of analyses of structure-functional relationships is constrained by the resolution of in vivo neuroimaging studies, which is in the millimeter range for the majorities of fMRI studies. This does not allow addressing the level of cortical layers, columns, and cells as structures relevant for brain activity and finally behavior. For this purpose, a resolution of 20 μm and less is mandatory, which captures details of laminar and columnar organization. Going to even higher resolution, light microscopic images on a scale of 1 μm allow detecting details of single cell morphology (for details see Fig. 2).

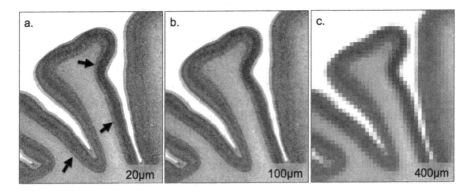

Fig. 2. Region of interest at various resolution levels. (a) A resolution of 20 μm enables a reliable identification of cortical layers and their regional differences (marked by the arrows), columns and cells. This becomes increasingly more difficult at a resolution of 100 μm (b) and is for most brain regions virtually impossible already at a resolution of 400 μm (c). Note that even this resolution is still more than twice as high as those used in many fMRI studies.

In 2013 we have introduced the BigBrain data set [2] with a spatial resolution of 20 μm isotropic. It is based on the 3D reconstruction of 7404 digitized histological sections, which were stained for cell bodies. This data set serves a new, microscopical reference space for neuroscience data and has become part of the HBP Human Brain Atlas [25]. In addition, it represents a basis for in-depths analyses of the cellular architecture. For example, the BigBrain data set has been used to extract parameters of brain organization such as cell densities, cortical thicknesses, the laminar pattern and cortical surface [14–16].

The generation of this BigBrain data set was extremely time-consuming and labor-intensive. Based on a 16-bit gray value coding, the total size of the original 7404 digitized histological sections with an in-plane resolution of 20 μm was between 0.6 and 1 TiB. The processing workflow for the 3D reconstruction included several steps: the reconstruction of blockface images, the registration of MR images of the formalin fixed brain to blockface images (obtained during histological sectioning), linear and nonlinear 2D alignment of histological sections to corresponding sections of the aligned MR-images, volume-to-volume registration of MR-images to stacked histological sections, and section-to-section alignment of histological sections to each other or to MR images [2].

In addition, the workflow was considerably complicated by the fact that many images of the histological sections were not successively processed through each processing step, but processed differently, for example to correct for distortions and histological artifacts affecting the images in a different degree. Histological artifacts are inevitably accompanied by cutting large human brain sections, the mounting of sections on glass slides and staining. This becomes particularly relevant at very high spatial resolutions, where even smallest artifacts become visible. Up to 40 % of the images required (time consuming) manual repair. The removal of artifacts in subsets of images was done in an iterative manner, to improve consecutively the quality of the 3D reconstructed data set.

The complex dependencies of the various data sets demand an efficient data management and processing system. It should be capable to facilitate the processing of those subsets of images, where artifact correction has been carried out to avoid a repetitive processing of the whole series of histological sections. In addition, it is necessary to report carefully the corrections in order to provide a detailed documentation of the modifications applied to each image. This is a prerequisite for reproducibility, and a reliable interpretation of measurement results. Due to the large amount of data in combination with the complexity of the reconstruction workflow, the processing of the BigBrain data set requires advanced HPC technology for both data management and computing in order to speedup the image processing.

Here, we introduce an efficient HPC-adapted processing workflow to 3D-reconstruct histological data sets of the human brain with a high quality $20\,\mu m$ resolution and with a scalability to be computed within a reasonable time frame. It includes a comprehensive documentation and provenance tracking of all processing steps as well as inter-dependencies of image and meta data at each level of the workflow. The new processing workflow was applied to 3D-reconstruct a new, second BigBrain data. The workflow has been developed on the multi-purpose HPC system JUROPA (Juelich Research on Petaflop Architectures) at the Juelich Supercomputing Centre (JSC). In 2015, it was necessary to migrate the complete workflow to JUROPA's successor JURECA (Juelich Research on Exascale Cluster Architectures).

2   Material and Overview of the Processing Workflow

A postmortem brain of a 30-year old male without any neurological or psychiatric diseases in clinical records was obtained through a body donor program in accordance to legal and ethical rules. It was fixed in 4 % buffered formalin

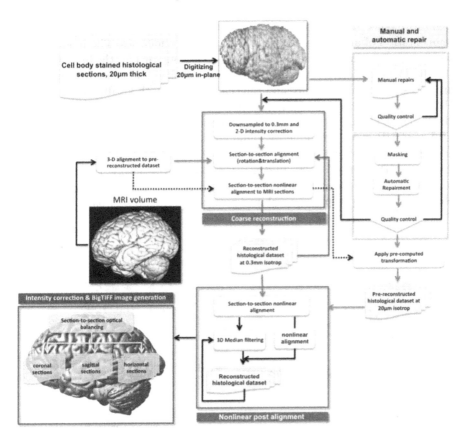

Fig. 3. HPC processing workflow for the 3D reconstruction of the second BigBrain data set. Gray colored boxes label different processing levels, which can be performed in parallel.

for several months. The fixed brain underwent MR-imaging with a resolution of $0.7 \times 0.7 \times 0.7$ mm. This MR data set served as an undistorted reference target for 3-dimensional reconstruction. The brain was embedded in paraffin, and serial coronal histological sections at 20 μm thickness were obtained with a large-scale microtome. 7676 sections were acquired, mounted, and stained for cell bodies. The stained sections were digitized using a flatbed scanner with a physical in-plane resolution of 10 μm and a dynamic range of 16 bits. All images were downscaled to 20×20 μm, framed to a uniform image size of 7000×6000 pixels and saved in png-format with lossless compression in order to generate an initial data set with isotropic resolution. All these steps were performed as described in our previous work [2]. In total, this raw data set occupied approximately 320 GiB of disk space.

To address the methodical data processing and managing challenges, we applied a simple, but efficient data provenance and tracking tool based on the

Open Provenance Model (OPM) [24] that provides a detailed and comprehensible documentation of all processing steps and data dependencies. The implementation permits a re-play of most of the processing scripts used for the first BigBrain data set. The tool does not require special prerequisites for the underlying hardware and software architecture and thus can be used both locally on a server as well as on a supercomputer. The processing steps include linear and nonlinear 2-dimensional alignments of histological sections to corresponding sections of the aligned MR images, volume-to-volume registration of MR images to stacked histological sections, section-to-section alignment of histological sections to each other or to MR images (Fig. 3). In contrast to our previous work, the new version specifies four interdependent processing levels executed in parallel. Sequentially executed processing steps are combined with those executed in parallel.

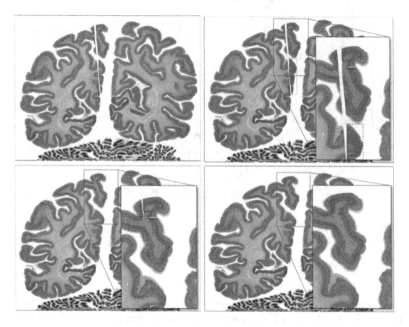

Fig. 4. Manual and automatic repair of displaced tissue pieces. Clockwise from top-left: Original section at 20 μm resolution, manual labeled misaligned/damaged ROIs, manual corrected ROIs, and automatically corrected ROIs using neighboring sections [11]. All processing steps were automatically documented and stored in an xml-file. This file can later be applied to the same images, e.g., those scanned with higher spatial resolution.

Processing level (i): Manual and automatic repair. Images of histological sections differ in the presence of artifacts and the severity of the artifacts. They include e.g., rips, tears, staining artifacts, folds, missing and displaced pieces, with different size and constitution. Fully automatic methods often fail in removing such artifacts. Thus, time and labor intensive manual repair steps are required. A trained expert can process approximately 20 to 30 sections per day. This manual repair is followed by an automatic artifact correction [11]. We have developed a new easy-to-use and effective tool, which also documents all steps (for some examples see Fig. 4).

Processing level (ii): Coarse reconstruction. A successive coarse-to-fine hierarchical framework was implemented for an efficient data processing and 3D-reconstruction, substantially accelerating the sequential data processing as used for the first BigBrain. A first coarse pre-reconstitution at a low in-plane resolution of 0.3 mm isotropic was computed, where the major part of the artifacts was negligible. Initially, every 15th section (section-to-section distance = 0.3 mm) was used, taking advantage of the postmortem MRI as an undistorted spatial reference [10]. The MRI was co-registered to this reconstructed histological data set and sampled up to the original number of sections using a B-spline imaging filter [13]. All down-sampled histological images were co-registered, section-by-section, to the coronal sections of the up-sampled co MR-volume using linear and non-linear registration tools [10]. Subsequently, the computed transformations were sampled up and applied to the original or to the repaired histological sections at a resolution of $20\,\mu$m. The second processing level was initially in parallel to the first level, but was re-executed, when new repaired sections were available. For example, the spatial resolution and the quality of the 3D-resonstruction were successively improved through newly incorporated repaired and corrected histological sections. In order to support this coarse-to-fine hierarchical processing, we employed a data flow management system, which provides an automatic monitoring of the processing steps and accounts for the complex dependencies of the data sets. In case of a modification of a certain number of input data sets only the modified images were re-computed, while non-modified data sets were not processed again.

Processing level (iii): Nonlinear post alignment. We computed at a (so far maximum) resolution of 40 m a section-to-section nonlinear alignment. This step required up to 8 h of computation time per image, and was the computationally most expensive part. In order to improve the quality of the 3D-reconstruction, we computed for every image i the nonlinear alignment to the median image of its $i \pm 3$ neighbors thus reducing minor local misalignments.

Processing level (iv): Intensity corrections and BigTIFF image generation. Finally, a further section-to-section optical imbalance correction was computed. A 3D-volume file (320 GiB) was created. In addition, two virtual section planes in horizontal and sagittal directions were generated respectively. They were saved as tiled BigTIFF images on the global GPFS file system at the Jülich Supercomputting Centre which has a dedicated 1-Gbit/s-Ethernet connection to our local web server.

Quality control throughout the whole workflow is mandatory to guarantee high accuracy of the 3D-reconstruction. Artifacts are immediately visible in the two virtual section planes at high spatial resolution (i.e., horizontal and sagittal planes). They appear, for example, as distortions of the laminar pattern of the

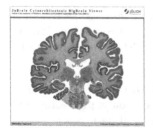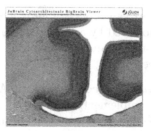

Fig. 5. Web-based online inspection of a processed histological section at different resolutions used for quality control.

cerebral cortex, or as distortions of the brain surface. Therefore, a web based visualization tool using the HTML5 standard was developed that is capable to visualize and explore even ultra-large tiled 2D data sets saved in the BigTIFF file format (see Fig. 5).

3   Computational Methods and Algorithms

In order to provide an automated workflow and data management system that efficiently utilizes advanced supercomputing infrastructures the provenance tracking systems documents every processing step automatically by creating a document file in xml data format. This document file contains detailed information about the compute node, the operating system, the time of creation, the software tools (name, revision, names of external library files, etc.), the processing parameters, and the input and output files (name, time, md5 checksum, etc.). Internally the workflow is implemented as a couple of Perl scripts, which call the executables that are written in C++. This was achieved by replacing the internal system command from Perl with a new, adapted system call command. By specifying program name, input options, name and type (regular or temporary file) of each input and output filename(s), the document file was automatically created for each output file and stored in its directory.

Data provenance and data management platforms become more important to facilitate a reproducible and effective neuroscience research [9]. The UNI-CORE (Uniform Interface to Computing Resources) grid middle ware offers a ready-to-run grid system that enables distributed computing on HPC and makes data resources available in a secure and user-friendly way in intranets and the internet [3]. However, like most of the platforms, it is not straightforward to integrate an already existing workflow package and to track all the processing steps carried out within the script. In order to meet the complexity of the present workflow and to re-use external workflow packages, we have developed a new in-house system. We used Python [18] powered by mpi4py [19] and graph-tool [20] for the programming of the processing workflows. In order to update a previously created data file, starting from the requested output file in a first run, a data dependency graph was created by backtracking and analyzing the created log files of all input files. Only those images that had to be re-processed with respect to the modified input data (check based on existence, time creation and md5 checksum) were transmitted to the allocated compute nodes in a second run. The large number of processing steps and the interdependence of a large number of files resulted in a data dependency graph containing approximately 260,000 nodes. To reduce the complexity, we computed for each execution level a data dependency graph independently and connected the individual graphs afterwards.

The processing pipeline used to 3D reconstruct the first BigBrain data set was based on the prominent MINC tool kit, a comprehensive collection of individual programs for medical image processing and analysis [23]. Most of the included programs are very selective; in order to realize a more complex computation, often, multiple calls of a couple of different programs are required, which leads to a comparatively high I/O. In order to minimize I/O operations, successive computing algorithms and highly specialized C++ programs were developed, which are based on the Insight Segmentation and Registration Toolkit (ITK) [21] and an internal image processing library. A B-spline transformation model was used in combination with a Limited memory Broyden-Fletcher-Goldfarb-Shannon (L-BFGS-B) optimizer and a L2 metric [12] for the section-to-section alignment. The parameter space of the B-spline transformation was composed of the set of all the deformations associated with the nodes of the grid. Thus, a wide variety of deformations is considered, requiring a rather large amount of computation time. Specialized programs, parallelized with MPI-2, were developed since the ITK library does not support distributed processing by MPI-2 and cannot be used for very memory intensive programs. These programs allowed processing the complete BigBrain data volume with 320 GiB, which is a prerequisite to generate virtual sectioning planes. To save and read 3D data sets from storage, we used the HDF5 library that provides optimized parallel I/O based on the MPI-2 library [22]. To provide a fast data visualization, final output images were stored in BigTIFF format that supports a tiled data organization facilitating a rapid access to single tiles.

4 HPC Computations on JUROPA and JURECA

All development and computations were done at the Jülich Supercomputing Centre on the HPC-system JUROPA and then migrated to its successor JURECA. JUROPA had 3288 compute nodes each with 2 Intel Xeon X5570 (Nehalem-EP) 2.93 GHz quad-core processors and 24 GiB of main memory. Approximately 22 GiB of memory per node were available for applications. In total, this led to a complete system of 26,304 cores, 79 TiB main memory, a peak performance of 308 Teraflops and a Linpack performance of 274.8 Teraflops. The batch system for managing jobs was Moab with the underlying resource manager TORQUE. The JURECA system, where so far 15 % of the computations have been carried out, has 1872 compute nodes each with 2 Intel Xeon E5-2680 v3 (Haswell) 2.5 GHz 12-core processors and 128 GiB of main memory. In total, this led to a complete system of 45,216 cores, 271 TiB main memory and a peak performance of 1.8 Petaflops. In contrast to JUROPA, the new system uses a Slurm batch system with Parastation resource management.

Python powered by mpi4py was used to implement the workflows, which scaled up well to the (so far) maximum allocation of 512 cores. Going from the bottom level to the highest stage of execution level that has already been reached for each execution level of the workflow, we executed a cold run, where no output files were generated. By analyzing previously created document files, the total number of images that had to be re-computed with respect to modified input data was determined. The required computation time was estimated using the documented execution time of the previous run. If no logging information was available, for example for the first run, the execution time was estimated based on past experience. Relative to the number of required computing cores and execution time, an appropriately adapted batch job was generated and sent to the batch system in a second run.

Each processing step was logged, including manual interventions. By analyzing data dependencies, only those images that had to be re-computed with respect to the modified original data were transmitted to the allocated compute nodes. The section-to-section, linear and nonlinear elastic alignment of all histological sections was hereby the most computational intensive part. For each section, the applied ITK registrations programs were called multiple times at different scale-levels with different parameter sets. In the more interactive, semi-automatic part of the removal of artifacts, only a limited number of sections (20) were processed at the same time whereas in the overall part all sections (7676) were affected. For most of our processing steps, each affected image was automatically transmitted by our data flow management system to a single core.

Table 1. Overview of the computation and processing time (including time spent for the manual repairs) for the individual processing levels presented in Fig. 3.

	Computation time	Processing time
Manual and automatic repair	20 %	85 %
Coarse reconstruction	5 %	1 %
Nonlinear post alignment	65 %	12 %
Intensity correction & BigTIFF image generation	10 %	2 %
In total	200,000 core-h	2.5 years

The maximum resolution for the nonlinear alignment, which was limited by the available amount of memory per core, was achieved on JUROPA at an in-plane resolution of 40 µm. In this case, the maximum amount of memory per core was about 2.1 GiB and was determined by the size of the input image, its internal data representation (which is unsigned integer), the number of internal scale levels (6 at maximum), the number and data representation of meta images (e.g. mask images), and the size and data type (which is double) of the nonlinear deformation vector field. Consuming about 200,000 core hours in 2.5 years (see Table 1) about 580,000 data files requiring 3.5 TiB of disk space have been computed while the original version of the first BigBrain required more than 2,000,000 core-h and 5 years of processing. Full spatial resolution of 20 μm will be achieved at JURECA where the work is continued.

5   Results

The second BigBrain has been 3D-resonstructed (Fig. 6). The quality of the reconstruction is high, as verified in the two virtual sectioning planes below. Minor structural imbalances are primarily due to the computation of the section-to-section alignment at a reduced resolution of 40 μm. They are currently corrected by re-computing the alignments at full resolution on JURECA.

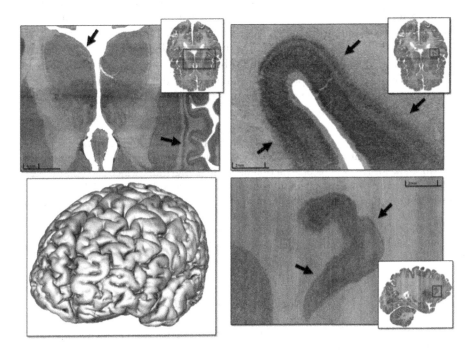

Fig. 6. Images of virtual section planes of the second BigBrain data. Note the smooth borders of the cerebral cortex and subcortical nuclei (arrow heads) in the virtual planes (horizontal upper row, sagittal lower right) as an indicator of the high quality of the 3D-reconstruction. The quality of the images is comparable to the results of the first BigBrain data set presented in 2013, but required much less computing time.

6 Conclusions

BigBrain data with microscopical resolutions are tools, that can be used by the neuroscience community for different purposes. They allow to generate morphometric parameters of brain organization, in form of an atlas, or can provide information for processing of in vivo data sets in order to constrain simulation. To facilitate the generation of such data sets, we have introduced a novel workflow for the 3D-reconstruction of serial histological sections using massively parallel supercomputers, thereby relying on our experience in generating the first BigBrain data set [2]. An efficient data processing performance is guaranteed by the data flow management system implemented that provides a detailed automatic documentation of the processing steps and the complex dependencies of the data sets at each level of the reconstruction workflow. In addition, this framework provides a necessary methodical prerequisite for future BigBrain data sets with even higher resolution. Such data sets pose significant challenges with respect to data handling, analysis, and storage capacities, i.e., Big Data Analytics. For example, images of whole brain histological sections scanned with $1\,\mu m$ in-plane resolution and 16-bit gray value would result in an image size of up to $120,000 \times 100,000$ pixels and 18 GiB per image for the BigTIFF data format. Thus, the total raw data set of a single brain will require about 180 TiB of storage space. The storage space of a human brain data set at $1\,\mu m$ isotropic will require several PiB. The workflow presented here opens new perspectives for analyzing human brain organization at the microscopical level.

Acknowledgments. The authors thank Claude Lepage and Alan C. Evans from the Montreal Neurological Institute, Montreal, Canada, for developing and providing the HPC workflow for the 3-D reconstruction of the first BigBrain, which served as a basis for the recent workflow and for many fruitful and inspiring discussions. We thank Ana Oros-Peusquens and Nadim J. Shah for their contribution in MR-imaging. Funding was provided for this study by the European Union Seventh Framework Programme (FP7/2007-2013) under grant agreement no. 604102 (Human Brain Project), and the Portfolio Theme Supercomputing and Modeling for the Human Brain of the German Helmholtz Association.

References

1. Zilles, K., Amunts, K.: Centenary of Brodmann's map - conception and fate. Nat. Rev. Neurosci. **11**(2), 139–145 (2010)
2. Amunts, K., Lepage, C., Borgeat, L., Mohlberg, H., Dickscheid, T., Rousseau, M., Bludau, S., Bazin, P., Lewis, L., Oros-Peusquens, A., Shah, N., Lippert, T., Zilles, K., Evans, A.C.: BigBrain: an ultrahigh-resolution 3D human brain model. Science **340**, 1472–1475 (2013)
3. Amunts, K., Bücker, O., Axer, M.: Towards a multiscale, high-resolution model of the human brain. In: Grandinetti, L., Lippert, T., Petkov, N. (eds.) BrainComp 2013. LNCS, vol. 8603, pp. 3–14. Springer, Heidelberg (2014). doi:10.1007/978-3-319-12084-3_1

4. Amunts, K., Hawrylycz, M., Van Essen, D., Van Horn, J.D., Harel, N., Poline, J.B., De Martino, F., Bjaalie, J.G., Dehaene-Lambertz, G., Dehaene, S., Valdes-Sosa, P., Thirion, B., Zilles, K., Hill, S.L., Abrams, M.B., Tass, P.A., Vanduffel, W., Evans, A.C., Eickhoff, S.B.: Interoperable atlases of the human brain. Neuroimage **99**, 525–532 (2014)
5. Brodmann, K.: Vergleichende Lokalisationslehre der Großhirnrinde in ihren Prinzipien dargestellt auf Grund des Zellbaues. Barth, Leipzig (1909)
6. Amunts, K., Malikovic, A., Mohlberg, H., Schormann, T., Zilles, K.: Brodmanns area 17 and 18 brought into stereotaxic space where and how variable? Neuroimage **11**(1), 66–84 (2000)
7. Eickhoff, S., Stephan, K.E., Mohlberg, H., Grefkes, C., Fink, G.R., Amunts, K., Zilles, K.: A new SPM toolbox for combining probabilistic cytoarchitectonic maps and functional imaging data. Neuroimage **25**(4), 1325–1335 (2005)
8. Evans, A.C., Janke, A.L., Collins, D.L., Bailllet, S.: Brain templates and atlases. Neuroimage **62**(2), 911–922 (2012)
9. Delescluse, M., Franconville, R., Joucla, S., Lieurya, T., Pouzat, C.: Making neurophysiological data analysis reproducible. Why and how? J. Physiol. Paris **106**, 159–170 (2011)
10. Hömke, L.: A multigrid method for anisotropic PDEs in elastic image registration. Numer. Linear Algebra Appl. **13**, 215–229 (2006)
11. Lepage, C., Mohlberg, H., Pietrzyk, U., Amunts, K., Zilles, K., Evans, A.C.: Automatic repair of acquisition defects in reconstruction of histology slices of the human brain. In: 16th Annual Meeting of the Organization for Human Brain Mapping (OHBM), Barcelona, 06. - 10.06.2010: available on CD-ROM (2010)
12. Zhu, C., Byrd, R.H., Nocedal, L.: L-BFGS-B: Algorithm 778: L-BFGS-B, FORTRAN routines for large scale bound constrained optimization. ACM Trans. Math. Softw. **23**(4), 550–560 (1997)
13. Thévenaz, P., Blu, T., Unser, M.: Interpolation revisited. IEEE Trans. Med. Imaging **19**(7), 739–758 (2000)
14. Lewis, L., Lepage, C., Fournier, M., Zilles, K., Amunts, K., Evans, A.C.: BigBrain: Initial tissue classification and surface extraction. In: 20th Annual Meeting of the Organization for Human Brain Mapping (OHBM), Hamburg (2014)
15. Liu, S., Azevedo, C., Pelletier, D.: The use of BigBrain in MS: An ultrahigh-resolution 3D template for grey matter MRI segmentation. Neurology **82**(10), 6.135 (2014)
16. Wagstyl, K., Lepage, C., Zilles, K., Amunts, K., Fletcher, P., Evans, A.: BigBrain: Automated analysis of laminar structure in the cerebral cortex. In: 22nd Annual Meeting of the Organization for Human Brain Mapping (OHBM), Geneva (2016)
17. JuBrain Cytoviewer: https://www.jubrain.fz-juelich.de/apps/cytoviewer/cytoviewer-main.php
18. Python Software Foundation: Python Language Reference, Version 2.7. http://www.python.org
19. MPI for Python. http://pypi.python.org/pypi/mpi4py
20. Graph-tool: Efficient network analysis with Python. http://www.graph-tool.org
21. Insight Segmentation and Registration Toolkit (ITK). http://www.itk.org
22. The HDF Group: Hierarchical data format (HDF), Version 5. http://www.hdfgroup.org/HDF5
23. Minc Tool Kit. http://www.bic.mni.mcgill.ca/ServicesSoftware/MINC
24. The Open Provenance Model (OPM). http://www.openprovenance.org
25. The Human Brain Project (HBP). https://www.humanbrainproject.eu

Towards Large-Scale Fiber Orientation Models of the Brain – Automation and Parallelization of a Seeded Region Growing Segmentation of High-Resolution Brain Section Images

Anna Lührs[1]([✉]), Oliver Bücker[2], and Markus Axer[3]

[1] Simulation Lab Neuroscience - Bernstein Facility for Simulation
and Database Technology, Institute for Advanced Simulation,
Jülich Aachen Research Alliance, Forschungszentrum Jülich, 52425 Jülich, Germany
a.luehrs@fz-juelich.de
[2] Jülich Supercomputing Centre, Institute for Advanced Simulation,
Forschungszentrum Jülich, 52425 Jülich, Germany
o.buecker@fz-juelich.de
[3] Institute of Neuroscience and Medicine (INM-1),
Forschungszentrum Jülich, 52425 Jülich, Germany
m.axer@fz-juelich.de

Abstract. To understand the microscopical organization of the human brain including cellular and fiber architectures, it is a necessary prerequisite to build virtual models of the brain on a sound biological basis. 3D Polarized Light Imaging (3D-PLI) provides a window to analyze the fiber architecture and the fibers' intricate inter-connections at microscopic resolutions. Considering the complexity and the pure size of the human brain with its nearly 86 billion nerve cells, 3D-PLI is challenging with respect to data handling and analysis in the TeraByte to PetaByte ranges, and inevitably requires supercomputing facilities. Parallelization and automation of image processing steps open up new perspectives to speed up the generation of new high resolution models of the human brain to provide groundbreaking insights into the brain's three-dimensional micro architecture. Here, we will describe the implementation and the performance of a parallelized semi-automated seeded region growing algorithm used to classify tissue and background components in up to one million 3D-PLI images acquired from an entire human brain. This algorithm represents an important element of a complex UNICORE-based analysis workflow ultimately aiming at the extraction of spatial fiber orientations from 3D-PLI measurements.

Keywords: Polarized light imaging · Fiber architecture · Human brain · Workflow · Region growing · Segmentation · Scaling · Supercomputing

1 Introduction

3D-Polarized Light Imaging (3D-PLI) is a microscopic neuroimaging technique that has opened up new avenues to study the complex fiber architecture in the

© Springer International Publishing AG 2016
K. Amunts et al. (Eds.): BrainComp 2015, LNCS 10087, pp. 28–42, 2016.
DOI: 10.1007/978-3-319-50862-7_3

human brain at micrometer scales [AAG+11, AGK+11]. 3D-PLI is applicable to unstained microtome sections of postmortem brains and utilizes the optical bire-fringence of nerve fibers, which basically arises from the highly ordered arrange-ment of lipid molecules in the myelin sheath surrounding most of the axons in the brain. Polarimetric setups (e.g., a polarizing microscope) are employed to carry out birefringence measurements and to give contrast to individual nerve fibers and their tracts. Supported by fundamental principles of optics and dedicated simulation approaches (cf. contribution of M. Menzel et al. in this book "Finite-Difference time-domain simulation for three-dimensional Polarized Light Imag-ing"), the measured signals are additionally interpreted in terms of spatial fiber orientations. Each tissue voxel defined by (*pixel size in x*) × (*pixel size in y*) × (*section thickness*) is assigned a unit orientation vector that reflects the net effect of all fibers comprised in the corresponding voxel. The assembly of all unit vectors is referred to as fiber orientation map.

Considering the vast complexity and the pure size of the human brain, it becomes obvious that both imaging of about 2,500 histological brain sections (each covering an area of up to $150\,cm^2$) with microscopic resolution and sub-sequent image processing require sophisticated data management and efficient computing strategies. A 3D-PLI analysis workflow has been set up that is capable of utilizing the supercomputing facilities provided by the Jülich Supercomputing Centre (JSC) at the Forschungszentrum Jülich, Germany [ABA14]. UNICORE (https://www.unicore.eu) represents a key element of 3D-PLI analysis, since it facilitates automated and distributed supercomputing of the complex workflow composed of parallelized software packages addressing signal and image process-ing tasks such as noise removal, segmentation, stitching, and signal interpreta-tion. Figure 1 illustrates the essential ingredients that make up 3D-PLI, starting from the polarimetric image acquisition and ending with a fiber orientation map of a histological brain section.

One important task within the 3D-PLI workflow is image segmentation to separate image pixels showing brain tissue from those representing unde-sired background or artifacts. A significant number of segmentation algorithms have been developed so far (e.g., [AB94, BJHD96, GSAW05, HFB+05, HFBF12, Hua92, HZ09, KB90, MG98, WMS09, ZCUM11]) and individually adopted to the characteristics of the input images, such as color mode and range, contrast, image size, texture. In the following, we will describe how we adopted the seeded region growing algorithm described in [AB94] for the specific requirements posed by 3D-PLI. We semi-automized and parallelized the algorithm in a flexible way enabling the usage of the same software on notebooks and desktop computers as well as on (GPU) clusters and supercomputers.

2   Methods

2.1   Tissue Preparation and Image Acquisition

An entire human brain was immersion fixed in 4 % paraformaldehyde. After cry-oprotection (20 % glycerin), the brain was deep frozen at $-70\,°C$ and stored till

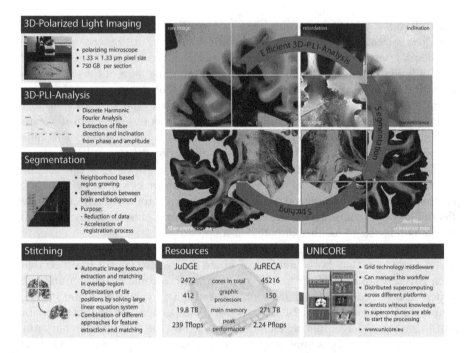

Fig. 1. Sketch of the 3D-PLI analysis workflow. For each field of view a series of 18 raw image tiles is acquired with the polarizing microscope providing a pixel size of $1.33\,\mu\text{m} \times 1.33\,\mu\text{m}$. A sinusoidal variation of the measured light intensity is observed in each image pixel. The individual sinusoidal course of the light intensity essentially depends on the local fiber composition within a tissue voxel and enables the extraction of different modalities such as birefringence (retardation), fiber orientation angles (in-plane fiber direction and out-of-plane fiber inclination), light extinction (transmittance), and fiber orientation (vector) map by means of fitting the sinusoidal signals with the used physical model (Efficient 3D-PLI Analysis, EPA). Afterwards image segmentation is applied to the still existing image tiles (up to 3,000 tiles per section) which are finally combined into a coherent single image of the section (up to $120,000 \times 100,000$ pixels) applying a stitching procedure. The involved software packages are managed by UNICORE and suited to be executed on supercomputers, such as the GPU cluster JuDGE (Juelich Deducated GPU Environment, http://www.fz-juelich.de/ias/jsc/judge).

further processing. The brain was serially sectioned (section thickness: $70\,\mu\text{m}$) using a large scale cryostat microtome (Polycut CM 3500, Leica, Germany), cover-slipped with glycerin, and scanned with a polarization microscope (PM, Taorad GmbH, Germany; pixel size: $1.33\,\mu\text{m} \times 1.33\,\mu\text{m}$). Because of the high resolution provided by the microscope, the field of view is restricted to an area of $2.7\,\text{mm} \times 2.7\,\text{mm}$ and makes single shot imaging of larger brain sections impossible. Therefore, the brain sections were scanned in tiles with overlapping fields of view using a motorized scanning stage (Märzhäuser, Germany). Image analysis was based on the implemented workflow [ABA14]. The segmentation procedure described here was optimized for the 3D-PLI modality referred to as transmittance map. A transmittance value reflects the average of the sinusoidal light intensity curve and is a direct measure of the local light extinction. The transmittance values vary over a whole brain section depending on fiber orientation and fiber density amongst others, which results in an image separating white matter from gray matter regions in the brain.

2.2 Basic Seeded Region Growing Algorithm

The fundamental algorithm adapted for 3D-PLI image segmentation has been introduced in [AB94] for the first time. It is a region growing algorithm based on seeds, which avoids over- and under-segmentation of the images, due to the fact that the number of classes in the resulting masks can be controlled.

The algorithm has been developed for gray-valued images. It divides the image into n classes $A_1, \ldots, A_n$ that are initially filled with the seeds. In every following region growing iteration, one of the remaining, unassigned pixels is added to one of the sets A_i, $i \in [1, n]$. The set T of all non-labeled pixels, defined in Eq. (1), contains all pixels which are not yet part of any class A_i, but which are directly adjacent to at least one. $N(x)$ is the set of all eight direct neighbors of a pixel at the one-dimensional position x.

$$T = \left\{ x \notin \bigcup_{i=1}^{n} A_i \mid N(x) \cap \bigcup_{i=1}^{n} A_i \neq \emptyset \right\} \tag{1}$$

If pixel $x \in T$ is adjacent to exactly one of the A_i, let $i(x)$ be the index for which $N(x) \cap A_{i(x)} \neq \emptyset$. Otherwise, if x is neighbor of two or more A_i, $i(x)$ is defined as the index for which $N(x) \cap A_{i(x)} \neq \emptyset$ and a measure $\delta(x)$ is minimized. The measure $\delta(x)$ defines how similar a pixel x is compared to the region it adjoins. It is defined as follows with $g(x)$ being the gray value of pixel x:

$$\delta(x) = \left| g(x) - \operatorname*{mean}_{y \in A_{i(x)}} \{g(y)\} \right| \tag{2}$$

Alternatively pixels adjacent to two or more of the A_i can be assigned to a set B of all boundary pixels. At the end of each iteration, the pixel $z \in T$ with

$$\delta(z) = \min_{x \in T} \{\delta(x)\} \tag{3}$$

is labeled corresponding to $A_{i(z)}$ and, hence, added to this class or to B. The definitions (2) and (3) assure that the regions A_i are as homogeneous as possible and, by the use of $N(x)$, each of the regions growing from a seed pixel is connected.

The evaluation of Eq. (3) can be accelerated by the use of a sequentially sorted list that contains the positions of all pixels $x \in T$ sorted by $\delta(x)$ so that the first pixel in the list is always the one with the largest similarity to one of the classes A_i.

2.3   Automating the Choice of Seeds

The seeded region growing algorithm requires at least one manually chosen seed per class as input, which means one seed per class and per image tile in case of 3D-PLI data. When automatizing the choice of seeds, it has to be kept in mind that some tiles show brain tissue and background, some show only tissue and some only background. In transmittance maps, the brain tissue is typically darker than the background. Air bubbles, artifacts inevitably introduced during tissue mounting, appear even darker. Therefore, it is possible to base the choice of seeds on the intensity histogram. Due to the different image contents, it is not possible to use only the histogram of one tile for its segmentation, but the joint histogram of a representative subset of all tiles must be considered instead. User intervention is required to define an initial threshold to differentiate between brain and background intensities. This effort is independent from the number of images to be processed, which means it has the complexity of $O(1)$. Consequently, we split the segmentation task into two steps: in the first step the joint intensity histogram is calculated and in the second step the histogram and the user-defined threshold are used to perform the region growing segmentation.

The threshold divides the intensities into two intervals. The median intensity $q_{0.5}$ and the quantiles q_α and $q_{1-\alpha}$ are calculated for every interval. Based on this information, the measure m_c defines the suitability of a pixel to become a seed for the respective class. $g(x, y)$ is the intensity of the pixel at position (x, y).

$$m_c(x, y) = \begin{cases} \frac{g(x,y)-q_{0.5}}{q_{0.5}-q_\alpha}, & g(x, y) \leq q_{0.5} \\ \frac{q_{0.5}-g(x,y)}{q_{1-\alpha}-q_{0.5}}, & g(x, y) > q_{0.5} \end{cases}$$

$$= \max\left(\frac{g(x, y) - q_{0.5}}{q_{0.5} - q_\alpha}, \frac{q_{0.5} - g(x, y)}{q_{1-\alpha} - q_{0.5}} \right) \qquad (4)$$

m_c is computed for every pixel and the measures of all pixels build up the so-called measure image. m_c is the normalized distance of a pixel's intensity to the median intensity of the respective class. In this case, normalization means that the measure is 0 for a pixel with the median intensity and 1 for pixels with an intensity at the quantiles q_α or $q_{1-\alpha}$. For all pixels outside the interval $[q_\alpha, q_{1-\alpha}]$, the measure value is greater than 1. With this definition, every pixel with $m_c(x, y) \leq 1$ is a candidate seed. The candidates with the smallest measure values are considered as the best seeds. Pixels with intensities similar to the threshold intensity are neither good seeds for the brain nor for the background region, because the intensity ranges of brain and background overlap.

The images are segmented into two classes, so that there are also two measure images computed per tile: one based on the brain and one based on the background intensity interval. If candidate seeds were chosen using these measure images without further modifications, also pixels with a variation in intensity or color as compared to neighboring pixels would be seed candidates. To overcome this issue, spatial information is also integrated into the definition of δ.

The measures are first computed independently for every pixel according to (4). Afterwards, a linear smoothing is applied to this first measure image to eliminate outlier pixels.

The calculation of the initial measure and the following smoothing operation can be combined into a single convolution, i.e., a linear filter. This accelerates the execution, because the image has to be traversed only once, which means that less memory access to slow storage components is needed (an image tile is too large to keep it in the cache as a whole). The tradeoff is that the measure value is computed multiple times for each pixel. Thus, the pre-final seed measure images m_p are computed using convolution Eq. (5).

$$m_p(x, y) = w(x, y) * m_c(x, y)$$

$$= \sum_{i=-l}^{l} \sum_{k=-n}^{n} w(i, k) \cdot m_c(x + i, y + k) \tag{5}$$

A weighted average smoothing filter w works best for 3D-PLI tiles, if for a central value p all other entries have the same value $\frac{1-p}{(2l+1)\cdot(2n+1)-1}$ assuming a kernel size of $(2l + 1) \times (2n + 1)$. This is equivalent to an average filter with a higher weighted central value. The central weight is chosen as $p = 0.1$ and $l = n = 4$. Figure 2 illustrates the measure images m_p for brain and background seeds of the example tiles. It is also observable that some of the artifacts in the background region of the image are erroneously labeled as seeds for the brain region. Since these artifacts result in isles of seeds that are much smaller than any brain region, they can be eliminated from m_p.

For all brain seeds, the number N of brain seeds within a square neighbor region with a size of $(\text{radius} \cdot 2 + 1) \times (\text{radius} \cdot 2 + 1)$ is determined. Furthermore, the sum S of the inverted measure values of these neighboring seeds is computed. $\mathbb{1}$ denotes the indicator function, r is the radius.

$$S(x, y) = \sum_{i,k=-r}^{r} (1.0 - m_p(x + i, y + k)) \cdot \mathbb{1}_{\{x \leq 1\}}(m_p(x + i, y + k)) \tag{6}$$

This sum is approximately $N \cdot 1.0 \approx N$ with N seeds in the defined neighborhood, given that the seeds are reliable with intensities similar to the median intensity, and $N \cdot 0.0 \approx 0$ if the seed intensities are close to the quantiles.

The number of neighboring seeds is evaluated to define a new measure value based on S as in Eq. (7). This way seeds are rated higher, i.e., they are more reliable, if they have good seeds in their surrounding. In case of the misclassified brain seeds caused by artifacts, the number of neighboring seeds does not exceed a defined threshold, which means that these pixels will finally not be used as seeds. It can be proven that the respective value of m_f is always greater than 1, in case that $\frac{N}{(2r+1)^2} < t$, threshold $t \in [0, 1]$.

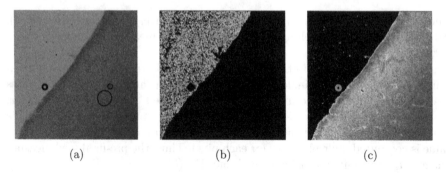

(a)   (b)   (c)

Fig. 2. Candidate seeds. 2a shows a transmittance tile, 2b the measure values for background seeds, and 2c the measure values for brain seeds. All pixels with a color deviating from black are used as seeds for the respective class; the brighter the grey value, the better the pixel is suited as a seed. Pixels with a measure value greater than 1 (black pixels) are not defined as seeds.

$$m_f\left(x,y\right) = \begin{cases} 1.0 - \frac{S(x,y)}{(2r+1)^2}, & \frac{N}{(2r+1)^2} \geq t \\ 1.0 + (1.0 - t) \cdot \frac{S(x,y)}{(2r+1)^2}, & \frac{N}{(2r+1)^2} < t \end{cases} \tag{7}$$

The final elimination of small seed isles is only done for the brain measure image, not for the background. The effect of this step is illustrated in Fig. 3. The definition (7) of a new brain seed measure has the side effect of smoothing the measure values of the remaining seeds.

2.4   Flexible Parallelization for Hybrid Architectures

The huge number of tiles can only be processed in a reasonable time frame, if the segmentation - as well as most other 3D-PLI workflow components - is parallelized and executed on a supercomputer. However, for the development of the software, for pre- and post-processing purposes, and for parameter optimization the seeded region growing segmentation was implemented and parallelized in a way that allows to execute the same code on different architectures. The software was realized in C++ and the parallelization was done based on the Message Passing Interface MPI (cf. [MS] for normal compute cores) and CUDA (cf. [NVI] for NVIDIA GPUs). A detailed description of the parallelization can be found in [Wes14].

Multi-core Parallelization Based on MPI. All tiles belonging to the same brain section can be segmented independently because neighboring tiles are captured with a large overlapping so that all required information is already present in the respective tile.

To port the seeded region growing segmentation to a supercomputer, the tiles of a section are cyclically distributed between all allocated processes. This

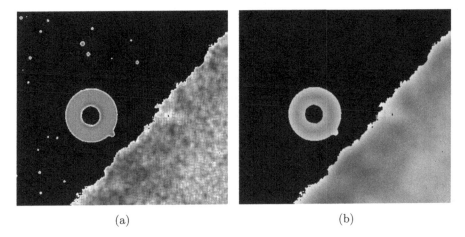

(a)   (b)

Fig. 3. Elimination of misclassified small isles of brain seeds. 3a shows the measure image before and 3b the measure image after elimination. Only big artifacts such as the large circular bubble are not affected. The smoothing of the remaining measure values is obvious.

distribution is used for the computation of the joint histogram as well as for the seeded region growing. In case of the joint histogram, every process first calculates the joint histogram of the tiles assigned to it, so that each process has got a part of the global joint histogram covering the whole intensity range but only a fraction of the tiles. Afterwards, the distributed histograms are collected by a master process using MPI and integrated into a global joint histogram. The seeded region growing of a tile can be done completely independent of the other tiles so that no MPI communication is required at all.

GPU Parallelization Based on CUDA. For the second level of parallelism, the required runtime per section of the different region growing steps was analyzed in a sequential execution, i.e., on a single core without MPI (cf. Table 1). We observed that the first two steps responsible for the choice of seeds consumed 96.67 % of the total runtime. Consequently, we focused on further optimization of the corresponding parts of the software, which appeared to require data parallel operations. Since all computations could be done independently for each pixel, they were perfectly suited for GPU usage. The code (re-)implementation was done based on CUDA with a one-to-one assignment of pixels to CUDA threads. We decided to use one-dimensional thread blocks in form of rows because this shape exploited the data locality of the operations best and the images were stored row-wise in C order. For the processing of two neighboring pixels, the required information of other pixels were almost the same, which also favored the one-dimensional shape of a thread block. Analysis of different thread block sizes showed that the optimal size for the JuDGE GPUs was at 256 threads per

Table 1. Proportions of runtime consumed by the different steps of the segmentation (listed in the order of execution).

Step of the Algorithm	Runtime
Calculation of the measure images m_c and m_p	48.46 %
Elimination of the seed isles out of $m_p \Rightarrow m_f$	48.21 %
Labeling of the seeds in the masks	0.11 %
Seeded region growing	3.21 %

block and $16,384$ blocks for the standard image tile size of 3D-PLI (2048×2048 pixels).

3   Results

3.1   Segmentation Masks

To enable evaluation of the segmentation quality by neuroanatomists, fusion of the input (transmittance) image and the border between classified mask regions appeared to be valuable (Fig. 4). In the selected examples, brain tissue regions were identified with high accuracy by our seeded region growing implementation. Apparently, even small tear-offs in the vicinity of the tissue region were assigned correctly (cf. the magnified regions of interest in Fig. 4). We observed for thousands of image tiles robust and reliable automated choices of seeds. This statement also held true for most small artifacts, which were successfully ignored during the seed determination.

3.2   Runtime and Speedup

Runtime and speedup behavior of both the multi-core and the GPU parallelizations were analyzed (Figs. 5 and 6).

Multi-core Parallelization Based on MPI. The speedup curve for the histogram calculation revealed a linear course for small numbers of processes and flattened out with increasing processes (Fig. 5a). In case of the seeded region growing algorithm, an optimal linear speedup was reached (Fig. 5b). The runtime of the histogram calculation was small as compared to the runtime of the region growing.

GPU Parallelization Based on CUDA. To evaluate the GPU parallelization, the runtimes required by the different steps of the algorithm were measured; the results are shown in Table 2. The proportion of runtime required for the choice of seeds was reduced from 96.67 % to 15.45 % by executing the CUDA

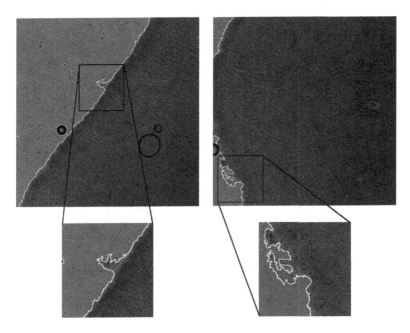

Fig. 4. Segmentation results. The white lines demonstrate the determined borders between tissue and background overlaid with the input transmittance images. The magnified images highlight the convincing accuracy of the segmentation. The extracted regions are connected and do not contain holes.

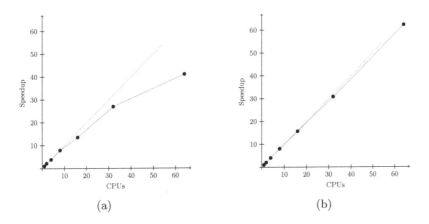

Fig. 5. Speedup curves measured per section on the JuDGE system with up to 64 processes for 5a the calculation of the joint intensity histogram of all image tiles and 5b the region growing.

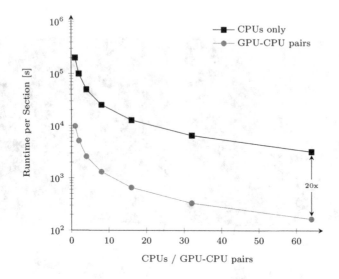

Fig. 6. Scaling behavior of the multi-core approach with and without the additional use of the GPU parallelization. Up to 64 processes or 64 pairs of CPUs and GPUs, respectively, were used.

code instead of the sequential version. This resulted in an increase of the proportion of the (not modified) region growing from 3.21 % to 81.24 %.

The segmentation algorithm was applied to one brain section image using up to 64 CPUs and up to 64 pairs of CPUs and GPUs, respectively, and the total runtime of the region growing implementation was measured (Fig. 6). The trends of the runtime curves were similar, but shifted with respect to each other. Apparently, the additional usage of one GPU per MPI process accelerated the region growing by a factor of about 20.

4   Discussion

One of the fundamental goals in neuroscience is to reveal the nerve fiber architecture, i.e., the structural connectome of the human brain at microscopic scales. 3D-Polarized Light Imaging is a microscopic approach applicable to unstained serial histological brain sections that allows to extract the three-dimensional orientation of fibers from birefringence measurements at micrometer resolution [AAG+11, AGK+11]. To carry out a whole brain analysis, about 2,500 sections have to be prepared (with 70 μm thickness) and imaged tile-wise with a polarizing microscope. Scanning a single coronal section from the central human brain region generates up to 3,000 image tiles, each with a size of 2048 × 2048 pixels. Apparently, any image processing technique (e.g., denoising, stitching, segmentation, registration) that has to be applied to the entire set of (about 1 million) images should provide a high degree of automation, performance, robustness, and reproducibility.

Table 2. Proportions of runtime required by the different steps of the segmentation with and without the GPU parallelization (listed in the order of execution).

Step of the Algorithm	Runtime	
	sequential	*GPU parallel*
Calculation of the measure images m_c and m_p	48.46 %	9.87 %
Elimination of the seed isles out of $m_p \Rightarrow m_f$	48.21 %	5.58 %
Labeling of the seeds in the masks	0.11 %	3.31 %
Seeded region growing	3.21 %	81.24 %

Here, we have presented our implementation of a parallel and semi-automated seeded region growing algorithm to efficiently classify brain tissue and background regions in a vast amount of images. This software can be used as a stand-alone tool, but it is also integrated in a complex UNICORE-based 3D-PLI analysis workflow [ABA14]. An essential element of the segmentation is the choice of seeds, which has been realized in a semi-automated way. The algorithm requires the manual selection of a single intensity threshold within the joint intensity histogram for an entire brain. Since the choice of threshold has to be done only once for the complete data set, this level of automation appeared to be sufficient for the time being. As intended, the seed algorithm identified at most two classes, brain tissue and background. In contrast to unseeded region growing segmentation approaches, such as [KB90, HFBF12], over- or under-segmentation of the images was successfully avoided by this means. Speedup analysis of the multi-core approach for the histogram calculation showed linear behavior only for small numbers of processes. This is due to the fact that for an increasing number of processes the efforts required for inter-process communication also increased while collecting the distributed histograms. Consequently, acceleration significantly slowed down, but the runtime required for the histogram calculation is negligible compared to the region growing.

The region growing algorithm itself was implemented to run efficiently, i.e., parallel, on different supercomputing facilities either in a multi-core setting or on a GPU cluster. Speedup measurements revealed linear scaling behavior for both cases (since no inter-process communication was required), but shifted with respect to each other by a factor of 20. This means that (i) the multi-core approach enables to perform large scale segmentation tasks, if the number of processes available is large enough and (ii) in case of utilizing GPUs in addition, the image processing is accelerated tremendously. To give an example: The segmentation of a whole human brain data set as described above takes about 300 days applying the sequential variant of the region growing algorithm. Using 64 cores reduces the runtime to 5 days and adding GPUs minimizes the runtime even to 6 h. This clearly demonstrates the potential gain of dedicated code parallelization capitalizing on individual computing capacities and capabilities. An acceleration by a factor of 20 appears to be outstanding as compared to reports on accelerations achieved by implementations of other segmentation algorithms, which were typically between 4.9 and 6.8 depending on the employed type of GPU (e.g., [HFBF12]). A multi-thread OpenMP paralleliza-tion [HFB+05] reached a speedup of 2.6 for 4 processes, i.e., an efficiency of 0.65, while a histogram-based clustering algorithm [KB90] showed a linear speedup similar to our approach.

The results of the seeded region growing were positively rated by neu-roanatomical experts. Irregular segmentations occurred in images where transi-tions from tissue into background were hardly detectable (even for the observer's eye) or superimposed intensity gradients across the image (e.g., due to inhomoge-nous embedding in glycerin and gradual diffusion of the glycerin into the tissue) impaired the joint histogram.

Future studies might focus at further optimizing the region growing process, which currently consumes more than 80 % of the total runtime in the GPU parallelized version. The division of each image tile into sub-tiles as described in [HFB+05, BJHD96, HZ09, ZCUM11, MG98] appears to be a reasonable step towards the next level of parallelization. In this case, the sub-tiles may then be processed either using again a multi-core variant (i.e., distributed memory) or a multi-threaded version with shared memory. However, such approach inevitably requires additional communication efforts, so that the perfect linear speedup achieved by the presented multi-core approach is likely to be unsustainable. Thus, the expected gain in runtime due to the new level of parallelism has to be demonstrated to at least compensate the induced communication or synchro-nization efforts. Since the region growing algorithm itself is computed on the CPU(s), a GPU-based parallelization is appealing, but the algorithm might not be well suited for this [HFBF12].

5   Conclusion

We successfully implemented a parallelized semi-automatic seeded region grow-ing algorithm optimized for the segmentation of high-resolution brain section images obtained from 3D-Polarized Light Imaging. Its runtime was minimized in way that the expenditure times required for whole brain sectioning and imag-ing at microscopic scales (months) have become much larger than the process of image segmentation (hours). I.e., the computation time of the segmentation is marginal as compared to the rates the input images become available. One essential strength of our approach is that the different levels of implemented par-allelism can be used in combination or as alternatives, depending on the available computation hardware.

Acknowledgement. This work was partially supported by the Helmholtz Association portfolio theme "Supercomputing and Modeling for the Human Brain" and by the European Union Seventh Framework Programme (FP7/2007-2013) under grant agreement no. 604102 (Human Brain Project).

References

[AAG+11] Axer, M., Amunts, K., Gräßel, D., Palm, C., Dammers, J., Axer, H., Pietrzyk, U., Zilles, K.: A novel approach to the human connectome: ultra-high resolution mapping of fiber tracts in the brain. NeuroImage **54**, 1091–1101 (2011)

[AB94] Adams, R., Bischof, L.: Seeded region growing. IEEE Trans. Pattern Anal. Mach. Intell. **16**(6), 641–647 (1994)

[ABA14] Amunts, K., Bücker, O., Axer, M.: Towards a multiscale, high-resolution model of the human brain. In: Grandinetti, L., Lippert, T., Petkov, N. (eds.) BrainComp 2013. LNCS, vol. 8603, pp. 3–14. Springer, Heidelberg (2014). doi:10.1007/978-3-319-12084-3_1

[AGK+11] Axer, M., Gräßel, D., Kleiner, M., Dammers, J., Dickscheid, T., Reckfort, J., Hütz, T., Eiben, B., Pietrzyk, U., Zilles, K., Amunts, K.: High-resolution fiber tract reconstruction in the human brain by means of three-dimensional polarized light imaging (3D-PLI). Front. Neuroinformatics **5**, 34 (2011)

[BJHD96] Bader, D.A., Jájá, J., Harwood, D., Davis, L.S.: Parallel algorithms for image enhancement and segmentation by region growing, with an experimental study. J. Supercomputing **10**(2), 141–168 (1996)

[GSAW05] Grady, L., Schiwietz, T., Aharon, S., Westermann, R.: Random walks for interactive organ segmentation in two and three dimensions: implementation and validation. In: Duncan, J.S., Gerig, G. (eds.) MICCAI 2005. LNCS, vol. 3750, pp. 773–780. Springer, Heidelberg (2005). doi:10.1007/11566489_95

[HFB+05] Happ, P.N., Ferreira, R.S., Bentes, C., Costa, G., Feitosa, R.Q.: Multiresolution segmentation: a parallel approach for high resolution image segmentation in multicore architectures. In: The International Archives of the Photogrammetry, Remote Sensing and Spatial Information Sciences, XXXVIII-4/C7, 28–32 (2005)

[HFBF12] Happ, P.N., Feitosa, R.Q., Bentes, C., Farias, R.: A parallel image segmentation algorithm on GPUs. In: Proceedings of the 4th GEOBIA, pp. 580–585, May 2012

[Hua92] Huang, C.-L.: Parallel image segmentation using modified Hopfield model. Pattern Recogn. Lett. **13**(5), 345–353 (1992)

[HZ09] Hagan, A., Zhao, Y.: Parallel 3D Image segmentation of large data sets on a GPU cluster. In: Bebis, G., et al. (eds.) ISVC 2009. LNCS, vol. 5876, pp. 960–969. Springer, Heidelberg (2009). doi:10.1007/978-3-642-10520-3_92

[KB90] Khotanzad, A., Bouarfa, A.: Image segmentation by a parallel, non-parametric histogram based clustering algorithm. Pattern Recogn. **23**(9), 961–973 (1990)

[MG98] Moga, A.N., Gabbouj, M.: Parallel marker-based image segmentation with watershed transformation. J. Parallel Distrib. Comput. **51**(1), 27–45 (1998)

[MS] ANL Mathematics and Computer Science. The Message Passing Interface (MPI) standard. http://www.mcs.anl.gov/research/projects/mpi/. Accessed 29 October 2015

[NVI] NVIDIA. CUDA Parallel Computing. http://www.nvidia.co.uk/object/cuda-parallel-computing-uk.html. Accessed 29 October 2015

[Wes14] Westhoff, A.: Hybrid parallelization of a seeded region growing segmentation of brain images for a GPU cluster. In: ARCS 2014: 27th International Conference on Architecture of Computing Systems - Workshop Proceedings, p. 8. Berlin, Lübeck (Germany), 25 Feb 2014–28 Feb 2014, VDE Verlag, February 2014

[WMS09] Wassenberg, J., Middelmann, W., Sanders, P.: An efficient parallel algorithm for graph-based image segmentation. In: Jiang, X., Petkov, N. (eds.) CAIP 2009. LNCS, vol. 5702, pp. 1003–1010. Springer, Heidelberg (2009). doi:10.1007/978-3-642-03767-2_122

[ZCUM11] Zhuge, Y., Cao, Y., Udupa, J.K., Miller, R.W.: Parallel fuzzy connected image segmentation on GPU. Med. Phys. 38(7), 4365–4371 (2011)

Including Gap Junctions into Distributed Neuronal Network Simulations

Jan Hahne[1(✉)], Moritz Helias[2,3,12], Susanne Kunkel[3,4,5], Jun Igarashi[6,7], Itaru Kitayama[7,8], Brian Wylie[9], Matthias Bolten[10], Andreas Frommer[1], and Markus Diesmann[2,11,12]

[1] School of Mathematics and Natural Sciences,
University of Wuppertal, Wuppertal, Germany
hahne@math.uni-wuppertal.de
[2] Institute of Neuroscience and Medicine (INM-6)
and Institute for Advanced Simulation (IAS-6)
and JARA BRAIN Institute I, Jülich Research Centre, Jülich, Germany
diesmann@fz-juelich.de
[3] RIKEN Advanced Institute for Computational Science,
Programming Environment Research Team, Kobe, Japan
[4] Department of Computational Science and Technology,
School of Computer Science and Communication,
KTH Royal Institute of Technology, Stockholm, Sweden
[5] Simulation Laboratory Neuroscience,
Bernstein Facility for Simulation and Database Technology,
Institute for Advanced Simulation, Jülich Aachen Research Alliance,
Jülich Research Centre, Jülich, Germany
[6] Okinawa Institute of Science and Technology,
Neural Computation Unit, Okinawa, Japan
[7] Laboratory for Neural Circuit Theory,
RIKEN Brain Science Institute, Wako, Japan
[8] HPC Usability Research Team,
RIKEN Advanced Institute for Computational Science, Kobe, Japan
[9] Jülich Supercomputing Centre, Jülich Research Centre, Jülich, Germany
[10] Institut für Mathematik, Universität Kassel, Kassel, Germany
[11] Department of Psychiatry, Psychotherapy and Psychosomatics, Medical Faculty,
RWTH Aachen University, Aachen, Germany
[12] Department of Physics, Faculty 1, RWTH Aachen University, Aachen, Germany

Abstract. Contemporary simulation technology for neuronal networks enables the simulation of brain-scale networks using neuron models with a single or a few compartments. However, distributed simulations at full cell density are still lacking the electrical coupling between cells via so called gap junctions. This is due to the absence of efficient algorithms to simulate gap junctions on large parallel computers. The difficulty is that gap junctions require an instantaneous interaction between the coupled neurons, whereas the efficiency of simulation codes for spiking neurons relies on delayed communication. In a recent paper [15] we describe a technology to overcome this obstacle. Here, we give an overview of the challenges to include gap junctions into a distributed simulation scheme

K. Amunts et al. (Eds.): BrainComp 2015, LNCS 10087, pp. 43–57, 2016.
DOI: 10.1007/978-3-319-50862-7_4

for neuronal networks and present an implementation of the new technology available in the NEural Simulation Tool (NEST 2.10.0). Subsequently we introduce the usage of gap junctions in model scripts as well as benchmarks assessing the performance and overhead of the technology on the supercomputers JUQUEEN and K computer.

Keywords: Computational neuroscience · Spiking neuronal network · Gap junctions · Waveform relaxation · Supercomputer · Large-scale simulation

1   Introduction

Electrical synapses, or gap junctions, are classically regarded as a primitive mechanism of neural signaling mainly of relevance in invertebrate neural circuits. Recently, advances in molecular biology revealed their widespread existence in the mammalian nervous system, such as visual cortex, auditory cortex, sensory motor cortex, thalamus, thalamic reticular nucleus, cerebellum, hippocampus, amygdala, and the striatum of the basal ganglia [8,21], which suggests their importance in brain processes as diverse as learning and memory, movement control, and emotional responses [8,9,21]. The functional roles of gap junctions in network behavior are still not fully understood, but are widely believed to be crucial for synchronization and the generation of rhythmic activity. Theoretical work suggests that the contribution of gap junctions to synchronization is versatile, as it depends on the intrinsic currents and the morphology of the neurons as well as on their interaction with inhibitory synapses [16].

Even though brain-scale neural network simulations approach the size of the brain of small primates [17] and many biophysical phenomena are already included, such as the layer-specific connectivity and spike-timing dependent synaptic plasticity, simulations with correct cell densities are still lacking gap junctions. The new technology presented in [15] will hopefully help to overcome these shortcomings. This chapter starts with a brief review of the challenges of including gap junctions into neuronal network simulators. On the basis of examples of increasing complexity we then discuss the user interface of the recently released implementation of the new technology in NEST 2.10.0 [3]. Finally we evaluate results on the performance of the implementation obtained on the JUQUEEN supercomputer and the K computer in comparison to the release (NEST 2.8.0) prior to the incorporation of the gap-junction framework. The conceptual and algorithmic work is a module in our long-term collaborative project to provide the technology for neural systems simulations [11].

2   The Challenge of Including Gap Junctions

To understand the challenge of including gap junctions into a neuronal network simulator such as NEST we need to take a look at the architecture of the simulation kernel and the underlying assumptions. Simulation codes for neuronal networks exploit the delayed and point-event like nature of the spike interaction between neurons. In a network with only chemical synapses with delays d_{ij}, the dynamics of all neurons is decoupled for the duration of the minimal delay $d_{\min} = \min_{ij}(d_{ij})$. The synaptic delays in networks of point-neuron models are the result of an abstraction of the axonal propagation time of the action potential and the time the postsynaptic potential needs to travel from the location of the synapse on the dendrite to the soma where postsynaptic potentials are assumed to interact. Hence, the dynamics of each neuron can be propagated independently for the duration $d_{\min}$ without requiring information from other neurons, such that in distributed simulations the processes need to communicate spikes only after this period [25]. Gap junctions, however, are typically represented by an instantaneous interaction between pairs of neurons of the form

$$I_{\text{gap},ij}(t) = g_{ij} \left(V_i(t) - V_j(t) \right),$$

with V_i and V_j denoting the membrane potentials of the involved neurons and g_{ij} the conductance of the gap junction, also called gap weight. The gap current I_{gap} occurs in both cells at the site of the gap junction. In point-neuron models that assume equipotentiality, the gap-junction current immediately affects the membrane potential. This is unlike the modeling of chemical synapses in point neurons, where any axonal and dendritic delays are subsumed in a retarded spike interaction. Implementing a gap junction between neuron i and j in a time-driven simulation scheme therefore requires that neuron i knows the membrane potential of neuron j and vice verse at all times. The direction of the influence mediated by a gap junction depends on the difference of the neurons' membrane potentials; one neuron is excited, the other one inhibited.

Figure 1 illustrates the effect of a gap junction on the system of ordinary differential equations (ODEs) describing the neuronal dynamics. The originally decoupled systems of ODEs of neurons i and j are combined to a system of ODEs and can only be solved along with each other. Any additional neuron with a gap-junction connection to either i or j adds a further set of equations to the coupled system. In a biologically realistic simulation of a local cortical network each neuron has a couple of tens of gap-junction connections. In consequence the dynamics of almost all neurons are likely interrelated by one large system of ODEs. Although there are solvers like PVODE [7] of the software package SUNDIALS [19], which are specialized to the parallel solution of very large systems of differential equations of the form

$$\dot{y} = f(t, y), \qquad y(t_0) = y_0, \qquad y \in \mathbb{R}^n,$$

they cannot be employed in the context of distributed neuronal network simulations, due to the incompatible overall workflow. These solvers receive the entire system of ODEs given by the n-dimensional function $f(t, y)$ and the initial conditions y_0 as an input and integrate the dynamics by some user specified numerical method. In the more common case of an implicit numerical method, the resulting system of nonlinear algebraic equations is either solved by fixed-point iteration or by Newton iteration. The latter requires the solution of a

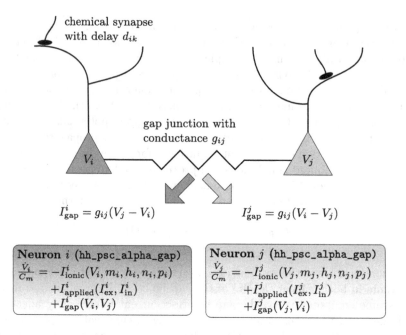

Fig. 1. Representation of two point neurons coupled by a gap junction.

linear system of equations. The idea of parallelization is to distribute the system
of ODEs over the available computation nodes such that each node is solving a
contiguous subset of the system. This is achieved by correspondingly distribut-
ing all vector operations (e.g. dot products, the calculation of norms, and linear
sums) over the computation nodes. Each node computes the local part of each
vector operation followed by a global MPI reduce operation for those operations
where it is needed (see [7] for further details on CVODE). Thus this software
conceptually uses one instance of the employed ODE solver and distributes its
vector computations across the computation nodes. Instead, parallel neuronal
network simulators distribute the neurons over the computation nodes. The parallelization makes use of the fact that the dynamics of the neurons without gap
junctions is decoupled for the duration of the minimal delay $d_{\min}$. The solver is
specified on the single-neuron level and may be different for different cell types.
The membrane potentials of the gap-junction coupled neurons in the I_{gap}-term
need to be approximated and communicated between the neurons at suitable
times. The MPI communication between compute nodes happens collectively
for all neurons on the node and only once for the duration of the minimal delay
$d_{\min}$. These fundamental structural decisions are crucial for the performance of
neuronal simulators and their scalability on supercomputers, where communication is expensive, because it is associated with considerable latency.

A simple approximate solution for this problem is to decrease the communication interval to the computation time step h and to communicate the membrane
potentials of gap-junction coupled neurons at the beginning of each time step.

This way gap currents are assumed to be constant for the duration of the time step when the ODE-system is solved. In [15] we show that the usage of this so called single-step method causes a shift in the membrane potential time course and errors in network spike rate and synchrony. An iterative framework using Jacobi waveform relaxation [24] avoids these shortcomings. The iterative method converges against the solution of the original large system and for a given integration error achieves higher performance. The framework is compatible with the propagation of neuron dynamics on the neuron level as well as communication in intervals of the $d_{\min}$.

3   Using Gap Junctions in NEST 2.10.0

The NEST `Connect` routine enables neuroscientists to express a partial network structure through the connections between two sets of neurons. One dictionary specifies the connection rule and the rule-specific parameters, a second the dynamics of the interaction. The present implementation [3] accepts various connection rules from simple ones, like `all_to_all` and `one_to_one`, to random connections between the sets, such as `fixed_indegree` and `fixed_total_number`. Chemical synapses, the original research domain of NEST, mediate a directed interaction. Therefore the `Connect` routine is designed to specify directed graphs. Gap junctions, however, mediate a bidirectional interaction. Simulation code for spiking neuronal networks exploits the directedness of chemical synapses by representing synapses only on the compute node where the postsynaptic neuron resides. This enables network creation to be organized as an ideally parallelized activity without communication between nodes [25]. In this framework gap junctions need partial representations on the postsynaptic as well as on the presynaptic side to mediate the bidirectional interaction on the undirected subgraph [15]. Hence, in order to connect two neurons through a gap junction, connections in both directions need to be created.   Script 1 shows corresponding code in the PyNEST [10] syntax to create two neurons connected by a single gap junction. The default algorithm of the `Connect` command is `all_to_all`. It connects the neurons specified as presynaptic (first argument) to all the neurons specified as postsynaptic. As each of the n-tuples `a` and `b` contains only a single neuron, the two `Connect` calls achieve the desired result of bidirectional connectivity. Script 2 creates the identical network in two alternative ways employing higher-level connection algorithms. The `one_to_one` algorithm connects neuron pairs specified by explicit corresponding lists of pre- and postsynaptic neurons. For our example of a single gap junction the two lists are formed from the tuple of two neurons `n` and its reverse. Line 9 again uses the algorithm `all_to_all` that has already been employed in Script 1. By using the same list for the pre- and postsynaptic neurons a fully connected network is created. Self connections are excluded by setting the `autapses` flag to false. This alternative generalizes to all-to-all connected networks of an arbitrary number of neurons independent of whether a network of chemical synapses or gap junctions is desired. All three

Script 1. Creation of a gap junction using the command for a directed interaction between two neurons. Two calls are required; one for each direction. Here and in the following scripts we use the syntax of the PyNEST interface [10] of the NEST simulation software as of version 2.10.0 [3]. By convention in Connect(i,j) the interaction is from i to j; i exerts an influence on j. This differs from the convention for connectivity matrices W_{ij} in computational neuroscience. Create returns an n-tuple and Connect accepts n-tuples, lists, and arrays of the numpy module as arguments for i and j. The third positional argument of Connect specifies the connection algorithm; it is not given here and hence falls back to its default value all_to_all. The fourth positional argument specifies the dynamics of the connection; as the third argument is omitted, the fourth argument needs to be assigned by its name syn_spec.

```
1   import nest
2
3   a = nest.Create('hh_psc_alpha_gap')
4   b = nest.Create('hh_psc_alpha_gap')
5   nest.Connect(a, b, syn_spec= 'gap_junction')
6   nest.Connect(b, a, syn_spec= 'gap_junction')
```

Script 2. Creation of a single gap junction using alternative algorithms for directed interactions between groups of neurons. Here n[::-1] is the Python notation for an n-tuple in reversed order. Use of a dictionary for the connection algorithm enables the specification of more details. An autapse is a connection a neuron forms with itself, which is forbidden here. Other notation as in Script 1. The first alternative is only meaningful for a single gap junction, the second generalizes to networks with all-to-all connectivity.

```
1    import nest
2
3    n = nest.Create('hh_psc_alpha_gap', 2)
4
5    # using algorithm 'one_to_one'
6    nest.Connect(n, n[::-1], 'one_to_one', 'gap_junction')
7
8    # alternative algorithm
9    nest.Connect(n, n, {'rule': 'all_to_all',
10            'autapses': False}, 'gap_junction')
```

variants ideally and automatically parallelize relying on the NEST implementation of Connect.

We need to take more care for more complex networks. Let us consider an example where the total number of gap junctions in a given volume of cortical tissue is known. These gap junctions are randomly distributed over all possible

Script 3. Creation of a network with a predetermined total number of gap junctions between randomly chosen pairs of neurons using a predefined connection algorithm. In a first step (line 16) the random network is created as a directed graph. The second step (lines 19–21) obtains the list of connected neuron pairs from the simulator and reshapes the data to corresponding lists of pre- and postsynaptic neurons. The final step (line 23) adds the transposed connectivity matrix to the network by supplying Connect with the lists of the pre- and postsynaptic neurons of the original network in reversed order. The parameters in the script result in a binomially distributed number of gap junctions per neuron with a mean of 60. The script does not work in a distributed simulation as the function GetConnections only returns the part of the network represented on the node executing the command; the set of incoming connections of the locally represented neurons.

```
1   import nest
2   import numpy as np
3
4   # total number of neurons
5   N = 100
6
7   # total number of gap junctions
8   K = 3000
9
10  n = nest.Create('hh_psc_alpha_gap', N)
11
12  r = {'rule':'fixed_total_number','N': K,'autapses':False}
13  g = {'model': 'gap_junction', 'weight': 0.5}
14
15  nest.Connect(n, n, r, g)
16
17  # get source and target of all connections
18  m = np.transpose(
19          nest.GetStatus(nest.GetConnections(n),
20          ['source', 'target']))
21
22  nest.Connect(m[1], m[0], 'one_to_one', g)
```

pairs of neurons in the volume without any further constraints. In particular, a neuron does not have a gap junction with itself, but a given pair of neurons may be coupled by more than one gap junction. Script 3 shows a script implementing this network using the algorithm fixed_total_number of the Connect command. At line 16 the network is created as a directed graph; the interaction is mediated only in one direction. Connect efficiently generates this network instantiating the relevant subgraphs in parallel on all of the compute nodes using parallel random number generators. Therefore on the level of the interpreter executing the script, the actual connectivity is not known. In order to create the complementary directed graph we need to retrieve the existing connections from the simulation kernel, exchange the roles of pre- and postsynaptic neurons, and create this subnetwork in addition. GetConnections, however, only returns the set of incoming connections of the neurons represented on the local compute node. The transpose of this subnetwork therefore, generally, has mainly non-local postsynaptic neurons which the Connect command ignores. Hence, Script 3 does not work in a distributed simulation. This problem occurs for any type of network where the realization is only known to the simulation engine. The alternative is to generate lists of neurons to be connected on the level of the interpreter executing the script before handing them down to the Connect command.

Script 4.Creation of a network with a predetermined total number of gap junctions using an explicit list of random neuron pairs. Same parameters as in Script 3. The random module of the Python Standard Library is used to independently draw K pairs of random samples from the list of all neurons (line 17). The data are in the same line reshaped into two corresponding lists of pre- and postsynaptic neurons. The first Connect command (line 19) interprets the first list (m[0]) as the presynaptic neurons. The second Connect command adds the transposed connectivity as in line 22 of Script 3. The script does work in a distributed simulation, but is inefficient as each compute node draws the full list of neuron pairs.

```
1   import nest
2   import random
3   import numpy as np
4
5   # total number of neurons
6   N = 100
7
8   # total number of gap junctions
9   K = 3000
10
11  n = nest.Create('hh_psc_alpha_gap', N)
12
13  g = {'model': 'gap_junction', 'weight': 0.5}
14
15  random.seed(0)
16
17  m = np.transpose([random.sample(n, 2) for _ in range(K)])
18
19  nest.Connect(m[0], m[1], 'one_to_one', g)
20  nest.Connect(m[1], m[0], 'one_to_one', g)
```

Script 4 illustrates this approach using the **random** module of the Python Standard Library. The drawback of this script is the serialization of the connection procedure in terms of computation time and memory. Each compute node participating in the simulation needs to draw the identical full set of random numbers and temporarily represent the total connectivity in variable m. In the two subsequent calls of connect, each compute node only considers those neuron pairs where the postsynaptic neuron is local.

4 Performance of the NEST Implementation

The gap-junction framework as described in [15] brings two major extensions to a simulation engine for biological neuronal networks such as NEST. Firstly a new event type, the so called secondary event. Secondary events are used to communicate approximations of the membrane potential time courses between neurons. They are emitted and communicated only at the end of the communication interval d_{min} and contain data for every computation time step within this interval. This data is used to approximate the membrane potential of the event-sending neuron in the event-receiving neuron. Secondly the simulation engine is extended by the ability to repeat the neuronal updates of a given time step multiple times until a stopping criterion is met. The latter is required for globally iterative solvers like the waveform relaxation scheme used here.

The design of the framework for gap junctions is guided by the requirement neither to impair code maintainability nor to impose penalties on run time or memory usage for simulations that exclusively use chemical synapses. The first requirement is addressed by the design choice to tightly integrate the novel framework with the existing connection and communication infrastructure of NEST instead of developing an independent pathway for gap-junction related data. To assess to what extent the second requirement is met we measure the performance of (i) simulations exclusively using chemical synapses and (ii) simulations including gap junctions. In this chapter we present benchmarks investigating the performance of NEST 2.10.0. The employed test cases are already included in [15] using a prototype branch of NEST and the JUQUEEN BlueGene/Q supercomputer at the Jülich Research Centre in Germany. For this chapter we rerun the benchmarks with NEST 2.10.0 and add results for the K computer at the Advanced Institute for Computational Science (AICS) in Kobe, Japan.

First we turn to the influence of the new capabilities of the simulation engine on simulations without gap junctions. We measure the deviation in simulation time and memory usage between the last release without the gap junction framework (NEST 2.8.0) and NEST 2.10.0. Although NEST 2.10.0 also contains other changes and new features like a framework for structural plasticity, the most time- and memory-sensitive changes are due to the gap-junction framework. The test case is a balanced random network model [5]. Figure 2 specifies the network model and presents results for a maximum-filling scenario, where for a given machine size VP we simulate the largest possible network that just fits into the memory of the machine (for a discussion of different scaling-scenarios

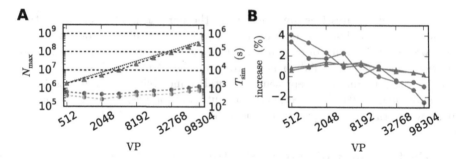

Fig. 2. Overhead of gap-junction framework for network with only chemical synapses. In this and all subsequent figures VP denotes the overall number of processes used in line with our distribution strategy (8 OpenMP threads per node). Shades of blue indicate the JUQUEEN supercomputer, while shades of red show data from the K computer. **(A)** Triangles show the maximum network size of a balanced random network model that can be simulated in the absence of gap junctions ([15], test case 3). The network consists of 80 % excitatory and 20 % inhibitory leaky integrate-and-fire model neurons with alpha-shaped post-synaptic currents. Each neuron has a total number of $11,250$ (9000 excitatory, 2250 inhibitory) incoming connections. Circles show the corresponding wall-clock time (averaged over three runs) required to simulate the network for 1s of biological time. Left semicircles indicate the results with NEST 2.8.0 without the gap-junction framework and right semicircles are obtained with the framework included (NEST 2.10.0). **(B)** Increase of time (circles) and memory consumption (triangles) of NEST 2.10.0 in percent as compared to NEST 2.8.0. (Color figure online)

and their interpretation in the context of neural network simulations see [1]). Although the simulation scenario is maximum filling, in the presence of the gap junction framework we are able to simulate the same network size as before; the increase in memory usage is within the safety margin of the maximum-filling procedure (see [23] for details). Measured in percentage of the prior memory usage (Fig. 2B) the consumption increases by 0.2 to 1.5 percent depending on the number of virtual processes VP. The small increase of memory usage is caused by the changes to the thread-local connection infrastructure and the communication buffer. The behavior on JUQUEEN and the K computer is almost identical. The run time of the simulation increases up to 4.0 percent for simulations with a low number of VPs with an average of 1.1 respectively 0.7 on JUQUEEN and the K computer. The simulation times on the K computer show slightly higher fluctuations, although the measurements are averaged over three runs on both supercomputers. One contribution to the increase in run time is an additional check for the existence of connections using secondary events during the event delivery. A further contribution are additional initializations in the beginning of the simulation. Therefore this increase reduces at higher numbers of virtual processes due to the prolonged simulation time of these simulations.

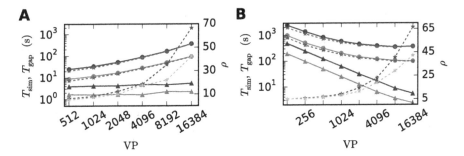

Fig. 3. Costs of gap-junction dynamics. All results are obtained with NEST 2.10.0 and communication is carried out in intervals of the minimal network delay $d_{\min}$ (here $d_{\min} = 1$ ms). The solid curves with circles show the simulation time T_{sim} of a network with Hodgkin-Huxley dynamics (test case 1b of [15]). The neurons have 60 gap-junctions and receive an additional current of 200.0 pA. The solid curves with triangles indicate the simulation time T_{sim} of the same network in the absence of gap junctions. The corresponding colored curves with asterisks show the ratio ρ of T_{sim} with and without gap junctions, while gray curves with asterisks show the difference T_{gap} of both simulation times. Simulations represent 50 ms of biological time at a step size of $h = 0.05$ ms. All simulations use only a single iteration per time interval. (**A**) Weak scaling with $N = 185 \cdot$ VP neurons. (**B**) Strong scaling with $N = 185 \cdot 16384 = 3,031,040$ neurons.

Figure 3 investigates the slowdown due to gap-junction dynamics. This is done by simulating a network with N neurons with Hodgkin-Huxley dynamics with alpha-shaped post-synaptic currents and gap-junction coupling. An additional current ensures realistic spiking behavior. For this test we only employ a single iteration per time interval, instead of using the entire iterative scheme. The obtained results are compared to the run time of a simulation without gap junctions, but otherwise identical setup. This way the difference of the two run times T_{gap} is the time required for the additional computational load and communication. Figure 3A is a weak-scaling scenario. It demonstrates that the scalability of the test case is impaired by the additional communication of the secondary events. Despite the constant number of neurons per virtual process the run time increases substantially. The reason is that NEST 2.10.0 employs global communication with MPI_Allgather to exchange events between computation nodes. Therefore the number of received events per compute node increases with the total number of neurons. The processing of these events combined with the increased communication time leads to a substantial increase in run time. Figure 3B studies the same setup in strong scaling with $N \approx 3 \cdot 10^7$ neurons. In this scenario the number of received events per computation node is constant, while the number of events produced by each compute node shrinks with increasing number of virtual processes. Here T_{gap} decreases at first and then almost stagnates for more than 2048 virtual processes. The saturation is explained by the processing and communication of the secondary events, which constitutes the major contribution to T_{gap} in this setup. As the simulation without gap junctions uses exactly the same pattern of MPI communication this is not an issue of latency, but an issue of bandwidth combined with the processing of the data. The initial decrease is due to the parallelization of the gap-junction dynamics: the computations on the single-neuron level, like the adaptive solution of the single-neurons ODE-system and the handling of incoming events are parallelized. For both scalings the behavior on JUQUEEN and the K computer is similar. The K computer benefits from the faster processors (2 GHz vs. 1.6 GHz) and the higher bandwidth per link (5 GB/s vs. 2 GB/s), but otherwise shows the same scaling behavior as JUQUEEN.

In conclusion the additional time required by simulations with gap junctions on both supercomputers is determined by the total number of neurons N. As the increase in run time is dominated by the processing and communication of the secondary events in combination with a global communication method it cannot be eliminated by using more virtual processes VP. Therefore it is advisable to use as few compute nodes as possible. In this optimal setting the communication required for gap junctions increases the simulation time of one iteration for a network of $N \approx 3 \cdot 10^7$ neurons by a factor of $\rho = 5.0$. This is, however, only the increase for a single iteration. For the accurate solution of simulations with gap junctions an iterative scheme is employed. Therefore one has to multiply the increase in simulation time T_{gap}, as displayed in Fig. 3, with the average number of iterations to receive an estimate of the overall increase in run time. For moderate gap weights the average number of iterations is about $3 - 6$ (for more details see [15]).

5   Conclusions

The framework for representing and simulating gap junctions in NEST 2.10.0 extends the capabilities of NEST, widens the domain of applications, and is available on supercomputers like JUQUEEN and the K computer. The iterative solver guarantees a high accuracy for network simulations with gap junctions regardless of the coupling strength. More generally, the new technology may serve as the foundation for other types of interactions requiring a continuous analog coupling as in so called rate or population models. The ability to roll backwards in time and repeat a propagation step including communication is a further generalization of the simulation engine. Nevertheless, there is still potential for optimization, both in terms of scalability and in terms of usability.

The limitation of the scalability of simulations with gap junctions arises from the need to communicate approximations of the membrane potential time courses between neurons. As the employed communication scheme uses collective MPI calls, these approximations are sent to all nodes that take part in the simulation irrespective of whether or not these nodes harbor neurons requiring this information. This situation is qualitatively similar to the spike times being collectively communicated. However, there are two quantitative differences, the number of connections per neuron (order 10,000 for chemical synapses vs. order 100 for gap junctions) and the amount of information communicated (4 Byte per spike vs. order 100 Bytes per minimum delay). Future work on the simulation code should assess the potential of targeted communication. Due to the low number of connections and their locality, directed communication may be particularly beneficial for gap-junction coupling.

In terms of usability the creation of complex bidirectional networks needs to be simplified. The present user interface requires all connected neuron pairs to be known beforehand at the level of the simulation language interpreter, for example Python, or the directed connections created by a previous `Connect` call to be obtained from the simulation engine using the `GetConnections` command. The former is inefficient as it leads to serialization, as demonstrated by Script 4. The latter, as demonstrated by Script 3, leads to code that is only correct for simulations using a single compute node; more disturbingly, distributed execution will result in incorrectly connected networks without a warning to the researcher. An exception are networks with all-to-all connectivity, as discussed in Script 2, for which a single call to connect produces the expected result for networks with chemical synapses (unidirectional interaction) as well as networks with gap junctions (bidirectional interaction). Future work should explore whether `Connect` can be informed about the intention to create unidirectional or bidirectional connections and whether the combination of specific connection dynamics with incompatible connectivity algorithms can be prevented.

Improvements to the user interface towards the expressive and safe handling of connection algorithms for networks with bidirectional connectivity have a wider scope than just networks with gap junctions. NEST already supports binary neuron models as documented in [14]. Early seminal works exploring fundamental properties of recurrently connected networks studied "symmetric", that is bidirectional, connectivity. A prominent example is the Hopfield network [20], employing binary units. Due to the symmetric connectivity, similar to spin-glass systems, an energy function can be defined and the dynamics is relaxational, approaching the minima of the energy. Functionally these models implement associative memories [2]. Their close relation to systems of classical statistical mechanics allows an analytical treatment and the transfer of earlier results from theoretical physics [18]. Networks of binary model neurons [13] have also played an important role for the development of the theory of fluctuating activity in neural networks [12]. In recent years they experienced a revival, because they enable a systematic fluctuation expansion [6]. Moreover, a fundamental link to spiking networks has been established: both model classes can, to some approximation, be mapped to networks of units that interact by analog variables in continuous time [14]. The implementation of the latter networks of so called rate or population models [4, for a recent review] requires only a moderate extension of the technology to exchange continuous signals, as presented here. However, further work is needed on the user interface and on the implementation of a set of canonical rate models treated in the literature.

The exercise of integrating a scheme for the simulation of gap junctions into an existing code for the distributed simulation of spiking neuronal networks has not only widened the scope of biophysical phenomena now accessible to large-scale simulation, but also taught us further lessons about useful abstractions of simulation engines, expanded our knowledge on the constraints of scaling, and opened a pathway towards the design of a unified simulation engine for some of the most classical neuronal network models.

Acknowledgements. We gratefully acknowledge the NEST core team for an in-depth discussion of the user interface and Mitsuhisa Sato for hosting our activities at RIKEN AICS. Computing time on the K computer was provided through early access in the framework of the co-development program, project hp130120 of the General Use Category (2013), the Strategic Program (project hp150236, Neural Computation Unit, OIST), and MEXT SPIRE Supercomputational Life Science. The authors gratefully acknowledge the computing time on the supercomputer JUQUEEN [22] at Forschungszentrum Jülich granted by JARA-HPC Vergabegremium (provided on the JARA-HPC partition, jinb33) and Gauss Centre for Supercomputing (GCS) (provided by John von Neumann Institute for Computing (NIC) on GCS share, hwu12). Partly supported by Helmholtz Portfolio Supercomputing and Modeling for the Human Brain (SMHB), the Initiative and Networking Fund of the Helmholtz Association, the Helmholtz young investigator group VH-NG-1028, the Next-Generation Supercomputer Project of MEXT, and EU grant agreement No 720270 (HBP SGA1). All network simulations carried out with NEST (http://www.nest-simulator.org).

References

1. Albada, S.J., Kunkel, S., Morrison, A., Diesmann, M.: Integrating brain structure and dynamics on supercomputers. In: Grandinetti, L., Lippert, T., Petkov, N. (eds.) BrainComp 2013. LNCS, vol. 8603, pp. 22–32. Springer, Heidelberg (2014). doi:10.1007/978-3-319-12084-3_3

2. Amit, D.J.: Modeling Brain Function. Cambridge University Press, Cambridge (1989)

3. Bos, H., Morrison, A., Peyser, A., Hahne, J., Helias, M., Kunkel, S., Ippen, T., Eppler, J.M., Schmidt, M., Seeholzer, A., Djurfeldt, M., Diaz, S., Morén, J., Deepu, R., Stocco, T., Deger, M., Michler, F., Plesser, H.E.: NEST 2.10.0 (Dec 2015). http://dx.doi.org/10.5281/zenodo.44222

4. Bressloff, P.C.: Spatiotemporal dynamics of continuum neural fields. J. Phys. A: Math. Theor. **45**(3), 33001 (2012). http://iopscience.iop.org/1751-8121/45/3/033001

5. Brunel, N.: Dynamics of sparsely connected networks of excitatory and inhibitory spiking neurons. J. Comput. Neurosci. **8**(3), 183–208 (2000)

6. Buice, M.A., Cowan, J.D., Chow, C.C.: Systematic fluctuation expansion for neural network activity equations. Neural Comput. **22**, 377–426 (2009)

7. Byrne, G.D., Hindmarsh, A.C.: PVODE, an ODE solver for parallel computers. Int. J. High Perform. Comput. Appl. **13**(4), 354–365 (1999). http://hpc.sagepub.com/content/13/4/354.short; http://acts.nersc.gov/sundials/documents/ucrl-jc-132361.pdf

8. Connors, B.W., Long, M.A.: Electrical synapses in the mammalian brain. Annu. Rev. Neurosci. **27**(1), 393–418 (2004)

9. Dere, E., Zlomuzica, A.: The role of gap junctions in the brain in health and disease. Neurosci. Biobehav. Rev. **36**, 206–217 (2011)

10. Eppler, J.M., Helias, M., Muller, E., Diesmann, M., Gewaltig, M.: PyNEST: a convenient interface to the NEST simulator. Front. Neuroinformatics **2**, 12 (2009)
11. Gewaltig, M.O., Diesmann, M.: NEST (NEural Simulation Tool). Scholarpedia **2**(4), 1430 (2007)
12. Ginzburg, I., Sompolinsky, H.: Theory of correlations in stochastic neural networks. Phys. Rev. E **50**(4), 3171–3191 (1994)
13. Glauber, R.: Time-dependent statistics of the Ising model. J. Math. Phys. **4**(2), 294–307 (1963)
14. Grytskyy, D., Tetzlaff, T., Diesmann, M., Helias, M.: A unified view on weakly correlated recurrent networks. Front. Comput. Neurosci. **7**, 131 (2013)
15. Hahne, J., Helias, M., Kunkel, S., Igarashi, J., Bolten, M., Frommer, A., Diesmann, M.: A unified framework for spiking and gap-junction interactions in distributed neuronal network simulations. Front. Neuroinform. **9**, 22 (2015)
16. Hansel, D., Mato, G., Pfeuty, B.: The role of intrinsic cell properties in synchrony of neurons interacting via electrical synapses. In: Schultheiss, N.W., Prinz, A.A., Butera, R.J. (eds.) Phase Response Curves in Neuroscience. SSCN, vol. 6, pp. 361–398. Springer, Heidelberg (2012). doi:10.1007/978-1-4614-0739-3_15
17. Herculano-Houzel, S.: The human brain in numbers: a linearly scaled-up primate brain. Front. Hum. Neurosci. **3**, 31 (2009)
18. Hertz, J., Krogh, A., Palmer, R.G.: Introduction to the Theory of Neural Computation. Perseus Books, New York (1991)
19. Hindmarsh, A.C., Brown, P.N., Grant, K.E., Lee, S.L., Serban, R., Shumaker, D.E., Woodward, C.S.: Sundials: Suite of nonlinear and differential/algebraic equation solvers. ACM Trans. Math. Softw. **31**(3), 363–396 (2005). http://dl.acm.org/citation.cfm?doid=1089014.1089020
20. Hopfield, J.J.: Neural networks and physical systems with emergent collective computational abilities. Proc. Natl. Acad. Sci. USA **79**, 2554–2558 (1982)
21. Hormuzdi, S., Filippov, M., Mitropoulou, G., Monyer, H., Bruzzone, R.: Electrical synapses: a dynamic signaling system that shapes the activity of neuronal networks. Biochim. Biophys. Acta **1662**, 113–137 (2004)
22. Jülich Supercomputing Centre: JUQUEEN: IBM Blue Gene/Q® supercomputer system at the Jülich Supercomputing Centre. J. Large-scale Res. Facil. 1 (2015). http://dx.doi.org/10.17815/jlsrf-1-18
23. Kunkel, S., Schmidt, M., Eppler, J.M., Masumoto, G., Igarashi, J., Ishii, S., Fukai, T., Morrison, A., Diesmann, M., Helias, M.: Spiking network simulation code for petascale computers. Front. Neuroinform. **8**, 78 (2014)
24. Lelarasmee, E.: The waveform relaxation method for time domain analysis of large scale integrated circuits: theory and applications. Memorandum p. No. UCB/ERL M82/40. (1982)
25. Morrison, A., Mehring, C., Geisel, T., Aertsen, A., Diesmann, M.: Advancing the boundaries of high connectivity network simulation with distributed computing. Neural Comput. **17**(8), 1776–1801 (2005)

Designing Workflows for the Reproducible Analysis of Electrophysiological Data

Michael Denker[1]([✉]) and Sonja Grün[1,2,3,4]

[1] Institute of Neuroscience and Medicine (INM-6) and Institute for Advanced
Simulation (IAS-6) and JARA BRAIN Institute I,
Jülich Research Centre, Jülich, Germany
{m.denker,s.gruen}@fz-juelich.de
[2] Osaka University, Osaka, Japan
[3] RIKEN Brain Science Institute, Wako, Japan
[4] Theoretical Systems Neurobiology, RWTH Aachen University, Aachen, Germany
http://www.fz-juelich.de/inm/inm-6

Abstract. The workflows that cover the experimental recording of neuronal data up to the publication of figures that illustrate neuroscientific analysis results are interwoven and complex. Unfortunately, current implementations of such workflows of electrophysiological research are far from being automatized, and software supporting such a goal is largely in development or missing. In consequence, the level of reproducibility of data analysis is poor compared to other scientific disciplines. Although the problem is well-known and leads to ineffective, unsustainable science, there is no solution in sight in terms of a complete, provenance-tracked workflow. Here, we outline principle challenges that complicate the design of workflows for electrophysiological research. We detail how existing tools can be integrated to form partial workflows which address some of the challenges. On the basis of a concrete workflow implementation we discuss open questions and urgently needed software components.

Keywords: Workflow · Electrophysiology · Metadata · Data analysis · Data storage · Reproducibility

1 Challenges of Storing, Describing, and Analyzing Complex Electrophysiological Experiments

Electrophysiological research has a rich history of more than a century to look back upon. Technological progress has constantly driven the field, enabling researchers to probe the activity of neuronal networks from population measures, such as the electroencephalogram (EEG) or the local field potential (LFP) [8], down to the level of nerve impulses of individual [2,12] cells, using techniques such as intra- and extracellular recordings or various dye-based [3,19], calcium-based [34] or intrinsic [13] imaging protocols. Over the years the technical capabilities to store experimental data signals in digital form has steadily grown, while the actual amount of data recorded from the brain had remained

© Springer International Publishing AG 2016
K. Amunts et al. (Eds.): BrainComp 2015, LNCS 10087, pp. 58–72, 2016.
DOI: 10.1007/978-3-319-50862-7_5

rather constant. Indeed, in the early days of readily available computer hardware, datasets rarely exceeded the scale of hundreds of megabytes, a dimension that was relatively easy to handle even on consumer hardware of the day. The reason for this was two-fold: on the one hand, the neurophysiological recording techniques rarely supported recording from more than a couple of electrodes. On the other hand, few scientists were actually interested in recordings from large neuronal ensembles of spiking cells, since the focus of scientific hypothesis building centered around the coding properties of the individual neurons [5]. Instead, the local field potential (LFP), which reflects to large degree the average synaptic input due to the network at the electrode location [22,23], was often seen as a sufficient description of the collective properties of the brain activity.

The new millennium saw a gradual shift in these paradigms as a result of the failure to explain a broad range of brain phenomena by looking at isolated cells only. This insight was paired with studies that provided experimental evidence for theoretical hypotheses on how the neuronal code of the brain may rely on an intricate population code that reflects neuronal processing by interactions in the network, e.g., population rate codes [16], neuronal assemblies of synchronized spiking [27,31], temporal sequences of spikes as exhibited by synfire chains [1,11,26], or descriptions based on on maximum-entropy models [28,30]. As a result, recording techniques were readily improved to record from up to hundreds of electrodes in parallel [7,38], in addition to technical improvements that allow to isolate the parallel spiking activity from massive populations in calcium imaging [21]. Together with an increase in typical signal sampling frequencies up to 30–40 kHz, the tendency to record sessions in their entirety including epochs outside the stimulations or behavioral trials, and the strict legal requirements to keep data for 10 or more years, we experience a massive increase of the data load that exceeds many commonly available solutions for data storage. Indeed, in modern projects it is not unusual for an experimental study to produce data on the scale of tens to hundreds of terrabytes. Consider, for instance, a study where each animal is recorded with a 64 channel recording device sampling at 30 kHz for 1 h per day, and the behavioral task consists of 10 different conditions, each of which is tested on 10 animals and on 14 days per animal. The expected size of the data will be in the range of 10 Tb.

While it is easy to focus on the sheer data size, a second and possibly even more problematic aspect faced with is the sheer complexity of such experimental data. In previous times, data was sparse enough that the experimenter could almost personally relate to each data trace and experimental peculiarity that may have come up during the experiment. For example, the experimenter would have known, maybe from his lab book or even his memory, that in session 15, the LFP on channel 2 was contaminated by a high-frequency noise and perhaps should be excluded for certain kinds of analyses. The researcher would then manually code the rejected LFP signal in his analysis script. In light of the complexity of modern data, this approach is no longer feasible or possible. Instead, the researcher needs to follow a strict protocol of post-processing steps on all recorded data traces and rely on this generated information along with any other metadata (i.e., the data that describe the generation of the principle data [18,39]) coming from the experiment in an automated fashion during the experiment. In the example above, the experimenter would run a post-processing step to identify unusual frequency contributions in the LFP, and store the resulting information. The code for loading the data would then have to query this information and make a decision on which data to include for the analysis based on all available information. The researcher would no longer actively know which data actually entered the analysis and must trust the automated process and his selection criteria. This is not a trivial step: in addition to the increase in the number of neurophysiological recordings, the intricate design of modern experimental designs also result in an increased information complexity. Additional signals (e.g., the x, y and z coordinates of the arm movement of a subject) may additionally constrain data selection (e.g., when the arm moves outside a predefined range), and need to be incorporated in such an automated mechanism for handling and selecting data.

Once the data is properly recorded, post-processed and selected, the next challenge is to identify analysis approaches that exploit the parallel nature of the data and probe its correlative structure. While a lot of theoretical research has gone in the development of suitable analysis approaches [6,33], e.g., [24,29,32,35,37] to name just a few, most of these methods are far more difficult to understand than methods based on the activity of single or few neurons only. In particular, they cover only partial aspects of the higher-order correlation, and often they require massive computational power, e.g., due to the combinatorial explosion of possible dynamical patterns of activity or the need for extensive Monte-Carlo methods in hypothesis testing ("surrogates", cf. [20]) to account for the non-stationary structure of neuronal activity data. Therefore, the analyst is faced with three challenges: (i) the analysis methods need to be readily implemented, by specialists for that particular method, in a framework that allows the experimenter to apply them in an easy fashion to his data selection, (ii) several different analyses methods need to be carried out in parallel to probe the full structure of the population activity by comparing the results against each other, and (iii) substantial computational resources with access to the high data volume need to be available to carry out the analysis. Luckily, it turns out that the analysis tasks are typically trivially parallelizable ("farming"), nevertheless, they require extensive knowledge on the analyst side on how to use such technology [10]. In addition, the output of many advanced methods for analyzing the activity of many neurons may also become large and requires reliable book-keeping, adding to the storage space requirements. Thus, the analyst must reconsider the strategy for data analysis. Whereas in the past, most computations were performed on the local machine, this approach is no longer feasible and the analyst must plan ahead on which high-performance compute infrastructure the analysis will be performed and where the results will be kept, and how they can be easily accessed for the interactive exploration of the results.

Lastly, it is the analyst's task to collect the various results and compile them into a comprehensive evaluation. Given all of the above mentioned sources of complexity in the acquisition and analysis workflow (data size, data complexity, data selection, the complexity of analysis tasks and their computational demand requiring the use of high-performance computers), it is difficult to keep track of which data were used, which analyses were run with which parameters, whereto analysis results have been copied, and – if analysis steps are interdependent – if they have been run in the appropriate order. Therefore, the availability of a software solution to record the complete provenance information in time (from experimental recording to publication) and across machines (from recording computer, post-processing computers, high-performance hardware, to the laptop on which the final manuscript is written) is in high demand for the scientist.

To investigate whether these theoretical considerations on the pressing practical challenges outlined above are in fact recognized by the community, we conducted a survey[1] among experimental and computational researchers in 2011 (see also [39]). Notably, of 50 responders, 48 % indicated that they saw their work "greatly" influenced by the complexity of datasets and analysis techniques, and 44 % saw their work at least "somewhat" influenced. In addition, the need for improving the current state of workflows and reproducibility in neurophysiology has been recognized by the International Neuroinformatics Coordination Facility (INCF), which has led to two sets of recommendations worked out by leading experts during the workshops on the validation of analysis methods [9] and on perspectives for workflows [4]. We conclude that, indeed, many neuroscientists face a number of serious challenges when it comes to tackling modern datasets with advanced methods for data analysis.

In the following, we will outline to which extent emerging solutions in neuroinformatics can be used to cover parts of a workflow that provides first solutions to some of these challenges (Sect. 2). Next, we will outline a concrete workflow, implemented in our lab, that shows how these parts can be stitched together to form a complete workflow (Sect. 3). Based on this model as an example, we discuss the challenges that are not yet adequately addressed, and we propose strategies for future development that could be used to tackle these shortcomings.

2   Emerging Software Tools for Electrophysiological Data

The challenges in defining workflows for the analysis of modern day electrophysiological datasets are in large due to a lack of a stack of cooperating software tools that complement the workflow in a domain-specific manner. Whereas some disciplines in neuroscience have a comparatively extensive history in developing viable solutions to the challenges for their domain, the long absence of large-scale datasets in electrophysiology has likely been a key factor that explains why only recently such efforts have been recognized as a necessity. In this section, we describe some of these efforts in order to outline how these tools can act together to form a complete workflow in Sect. 3.

---

[1] http://www.csn.fz-juelich.de/survey.

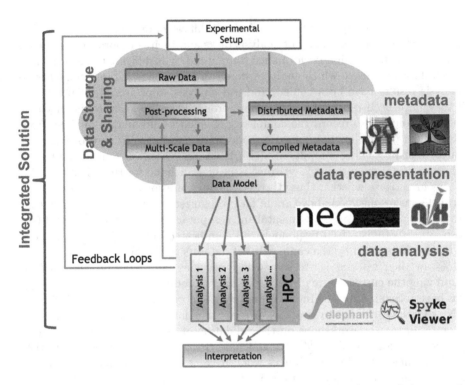

Fig. 1. Construction of a generic workflow for electrophysiological research by way of combining of multiple software tools. The experiment yields principle raw data which typically undergo a series of post-processing steps. In parallel, metadata obtained from the experiment and the post-processing steps are distributed across a number of metadata sources. Using tools for metadata handling, these metadata are collected and organized in a centrally compiled metadata collection. Data and metadata are stored in a location accessible to all collaborators. In a next step, data are read into a standard data representation for neurophysiological data, and individual data records are semantically enriched by relevant metadata (e.g., the stereotactic coordinate of the electrode from which a certain signal was recorded). Finally, a series of analyses is conducted, in part on high-performance computers (HPC), using standard software tools built on top of the standard data representation. By combination of the results, an interpretation of the results is gained, often leading to future changes in the experimental design or post-processing steps. Right: Examples of software tools (identified by their logos) serving the 3 categories: metadata management, data representation, and data analysis.

In Fig. 1 we show a typical generic workflow in electrophysiological research. Experiments typically lead to the data acquisition of principle raw data, consisting of neurophysiological signals, possibly time-dependent descriptions of features of the experimental protocol (e.g., stimuli delivered to the subject), and the read-out of behavioral or response information (e.g., button presses or movement information). Due to the large diversity of the conducted research and experimental setups, these data are typically scattered in a heterogeneous zoo of file formats. Neuronal data is often stored in proprietary formats specific to the manufacturer of the recording system. The large number of vendors of such systems and the lack of a common standardized interface to the data – if any – poses a large problem in exchanging data. Previous attempts to alleviate the situation, such as the *neuroshare*[2] initiative, were unable to provide a common format or a vendor-maintained data access across file formats, programming languages and platforms. Recently, the NWB initiative[3] has developed a novel file format aimed to accommodate for the data structures prevalent in common types of experiments. The increased awareness for the need of scientists to exchange data easily gives hope that vendors should embrace such community efforts to reduce the clutter of different, yet similar file formats.

Meanwhile, a community-driven effort to circumvent the situation of heterogeneous file formats has been put forth by the *Neo*[4] project [15]. At the heart of this Python library lies a hierarchical data model designed to represent generic neurophysiological datasets. A number of community-provided file input/output (I/O) modules are part of the *Neo* library. These enable users to construct such data representations from proprietary and generic source files. On the consumer end, applications that process neurophysiological data can build on data represented by the *Neo* model through the library. Thus, the *Neo* model provides a strong bridge between data and applications, but the need for the community to maintain the file I/O modules is a significant problem in light of the often poorly documented and frequently modified file format specifications set forth by recording hardware manufacturers.

Next to the principle raw data, a second type of data generated by electrophysiological experiments is commonly referred to as "metadata". This somewhat diffuse term refers to all other data that can be collected from the experiment, including such diverse aspects as information on the hardware (e.g., amplifier gains, filter settings), experimental task design (e.g., experimental stimuli used), external variables (e.g., temperature), personal observations by the experimenter (e.g., behavioral anomalies of the subject), or information gathered during post-processing procedures after the actual experiment (e.g., analysis of electrical artifacts in the recorded time series). While the detail and method by which to collect such information has long been the sole responsibility of the experimentalist, for the reasons detailed in Sect. 1 such individual and poorly defined procedures are no longer feasible. First, metadata is typically scattered across multiple files, in a large number of file formats. Second, some metadata may be recorded only on paper or is implicit knowledge carried by the experimenter, and thus not available electronically. A solution proposed by [18] is the open metadata markup language (*odML*) for the hierarchical representation and storage of metadata. In *odML* all metadata are stored in a key-value paradigm queryable via an API available for three of the most commonly used programming

---

[2] http://neuroshare.sourceforge.net/index.shtml.
[3] https://crcns.org/NWB.
[4] http://neuralensemble.org/neo.

languages in the analysis of neuronal data. *odML* therefore provides a practical solution to the problems of data selection on the basis of available metadata. Nevertheless, a major challenge remains the compilation of the various metadata sources into a useful metadata collection in the first place. Recent work [39] demonstrates by practical example how such a compilation process can be accomplished for a realistic, complex neurophysiological experiment in the *odML* framework. The recently initiated complementary *odML-tables* library[5] provides support for user-friendly, GUI-driven entry of metadata into a flat tabular representation (e.g., using spreadsheet applications such as Excel) and conversion to the hierarchical *odML* format. Still, a situation where also data acquisition systems would directly record metadata in a standardized format would provide a significant advantage for the researcher, and guarantee a less error-prone acquisition of information.

The experimenter is now in a position to share with his collaborators (or beyond) a completely post-processed dataset, including a rich metadata collection describing this data. Up to now, we have discussed data and metadata as separate processing streams, yet in an analysis the metadata pertaining to a specific data artifact need to be known and serve as potential query criteria. For instance, data objects holding the spiking activity of a specific neuron should be aware of the signal quality assigned to the corresponding recording electrode during a post-processing step, which is available as metadata. A mechanism to accomplish this goal is the ability to annotate data represented in the *Neo* object model by additional information as key-value pairs, implemented by Python `dict` structures. Therefore, given *odML* and *Neo* as available technologies, we propose here an approach where the experimenter subclasses the *Neo* file I/O class covering the file format in which the primary data is available. The child class is then extended by functionality that additionally reads corresponding metadata information using the *odML* API and appends this semantic information as annotations to the generic *Neo* data object returned by the parent class. By doing so, each experiment is provided with a specific I/O that returns a data object combining data and metadata. Specific parts of this data object can be extracted using operations, such as filtering or cutting, of the *Neo* API. If deemed practical, a number of *Neo* file I/Os can be used to serialize this semantically enriched data object to disk. In this context, *NIX*[6] is an emerging file format that puts a special focus on storing such data/metadata associations in an easily accessible manner.

Now that the experimenter is equipped with a standard data object that contains queryable metadata information and is independent of the original format of the data, he needs access to tools that can be used to perform the actual analysis. A number of applications have emerged in the past years that are based on the *Neo* data model. Of particular interest are applications to perform data analysis. Here, the Electrophysiological Analysis Toolkit[7] (*Elephant*) is a recent

---

[5] https://github.com/INM-6/python-odmltables.

[6] https://github.com/G-Node/nix.

[7] http://neuralensemble.org/elephant.

community-driven effort to establish a library of standard and advanced analysis tools, with a focus on tools that analyze the concerted activity of neuronal populations. The effort is a direct continuation of the *Neurotools*[8] project, which has also served as a the source of inspiration for the *Neo* library. The software *Spyke Viewer* [25] represents a graphical viewer to browse neuronal data stored in the *Neo* data model, and comes with both, a standard analysis library (*spykeutils*), and a plug-in architecture to allow custom code to be applied to the data. On a higher level, *OpenElectrophy*[9] [14] represents a full graphical interface to perform a selected set of interactive analyses. Indeed, even toolkits that provide methods originally targeted at a different scientific community have been effectively linked to the *Neo* data object model in order to make available relevant analysis methods, as can be seen by example of the *MNE*[10] toolbox [17] that is able to process *Neo* data via its `RawArray` component[11]. In summary, already to date, a number of tools exist to perform functional analysis in the domain of electrophysiological research, ranging from data and metadata acquisition to data representation and data analysis.

3   Envisioning an Integrated Workflow for Reproducible Data Analysis

Despite the rapid development of software tools to support the vision of a comprehensive data acquisition and analysis workflow, a number of issues mentioned in Sect. 1 remain as open problems. It may be argued that the most severe of these remaining challenges require nothing less than restructuring the way in which scientists use computers to analyze electrophysiological data. In other words, this is a radical change in the principle workflows that have evolved in labs over the last decades. The inevitability of this shift of paradigms is most vividly justified by the increase in data volume and the increase in computational complexity that goes along with it. While previously data could be stored and analyzed on the personal computers of the scientists, nowadays carrying such large datasets around on one's own laptop or workstation is cumbersome, if not . impossible. The insanity of such an approach becomes even more evident when considering that (large) collaborative efforts to analyze a single dataset become of increasing interest due to the plethora of available methods, and the richness of such datasets. In this light, the concept of collaborators carrying around multiple copies of terrabytes of data, and more so, keeping this data in sync among collaborators as new post-processing steps (e.g., artifact analyses or spike sorting analysis) become available, is impossible.

The natural solution is to have data stored in a central server-based location that is accessible to all collaborators. Indeed, assuming that a compute cluster

---

[8] https://github.com/NeuralEnsemble/NeuroTools.
[9] https://pythonhosted.org/OpenElectrophy.
[10] http://www.martinos.org/mne/stable/index.html.
[11] http://martinos.org/mne/dev/auto_examples/io/plot_objects_from_arrays.html.

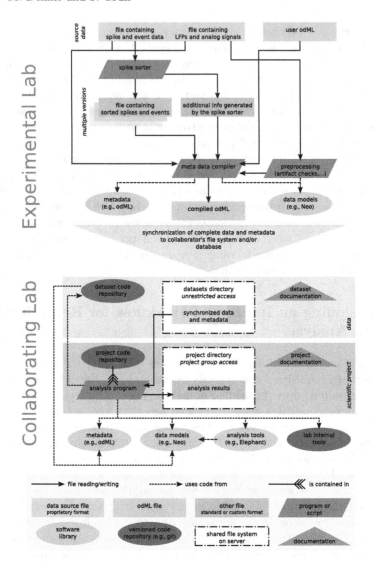

Fig. 2. Concrete illustration of a workflow built on available software tools covering data acquisition and post-processing by the experimenter (upper part of figure), and the server-based data analysis by a group of collaborating theoretical neuroscientists (lower part). The illustration follows the description of the workflow given in the text. Bottom box: description of individual workflow components.

with attached storage is available to the scientists, it is possible to build a workflow based on such a shared resource that embeds the analysis tools described in Sect. 2. As an example, in Fig. 2 we show how the data of one particular experiment is handled and analyzed (modeled after workflows established in our own lab). In this scenario, the data is collected in the experimental lab (upper part of Fig. 2), and a copy of the data is transferred to a collaborating theoretical lab performing the data analysis (lower part). In order to guarantee consistency of the dataset even in a situation where multiple collaborators have access to the data, all data post-processing is performed centrally on the experimentalist side. The source data is spike sorted (a common post-processing step to single out the activity of individual putative nerve cells [12]), leading to a new set of files containing the sorted spikes. In addition, quality assurance tests are performed on this post-processing step. In parallel, the raw recordings are post-processed in a number of other ways, for e.g. trigger detection, artifact rejection and others. Finally, a program, termed "metadata compiler", collects all metadata generated from the experimental data, the metadata entered manually by the user ("user odml"), and obtained from the post-processing steps, and generates from this one final metadata collection using the *odML* library.

The complete set of data and metadata is then synchronized to the collaborator's file server at a different physical location. On the server, the data is accessible to all collaborating scientists working on the data. Thus, only two copies of the data exist – one at the experimentalist's and one at the collaborator's site – avoiding data duplication in situations where multiple scientists or projects depend on the dataset. In addition, dataset specific code is kept in a version-controlled code repository, e.g., for loading the data and semantically annotating it, or cutting data into specific definitions of trials. Bundling such code in a repository guarantees that all researchers may enter the same parameters in their analysis, such as data selections, filter properties, ... The actual research is divided into projects, each typically headed by one scientist. Each project itself has a directory that is used to store analysis results. The analysis scripts for each project are stored in a code repository themselves, and utilize code from the corresponding dataset library, and from the generic metadata (e.g., *odML*), data model (e.g., *Neo*), and analysis libraries (e.g., *Elephant*). The analysis scripts themselves are executed on the compute cluster, which provides adequate resources to perform the analysis. Lastly, both datasets and projects are openly documented by the researchers, using a common blog or other documentation systems of this kind.

While this workflow presents a solution to perform the data analysis, it moves work completely to a remote compute server infrastructure. While this is a viable approach in research disciplines where standardized procedures are blindly applied to the data, an exploratory approach to view and analyze datasets is common and necessary practice in neurophysiology. The reason for this is the highly non-stationary and variable nature of the data that makes frequent inspection of primary data and intermediate analysis results a necessity. To this end, neuroscientists will often scan parameters to see their effect on the data, or visualize results in different ways in order to probe the data for interesting features. The move towards compute cluster-based workflows significantly suppresses the opportunities for scientists to perform such types of analyses due to the difficulty in running visual or even interactive processes – be it due to connection speed, missing graphics packages, or the inability to reserve interactive access to a compute node. Thus, in practice this means that the scientist is forced to revert to copy datasets to the personal computer to perform these exploratory analyses. In addition to the problems of data duplication, the need to keep primary data synchronized locally, and the need to manually copy files, another problem also occurs by the fact that the scientist has to manage the result data and sync it to and from the server in a reproducible, reliable manner.

Two solutions could be envisioned to remedy this situation. First, interactive analysis work could become better supported by the available compute infrastructure by providing the flexibility, ease-of-use and responsiveness comparable to the laptop ("Interactive Supercomputing"). Nonetheless, this solution will always limit researchers to have a high-performance internet connection available. A second option would be to establish the personal computer as an integrated part of the above workflow. To this end, synchronization of data and analysis results to and from the personal device would be performed by corresponding software backends on-demand in the background. Projects such as the git-annexed based *datalad*[12] for version-controlled data records or full-scale workflow engines (e.g., *Vistrails*[13], *LONI Pipeline*[14]), combined with workflow-aware distributed computing systems (e.g., *UNICORE*[15]), present first steps towards such a technology. In order to improve performance and responsiveness in the light of large datasets, the system to manage data should be aware of the internal structure of the data and metadata, such that only selected parts of the primary data, metadata and results (e.g., data from a specific neuron) must be transferred. The formulation of formal data models, such as through *Neo*, are a crucial requisite towards developing such methods for a generic data access.

A further draw-back of the approach in Fig. 2 is that it scales poorly in collaborative settings. First, the method of data sharing is a custom-tailored solution for the specific storage options available to the experimenter and the collaborating lab, and may not be transferable to the scenario that is encountered in a second collaboration. Once data has reached the collaborator's storage, it is then difficult to practically work jointly on a collection of data due to issues caused by the file system, such as access right problems. Moreover, collecting, structuring and visualizing the information about the methods by which analysis results are created across machines by multiple collaborators is a necessity for researchers to manage the data analysis process, but these issues are not addressed in Fig. 2. At the moment only isolated solutions for specific applications exist (e.g., *sumatra*[16]), making it difficult to follow what collaborators are doing due to the incompleteness of provenance information. This holds especially for the experimental lab, which has no access to the work on the collaborator's side. However, solutions for managing data and analysis results, as envisioned above, may also provide a foundation for gathering and synchronizing the

---

[12] http://datalad.org.

[13] http://www.vistrails.org.

[14] http://pipeline.loni.ucla.edu.

[15] https://www.unicore.eu.

[16] http://neuralensemble.org/trac/sumatra.

corresponding provenance tracks from exploratory work and batch analyses. A recent trend goes toward the development of platforms that attempt to address the requirements on data and results storage and synchronization (e.g., $CRCNS^{17}$, [36]) combined with basic analysis capabilities (e.g., $CARMEN^{18}$). Beyond these efforts, platforms emerge that provide a resource for an on-line collaborative exchange by organizing data, analysis results, code, provenance and documentation within groups of collaborators, while retaining access to data and computational infrastructures from supercomputers down to the individual laptop (e.g., the *Collaboratory* of the *Human Brain Project*[19]). From such projects, we can expect to see the development of a large array of tools that will enable to bridge the gaps that currently still prevent a smooth analysis workflow with the increasing access to high-performance computing infrastructure.

Despite these problems centered on the computer science side, Fig. 2 reveals another, more domain-specific challenge: The complex process of data acquisition, metadata agglomeration, and post-processing. While standards, such as *odML*, are useful to represent data in these various steps, the software tools generating data, such as recording software or post-processing tools, do not take advantage of such approaches. In particular, hardware vendors and their acquisition systems must recognize the need to embrace open standards and provide reliable metadata information in an easy format. However, also the individual data formats and tools need to interconnect more tightly. For instance, in Fig. 2 there is still the need for the dataset specific functions, which in large combine the neurophysiological primary data with corresponding metadata in a tedious, manual fashion. A better approach would be a mechanism to perform this step in an automated fashion. Standardized representations of both data and metadata, could facilitate the process (e.g., *NIX*).

The constant improvement and consolidation of tools into one consistent software framework is the key step to provide a convincing argument for experimenters to base their research on these emerging technologies instead of the inferior, but known-to-work home-brew solutions that currently dominate lab work. We recommend that some of the most pressing future work rests in (i) the development of platforms to easily share, access and query primary data and its accompanying metadata from multiple locations, (ii) libraries and applications that facilitate the process of metadata acquisition during the experiment and post-processing, (iii) systems that provide automated, yet understandable documentation and provenance tracks of the analysis to all collaborators in a project, and (iv) making the power of high-performance computing available to a broader community for both, batch processing and interactive exploratory work. A more productive, more reproducible, and ultimately, more fun way of doing science is the likely reward for following this road.

---

[17] https://crcns.org.
[18] http://www.carmen.org.uk.
[19] https://www.humanbrainproject.eu.

Acknowledgments. This work was supported by the Helmholtz Portfolio Theme Supercomputing and Modeling for the Human Brain (SMHB), EU grant 604102 (Human Brain Project, HBP) and FP7-ICT-2009-6 (BrainScales), Priority Program 1665 of the DFG (DE 2175/1-1 and GR 1753/4-1).

References

1. Abeles, M.: Corticons: Neural Circuits of the Cerebral Cortex. Cambridge Univ Press, New York (1991)
2. Abeles, M., Goldstein Jr., M.H.: Multispike train analysis. Proc. IEEE **65**(5), 762–773 (1977)
3. Arieli, A., Sterkin, A., Grinvald, A., Aertsen, A.D.: Dynamics of ongoing activity: explanation of the large variability in evoked cortical responses. Science **273**(5283), 1868–1871 (1996)
4. Badia, R., Davison, A., Denker, M., Giesler, A., Gosh, S., Goble, C., Grewe, J., Grün, S., Hatsopoulos, N., LeFranc, Y., Muller, J., Pröpper, R., Teeters, J., Wachtler, T., Weeks, M., Zehl, L.: Report: INCF Program on Standards for data sharing: new perspectives on workflows and data management for the analysis of electrophysiological data (2015). https://www.incf.org/about-us/history/incf-scientific-workshops
5. Barlow, H.B.: Single units and sensation: a neuron doctrine for perceptual psychology? Perception **1**(4), 371–394 (1972)
6. Brown, E.N., Kass, R.E., Mitra, P.P.: Multiple neural spike train data analysis: state-of-the-art and future challenges. Nat. Neurosci. **7**(5), 456–461 (2004)
7. Buzsáki, G.: Large-scale recording of neuronal ensembles. Nat. Neurosci. **7**(5), 446–451 (2004)
8. Buzsáki, G., Anastassiou, C.A., Koch, C.: The origin of extracellular fields and currents — EEG, ECoG. LFP and spikes. Nat. Rev. Neurosci. **13**(6), 407–420 (2012)
9. Denker, M., Einevoll, E., Franke, F., Grün, S., Hagen, E., Kerr, J., Nawrot, M., Ness, T., Ritz, R., Smith, L., Wachtler, T., Wójcik, D.: Report: 1st INCF workshop on validation of analysis methods (2014). https://www.incf.org/about-us/history/incf-scientific-workshops
10. Denker, M., Wiebelt, B., Fliegner, D., Diesmann, M., Morrison, A.: Practically trivial parallel data processing in a neuroscience laboratory. In: Grün, S., Rotter, S. (eds.) Analysis of Parallel Spike Trains. Springer Series in Computational Neuroscience, vol. 7, pp. 413–436. Springer, Heidelberg (2010)
11. Diesmann, M., Gewaltig, M.O., Aertsen, A.: Stable propagation of synchronous spiking in cortical neural networks. Nature **402**(6761), 529–533 (1999)
12. Einevoll, G.T., Franke, F., Hagen, E., Pouzat, C., Harris, K.D.: Towards reliable spike-train recordings from thousands of neurons with multielectrodes. Curr. Opin. Neurobiol. **22**(1), 11–17 (2012)
13. Frostig, R.D., Lieke, E.E., Ts'o, D.Y., Grinvald, A.: Cortical functional architecture and local coupling between neuronal activity and the microcirculation revealed by in vivo high-resolution optical imaging of intrinsic signals. Proc. Natl. Acad. Sci. **87**(16), 6082–6086 (1990)
14. Garcia, S.: OpenElectrophy: an electrophysiological data and analysis sharing framework. Front. Neuroinf. **3**, 14 (2009)

15. Garcia, S., Guarino, D., Jaillet, F., Jennings, T., Pröpper, R., Rautenberg, P.L., Rodgers, C.C., Sobolev, A., Wachtler, T., Yger, P., Davison, A.P.: Neo: an object model for handling electrophysiology data in multiple formats. Front. Neuroinf. **8**, 10 (2014)

16. Georgopoulos, A.P., Kalaska, J.F., Caminiti, R., Massey, J.T.: On the relations between the direction of two-dimensional arm movements and cell discharge in primate motor cortex. J. Neurosci. **2**(11), 1527–1537 (1982)

17. Gramfort, A.: MEG and EEG data analysis with MNE-Python. Front. Neurosci. **7**, 267 (2013)

18. Grewe, J., Wachtler, T., Benda, J.: A bottom-up approach to data annotation in neurophysiology. Front. Neuroinf. **5**, 16 (2011)

19. Grinvald, A., Anglister, L., Freeman, J.A., Hildesheim, R., Manker, A.: Real-time optical imaging of naturally evoked electrical activity in intact frog brain. Nature **308**(5962), 848–850 (1984)

20. Grün, S.: Data-driven significance estimation for precise spike correlation. J. Neurophysiol. **101**(3), 1126–1140 (2009)

21. Kerr, J.N.D., Denk, W.: Imaging in vivo: watching the brain in action. Nat. Rev. Neurosci. **9**(3), 195–205 (2008)

22. Logothetis, N.K., Wandell, B.A.: Interpreting the BOLD signal. Annu. Rev. Physiol. **66**(1), 735–769 (2004)

23. Mitzdorf, U.: Current source-density method and application in cat cerebral cortex: investigation of evoked potentials and EEG phenomena. Physiol. Rev. **65**(1), 37–100 (1985)

24. Peyrache, A., Benchenane, K., Khamassi, M., Wiener, S.I., Battaglia, F.P.: Principal component analysis of ensemble recordings reveals cell assemblies at high temporal resolution. J. Comput. Neurosci. **29**(1–2), 309–325 (2010)

25. Pröpper, R., Obermayer, K.: Spyke viewer: a flexible and extensible platform for electrophysiological data analysis. Front. Neuroinf. **7**, 26 (2013)

26. Prut, Y., Vaadia, E., Bergman, H., Haalman, I., Slovin, H., Abeles, M.: Spatiotemporal structure of cortical activity: properties and behavioral relevance. J. Neurophysiol. **79**(6), 2857–2874 (1998)

27. Riehle, A., Grün, S., Diesmann, M., Aertsen, A.: Spike synchronization and rate modulation differentially involved in motor cortical function. Science **278**(5345), 1950–1953 (1997)

28. Schneidman, E., Berry, M.J., Segev, R., Bialek, W.: Weak pairwise correlations imply strongly correlated network states in a neural population. Nature **440**(7087), 1007–1012 (2006)

29. Shimazaki, H., Amari, S., Brown, E.N., Grün, S.: State-space analysis of time-varying higher-order spike correlation for multiple neural spike train data. PLoS Comput. Biol. **8**(3), e1002385 (2012)

30. Shlens, J., Field, G.D., Gauthier, J.L., Grivich, M.I., Petrusca, D., Sher, A., Litke, A.M., Chichilnisky, E.J.: The structure of multi-neuron firing patterns in primate retina. J. Neurosci. **26**(32), 8254–8266 (2006)

31. Singer, W.: Neuronal synchrony: a versatile code for the definition of relations? Neuron **24**(1), 49–65 (1999)

32. Staude, B., Rotter, S., Grün, S.: CuBIC: cumulant based inference of higher-order correlations in massively parallel spike trains. J. Comput. Neurosci. **29**(1–2), 327–350 (2010)

33. Stevenson, I.H., Kording, K.P.: How advances in neural recording affect data analysis. Nat. Neurosci. **14**(2), 139–142 (2011)

34. Stosiek, C., Garaschuk, O., Holthoff, K., Konnerth, A.: In vivo two-photon calcium imaging of neuronal networks. Proc. Natl. Acad. Sci. **100**(12), 7319–7324 (2003)
35. Takahashi, K., Kim, S., Coleman, T.P., Brown, K.A., Suminski, A.J., Best, M.D., Hatsopoulos, N.G.: Large-scale spatiotemporal spike patterning consistent with wave propagation in motor cortex. Nat. Commun. **6**, 7169 (2015)
36. Teeters, J.L., Harris, K.D., Millman, K.J., Olshausen, B.A., Sommer, F.T.: Data sharing for computational neuroscience. Neuroinformatics **6**(1), 47–55 (2008)
37. Torre, E., Picado-Muiño, D., Denker, M., Borgelt, C., Grün, S.: Statistical evaluation of synchronous spike patterns extracted by frequent item set mining. Front. Comput. Neurosci. **7**, 132 (2013)
38. Velliste, M., Perel, S., Spalding, M.C., Whitford, A.S., Schwartz, A.B.: Cortical control of a prosthetic arm for self-feeding. Nature **453**(7198), 1098–1101 (2008)
39. Zehl, L., Jaillet, F., Stoewer, A., Grewe, J., Sobolev, A., Wachtler, T., Brochier, T., Riehle, A., Denker, M., Grün, S.: Handling metadata in a neurophysiology laboratory. Front. Neuroinform. **10**, 26 (2016)

Finite-Difference Time-Domain Simulation for Three-Dimensional Polarized Light Imaging

Miriam Menzel[1]([envelope]), Markus Axer[1], Hans De Raedt[2], and Kristel Michielsen[3]

[1] Institute of Neuroscience and Medicine (INM-1),
Forschungszentrum Jülich, 52425 Jülich, Germany
{m.menzel,m.axer}@fz-juelich.de
[2] Zernike Institute for Advanced Materials,
University of Groningen, 9747 AG Groningen, The Netherlands
h.a.de.raedt@rug.nl
[3] Jülich Supercomputing Centre (JSC),
Forschungszentrum Jülich, 52425 Jülich, Germany
k.michielsen@fz-juelich.de

Abstract. Three-dimensional Polarized Light Imaging (3D-PLI) is a promising technique to reconstruct the nerve fiber architecture of human post-mortem brains from birefringence measurements of histological brain sections with micrometer resolution. To better understand how the reconstructed fiber orientations are related to the underlying fiber structure, numerical simulations are employed. Here, we present two complementary simulation approaches that reproduce the entire 3D-PLI analysis: First, we give a short review on a simulation approach that uses the Jones matrix calculus to model the birefringent myelin sheaths. Afterwards, we introduce a more sophisticated simulation tool: a 3D Maxwell solver based on a Finite-Difference Time-Domain algorithm that simulates the propagation of the electromagnetic light wave through the brain tissue. We demonstrate that the Maxwell solver is a valuable tool to better understand the interaction of polarized light with brain tissue and to enhance the accuracy of the fiber orientations extracted by 3D-PLI.

Keywords: Polarized Light Imaging · Nerve fiber architecture · Optics · Birefringence · Jones matrix calculus · Maxwell solver · Finite-Difference Time-Domain algorithm · Computer simulation

1 Introduction

One of the greatest challenges that neuroscientists are facing today is to decode the highly complex architecture and connectivity of nerve fibers in the human brain, the so-called *connectome* [1–3]. In recent years, the neuroimaging technique *Three-dimensional Polarized Light Imaging (3D-PLI)* has proven its potential to reconstruct the spatial fiber architecture of human post-mortem brains with a resolution of a few micrometers [4,5]. It enables not only to investigate the course of long-range fiber bundles but also of single fibers, which makes 3D-PLI a bridging technology between the macroscopic and the microscopic scale.

© Springer International Publishing AG 2016
K. Amunts et al. (Eds.): BrainComp 2015, LNCS 10087, pp. 73–85, 2016.
DOI: 10.1007/978-3-319-50862-7_6

To validate the reconstructed fiber orientations, numerical simulations are used. By comparing the known underlying fiber architecture of the simulation model with the fiber orientations derived in a 3D-PLI measurement, possible misinterpretations in the fiber reconstruction process can be identified. The simulations also help to gain a better theoretical understanding of the interaction of polarized light with brain tissue and to improve the accuracy and reliability of the reconstructed fiber orientations.

2   Three-Dimensional Polarized Light Imaging (3D-PLI)

The measurement and signal analysis of 3D-PLI have been described in detail by Axer et al. [4,5]. Here, we describe only the basic principles that are needed for the presented simulation approaches.

2.1   Measurement

Post-mortem brains are fixated, frozen, and cut with a cryotome into histological sections with a thickness of about $d = 70\,\mu$m. The brain sections are embedded in a glycerin solution and placed in a polarimeter that measures the birefringence (optical anisotropy) of the brain tissue. Part of the birefringence arises from the highly ordered arrangement of lipid molecules in the myelin sheath – an insulating layer which surrounds most of the axons in white matter [6–8]. The polarimeter consists of a pair of crossed linear polarizers and a quarter-wave retarder which are rotated by angles $\rho \in \{0°, 10°, \ldots, 170°\}$ around the stationary brain section (see Fig. 1a). The setup is illuminated by a light source with wavelength $\lambda = 525$ nm and the transmitted light intensity is recorded by a CCD camera for each rotation angle.

2.2   Signal Analysis

Jones Matrix Calculus. For the analysis of the resulting light intensity profile $I(\rho)$, the *Jones matrix calculus* is used [9,10]: Each optical element of the polarimeter is represented by a 2×2 matrix (Jones matrix) and the electric field vector of the outgoing light $\boldsymbol{E}$ is computed by multiplying the associated Jones matrices:

$$\boldsymbol{E} = P_y \cdot M_{\text{tissue}} \cdot M_{\lambda/4} \cdot P_x \cdot \boldsymbol{E}_0. \tag{1}$$

Here, $\boldsymbol{E}_0$ represents the electric field vector of the incident light. P_x, P_y, and $M_{\lambda/4}$ are the Jones matrices of the linear polarizers and the quarter-wave retarder, respectively (see Fig. 1a for definition). The birefringent brain tissue is represented by the Jones matrix of an optical retarder (M_{tissue}) that introduces a phase shift δ between the polarization component along the retarder axis and the polarization component perpendicular to it. The retarder axis (optic axis) is considered to be oriented in direction of the nerve fibers (with in-plane direction angle ϕ and out-of-plane inclination angle α, in the following referred to as *direction* and *inclination*). Relative to the axis of the rotating polarizers, the retarder axis describes an in-plane rotation with rotation angle $\beta = \phi - \rho$:

$$
\begin{aligned}
M_{\text{tissue}} &= R(\beta) \cdot M_\delta \cdot R(-\beta) \\
&= \begin{pmatrix} \cos\beta & -\sin\beta \\ \sin\beta & \cos\beta \end{pmatrix} \begin{pmatrix} e^{\mathrm{i}\,\delta/2} & 0 \\ 0 & e^{-\mathrm{i}\,\delta/2} \end{pmatrix} \begin{pmatrix} \cos\beta & \sin\beta \\ -\sin\beta & \cos\beta \end{pmatrix},
\end{aligned}
\tag{2}
$$

$$
\delta \approx \frac{2\pi}{\lambda} d\,\Delta n \cos^2\alpha,
\tag{3}
$$

with λ being the wavelength of the light source, d the thickness of the measured brain section, and Δn the local birefringence of the brain tissue [4,5,11].

The transmitted light intensity per pixel can be computed using $I_{\text{theo}} \propto |\boldsymbol{E}|^2$ and Eqs. (1) and (2):

$$
I_{\text{theo}}(\rho) = \frac{I_T}{2}\left(1 + \sin\left(2(\rho - \phi)\right)\sin\delta\right).
\tag{4}
$$

Here, $I_T \propto |\boldsymbol{E}_0|^2$ is twice the average transmitted light intensity per pixel (in the following referred to as *transmittance*) and $|\sin\delta|$ the *retardation* per pixel.

Fourier Analysis. To derive the spatial fiber orientation (ϕ, α) for each image pixel, the measured intensity profile $I(\rho)$ is analyzed by means of a discrete harmonic Fourier analysis.

Every set of N data points can be represented by a Fourier series with at most N coefficients ($N/2^{\text{th}}$ order):

$$
I(\rho) = a_0 + \sum_{n=1}^{N/2}\left(a_n \cos(n\rho) + b_n \sin(n\rho)\right),
\tag{5}
$$

$$
a_0 = \frac{1}{N}\sum_{i=1}^{N} I(\rho_i), \quad a_n = \frac{2}{N}\sum_{i=1}^{N} I(\rho_i)\cos(n\rho_i), \quad b_n = \frac{2}{N}\sum_{i=1}^{N} I(\rho_i)\sin(n\rho_i).
\tag{6}
$$

Using $\sin(x - y) = \sin x \cos y - \cos x \sin y$, Eq. (4) can be written in terms of a Fourier series with Fourier coefficients of zeroth and second order [4,12]:

$$
\begin{aligned}
I_{\text{theo}}(\rho) &= \frac{I_T}{2} + \frac{I_T}{2}\sin\delta\,\cos(2\phi)\sin(2\rho) - \frac{I_T}{2}\sin\delta\,\sin(2\phi)\cos(2\rho) \tag{7} \\
&\equiv a_0' + a_2'\cos(2\rho) + b_2'\sin(2\rho), \tag{8}
\end{aligned}
$$

$$
a_0' = \frac{I_T}{2}, \quad a_2' = -\frac{I_T}{2}\sin\delta\,\sin(2\phi), \quad b_2' = \frac{I_T}{2}\sin\delta\,\cos(2\phi).
\tag{9}
$$

To determine the transmittance I_T, the direction angle ϕ, and the retardation $|\sin\delta|$ from the light intensities $I(\rho_i)$ measured at rotation angles $\rho_i \in \{0, 10°, ..., 170°\}$, we assume $a_0 = a_0'$, $a_2 = a_2'$, $b_2 = b_2'$, and $b_4 = b_4'$, whereby the

Fourier coefficients a_0, a_2, and b_2 are computed using Eq. (6), with $n = 2$ and $N = 18$. By rearranging Eq. (9), we obtain:

$$I_T = 2\,a_0 \,, \tag{10}$$

$$\phi = \frac{\text{atan2}(-a_2, b_2)}{2} \,, \tag{11}$$

$$|\sin\delta| = \frac{\sqrt{a_2^2 + b_2^2}}{a_0} \,, \tag{12}$$

where atan2 is the arctangent with two arguments.[1] The inclination angle α can be calculated from the retardation $|\sin\delta|$ by rearranging Eq. (3).

The computed fiber orientations (ϕ, α) of the measured brain section are visualized in a so-called *fiber orientation map (FOM)* (cf. Fig. 2).

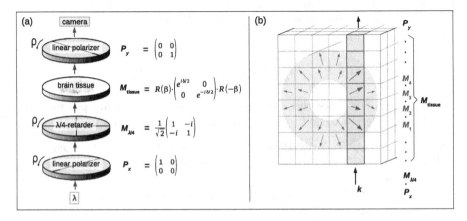

Fig. 1. (a) Experimental setup of 3D-PLI and associated Jones matrices of the optical elements (b) Simulation of 3D-PLI by means of the Jones matrix calculus illustrated for a large fiber: Each myelin voxel (gray) is represented by the Jones matrix of an optical retarder (M_j) whose axis is oriented in direction of the optic axis (arrows). All Jones matrices along the optical path of one image pixel (highlighted column) are multiplied. (Source: Menzel et al. [13])

3   Simulation of 3D-PLI by Means of the Jones Matrix Calculus

One possibility to simulate the interaction of polarized light with brain tissue is by using the Jones matrix calculus. Instead of representing the whole brain tissue (per pixel) by a single retarder matrix (as in Eq. (2)), the birefringence of the myelin sheaths is modeled by multiple optical retarder elements (Jones matrices). For more details, see Menzel et al. [11] and Dohmen et al. [14].

---

[1] The function atan2(x, y) denotes the angle (in radians) between the positive x-axis and the point (x, y). The angle is positive for $y > 0$ and negative for $y < 0$.

3.1   Simulation Method

For the simulation, the nerve fibers are replaced by hollow tubes representing the surrounding myelin sheaths. The simulation volume is discretized into small cubic volume elements (voxels, indicated by the gray mesh in Fig. 1b) and each myelin voxel is represented by the Jones matrix of an optical retarder with the retarder axis oriented along the optic axis of the myelin sheath (indicated by the arrows in Fig. 1b).

To generate a synthetic 3D-PLI image series, a modified version of the Jones matrix calculus described in Sect. 2 is used whereby M_{tissue} in Eq. (2) is replaced by the product of N retarder matrices that represent the myelin voxels along the optical path of one image pixel (indicated by the highlighted column in Fig. 1b):

$$E = P_y \cdot (M_N \cdot M_{N-1} \cdots M_1) \cdot M_{\lambda/4} \cdot P_x \cdot E_0. \tag{13}$$

The synthetic 3D-PLI image series is interpreted by applying the same Fourier analysis as for the experimental data (see Sect. 2). The generated FOM can directly be compared to experimental results.

3.2   Results

A comparison of a measured and a simulated FOM of the optic chiasm of a hooded seal (see Fig. 2) demonstrates that the simulation approach based on the simple Jones matrix calculus can be used to make hypotheses on the underlying fiber structure [14]. Even though the employed model of crossing and non-crossing fibers is quite simple, the most dominant features of the measured FOM are reproduced.

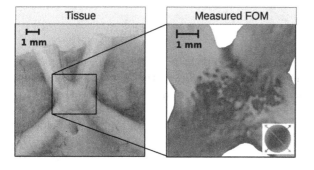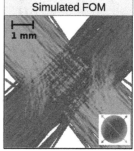

Fig. 2. Measured and simulated FOMs of the optic chiasm of a hooded seal, adapted from Dohmen et al. [14] (Color figure online)

4   Simulation of 3D-PLI by Means of a 3D Maxwell Solver

Although the previous simulation approach is already quite successful in reproducing 3D-PLI measurements, it is limited by the assumptions made in the Jones matrix calculus and the fact that only the molecular birefringence of the myelin sheaths is considered. To account for scattering and interference, we use a more sophisticated simulation approach: The propagation of the polarized light wave through the brain tissue is simulated by a massively parallel 3D Maxwell solver based on an unconditionally stable *Finite-Difference Time-Domain (FDTD)* algorithm [15].

4.1   Simulation Method

Finite-Difference Time-Domain (FDTD) Algorithm. The FDTD algorithm [15] numerically computes the components of the electromagnetic field by discretizing space and time and approximating Maxwell's curl equations by so-called *finite differences*: The Maxwell equations are discretized using the Yee cell [16], see top panel Fig. 3b, such that each component of the electric field E is surrounded by four components of the magnetic field H and vice versa. The propagation of the electromagnetic field in time is computed iteratively using a *leapfrog time-stepping scheme* (see lower Fig. 3b): The components of the E-field at a given time t are computed from the values of the H-field at time $(t - \Delta t/2)$ and from the values of the E-field at time $(t - \Delta t)$, where Δt is a globally defined time step. The components of the H-field at time $(t + \Delta t/2)$ are computed analogously from the values of the E-field at time t and from the values of the H-field at time $(t - \Delta t/2)$. The time-dependent electromagnetic fields are computed at every point in space using Maxwell's curl equations:

$$\frac{\partial E}{\partial t} = \frac{1}{\epsilon}\left[\nabla \times H - (J_{\text{source}} + \sigma_e E)\right], \tag{14}$$

$$\frac{\partial H}{\partial t} = -\frac{1}{\mu}\left[\nabla \times E + (M_{\text{source}} + \sigma_m H)\right], \tag{15}$$

where ϵ and μ are the electric permittivity and the magnetic permeability, J_{source} and M_{source} are the electric and magnetic current densities acting as independent sources of the electric and magnetic field energy, and σ_e and σ_m are the electric conductivity and the equivalent magnetic loss, respectively.

The spatial and temporal derivatives of the electric and magnetic fields are approximated by *second-order central differences*:

$$\frac{\partial u_{i,j,k}^n}{\partial x} = \frac{u_{i+\frac{1}{2},j,k}^n - u_{i-\frac{1}{2},j,k}^n}{\Delta x} + O\left[(\Delta x)^2\right], \tag{16}$$

$$\frac{\partial u_{i,j,k}^n}{\partial t} = \frac{u_{i,j,k}^{n+\frac{1}{2}} - u_{i,j,k}^{n-\frac{1}{2}}}{\Delta t} + O\left[(\Delta t)^2\right], \tag{17}$$

where $u_{i,j,k}^n$ represents the electric and magnetic fields evaluated at a discrete point in space $(i\Delta x, j\Delta y, k\Delta z)$ and a discrete point in time $(n\Delta t)$. This approximation allows to interleave the electric and magnetic field components in space

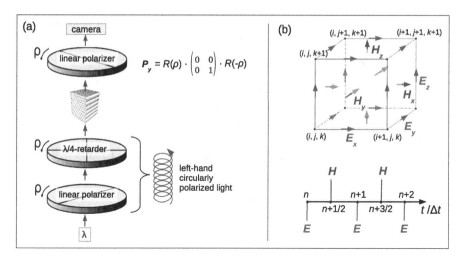

Fig. 3. Simulation principles of the 3D Maxwell solver: (a) The software TDME3D simulates the propagation of left-hand circularly polarized light through a given fiber configuration. The resulting electric field components are multiplied with the Jones matrix of a rotated linear polarizer. (b) The upper figure shows a unit cell of the cubic Yee grid used for the discretization of space (After: Yee [16]). The lower figure illustrates the leapfrog time-stepping scheme used for the discretization of time.

and time at intervals of $\Delta x/2$ and $\Delta t/2$ and thus to implement the leapfrog time-stepping algorithm.

Maxwell Solver Software. For the simulations, we use the software *TDME3D* − a massively parallel 3D Maxwell solver that is based on an unconditionally stable FDTD algorithm. The algorithm makes use of the formal solution of Maxwell's equations in matrix form and the *Lie-Trotter-Suzuki product formula approach*. For more details, see De Raedt [17].

The software solves Maxwell's equations for arbitrary (non-)periodic structures that are illuminated by arbitrary incident plane waves and that consist of linear, isotropic, lossy materials with known permeability, permittivity, and conductivity. The simulations are performed on the *JUQUEEN* supercomputer [18] at the Forschungszentrum Jülich, Germany.

Simulation of the Polarimetric Setup. The Maxwell solver computes the electromagnetic field behind a tissue sample from the given geometric and optical properties of the sample and the incident plane wave. In order to simulate a standard 3D-PLI measurement, the polarimetric setup needs to be taken into account (see Fig. 3a): After passing the first linear polarizer and the quarter-wave retarder, the light is left-hand circularly polarized. The propagation of this light wave through the sample is computed by TDME3D. The resulting electric field components (E_x, E_y, E_z) are then processed by a second linear polarizer rotated by angles ρ, yielding $\tilde{E}_x(\rho)$, $\tilde{E}_y(\rho)$, and $\tilde{E}_z(\rho)$. The x- and y-components of $\tilde{\boldsymbol{E}}$ are computed by multiplying $\boldsymbol{E}$ with the Jones matrix of a rotated linear polarizer $(R(\rho) \cdot P_y \cdot R(-\rho)$, cf. Sect. 2):

$$\begin{pmatrix} \tilde{E}_x \\ \tilde{E}_y \end{pmatrix} = \begin{pmatrix} \cos\rho & -\sin\rho \\ \sin\rho & \cos\rho \end{pmatrix} \begin{pmatrix} 0 & 0 \\ 0 & 1 \end{pmatrix} \begin{pmatrix} \cos\rho & \sin\rho \\ -\sin\rho & \cos\rho \end{pmatrix} \begin{pmatrix} E_x \\ E_y \end{pmatrix} \tag{18}$$

$$= \begin{pmatrix} \cos\rho(E_x \cos\rho + E_y \sin\rho) \\ \sin\rho(E_x \cos\rho + E_y \sin\rho) \end{pmatrix}. \tag{19}$$

The z-component of $\tilde{\boldsymbol{E}}$ is computed by applying Maxwell's equation in free space:

$$\operatorname{div}\tilde{\boldsymbol{E}} = 0 \Leftrightarrow \tilde{E}_z = -\frac{1}{k_z}(k_x \tilde{E}_x + k_y \tilde{E}_y) \tag{20}$$

$$\stackrel{(19)}{=} -\frac{k_x \cos\rho + k_y \sin\rho}{k_z}(E_x \cos\rho + E_y \sin\rho), \tag{21}$$

where $\tilde{\boldsymbol{E}} = \tilde{\boldsymbol{E}}_0\, e^{i(\boldsymbol{k}\cdot\boldsymbol{r}-\omega t+\varphi)}$ (monochromatic plane wave) has been used.

The light intensity recorded by the camera is given by the absolute squared value of the electric field vector:

$$I \propto |\tilde{E}_x|^2 + |\tilde{E}_y|^2 + |\tilde{E}_z|^2. \tag{22}$$

The x- and y-components of the electric field yield Fourier coefficients of zeroth and second order in ρ:

$$|\tilde{E}_x|^2 + |\tilde{E}_y|^2 \stackrel{(19)}{=} \cos^2\rho\,|E_x|^2 + \sin^2\rho\,|E_y|^2 + \sin\rho\cos\rho\big(E_x E_y^* + E_x^* E_y\big) \tag{23}$$

$$= \frac{1}{2}\Big(|E_x|^2 + |E_y|^2\Big) + \frac{1}{2}\Big(|E_x|^2 - |E_y|^2\Big)\cos(2\rho) \tag{24}$$

$$+ \frac{1}{2}\Big(E_x E_y^* + E_x^* E_y\Big)\sin(2\rho) \tag{25}$$

$$\equiv c_0 + c_2\,\cos(2\rho) + d_2\,\sin(2\rho). \tag{26}$$

Similar analytical calculations show that the z-component of the electric field yields Fourier coefficients of zeroth, second, and fourth order in ρ:

$$|\tilde{E}_z|^2 \stackrel{(21)}{=} e_0 + e_2\,\cos(2\rho) + f_2\,\sin(2\rho) + e_4\,\cos(4\rho) + f_4\,\sin(4\rho), \tag{27}$$

where e_n and f_n are analytical functions of the wave vector $\boldsymbol{k}$ and $E_{x,y}$.

The transmitted light intensity $I(\rho)$ can therefore be represented by means of a Fourier series with Fourier coefficients a_0, a_2, b_2, a_4, and b_4:

$$I(\rho) = a_0 + a_2\,\cos(2\rho) + b_2\,\sin(2\rho) + a_4\,\cos(4\rho) + b_4\,\sin(4\rho), \tag{28}$$

$$a_0 = c_0 + e_0, \quad a_2 = c_2 + e_2, \quad b_2 = d_2 + f_2, \quad a_4 = e_4, \quad b_4 = f_4. \tag{29}$$

From the five Fourier coefficients, the light intensity profile $I(\rho)$ is derived for arbitrary rotation angles ρ.

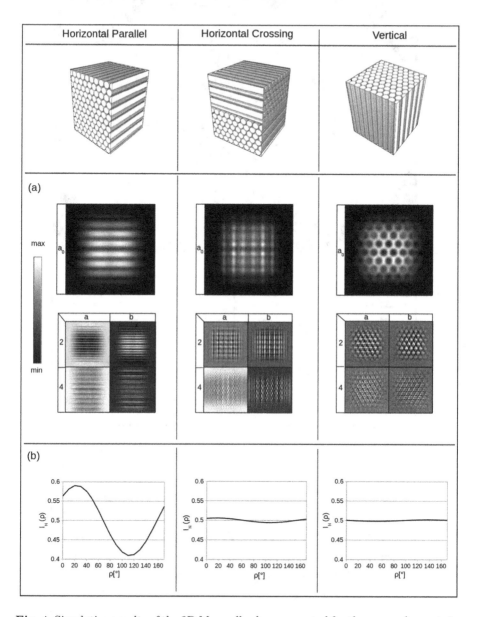

Fig. 4. Simulation results of the 3D Maxwell solver computed for three samples containing horizontal parallel, horizontal crossing, and vertical fibers, respectively: (a) Fourier coefficient maps (a_0, a_2, a_4, b_2, b_4; cf. Eq. (29)) (b) Light intensity profiles (averaged and normalized recorded light intensity plotted against the rotation angle ρ)

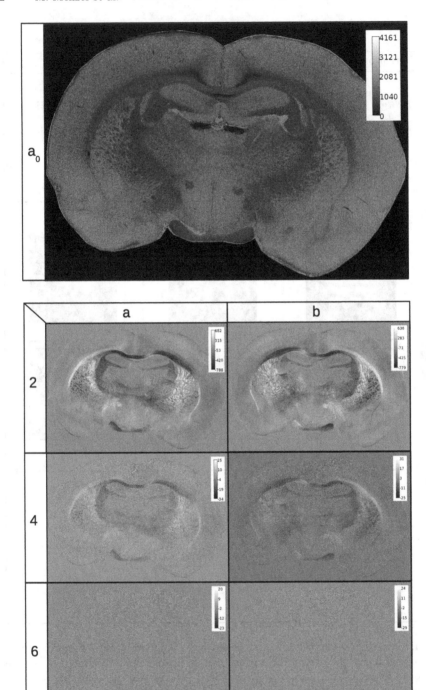

Fig. 5. Fourier coefficient maps (a_0, a_2, a_4, a_6, b_2, b_4, b_6; cf. Eq. (6)) of a coronal rat brain section measured with 3D-PLI

4.2   Results

Simulated Data. Figure 4 shows the computed Fourier coefficients and light intensity profiles for three samples containing horizontal parallel, horizontal crossing, and vertical fibers, respectively. The fibers were simulated as solid cylinders with diameters of $1\,\mu$m and arranged in hexagonal bundles with inter-fiber distances of $0.1\,\mu$m in a box of $10 \times 10 \times 12\,\mu$m^3. The simulations were performed with uniaxial perfectly matched layer absorbing boundary conditions [19], a Yee cell of 25 nm side length, and $\lambda = 525$ nm. The refractive indices of the fibers and the surroundings were chosen as 1.47 and 1.37 (according to measurements of the refractive indices of myelin and the embedding glycerin solution).

Similar to a 3D-PLI measurement, the transmittance $I_T \propto a_0$ shows the underlying fiber structure (see Fig. 4a). The (averaged and normalized) light intensity profiles $I(\rho)$ show a strong sinusoidal signal for horizontal parallel fibers, whereas the signal amplitude for horizontal crossing and vertical fibers is very small (see Fig. 4b) – an effect that can also be observed in a standard 3D-PLI measurement [4,5,14]. This demonstrates that the Maxwell solver is able to reproduce the most dominant effects of the 3D-PLI measurement without assuming any intrinsic birefringence of the nerve fibers.

Experimental Data. To derive the spatial fiber orientations in a standard 3D-PLI analysis, only the Fourier coefficients of zeroth and second order are extracted from the measured signal (see Eqs. (10)–(12)). However, the simulations with the Maxwell solver suggest that for non-normal incident light ($E_z \neq 0$), Fourier coefficients of fourth order will also be generated (cf. Eq. (27)).

Figure 5 shows the Fourier coefficient maps (up to the sixth order) computed from a 3D-PLI measurement of a coronal rat brain section. As can be seen, the Fourier coefficients of fourth order are smaller than the Fourier coefficients of second order, but they still show the underlying tissue structure. Fourier coefficients of higher orders do not contain valuable tissue information and are probably due to noise. This suggests that non-normal incident light (e.g. caused by scattering) leads to Fourier coefficients of fourth order which contain valuable signal information. Therefore, a_4 and b_4 should also be taken into account when computing the fiber orientations from the measured 3D-PLI light intensity profile.

5   Conclusion

The 3D Maxwell solver has proven to be a valuable tool for simulating 3D-PLI. It models the interaction of polarized light with brain tissue without assuming any intrinsic birefringence of the nerve fibers. Nevertheless, the Maxwell solver reproduces the most dominant features observed in a 3D-PLI measurement and opens up new ways to improve the accuracy of the extracted fiber orientations: The FDTD simulations suggest, for example, that the Fourier coefficients of fourth order contain valuable structural information and should be incorporated in an enhanced signal analysis of 3D-PLI.

Acknowledgments. Our work has been supported by the Helmholtz Association portfolio theme 'Supercomputing and Modeling for the Human Brain', by the European Union Seventh Framework Programme (FP7/2007-2013) under grant agreement No. 604102 (Human Brain Project), and partially by the National Institutes of Health under grant agreement No. R01MH 092311.

We gratefully acknowledge the computing time granted by the JARA-HPC Vergabegremium and provided on the JARA-HPC Partition part of the supercomputer JUQUEEN [18] at Forschungszentrum Jülich.

We would like to thank M. Cremer, Ch. Schramm, and P. Nysten for the preparation of the histological brain sections.

References

1. Behrens, T.E.J., Sporns, O.: Human connectomics. Current Opin. Neurobiol. **22**(1), 144–153 (2012). doi:10.1016/j.conb.2011.08.005
2. Sporns, O., Tononi, G., Kötter, R.: The human connectome: a structural description of the human brain. PLoS Comput. Biol. **1**(4), 245–251 (2005). doi:10.1371/journal.pcbi.0010042
3. Sporns, O.: The human connectome: linking structure and function in the human brain. In: Johansen-Berg, H., Behrens, T.E.J. (eds.) Diffusion MRI: From Quantitative Measurement to in vivo Neuroanatomy, pp. 309–332, 1st edn. Academic Press, Amsterdam (2009). doi:10.1371/journal.pcbi.0010042.
4. Axer, M., Amunts, K., Grässel, D., Palm, C., Dammers, J., Axer, H., Pietrzyk, U., Zilles, K.: A novel approach to the human connectome: Ultra-high resolution mapping of fiber tracts in the brain. NeuroImage **54**(2), 1091–1101 (2011). doi:10.1016/j.neuroimage.2010.08.075
5. Axer, M., Grässel, D., Kleiner, M., Dammers, J., Dickscheid, T., Reckfort, J., Hütz, T., Eiben, B., Pietrzyk, U., Zilles, K., Amunts, K.: High-resolution fiber tract reconstruction in the human brain by means of three-dimensional polarized light imaging. Frontiers Neuroinform. **5**(34), 1–13 (2011). doi:10.3389/fninf.2011.00034
6. Göthlin, G.F.: Die doppelbrechenden Eigenschaften des Nervengewebes - ihre Ursachen und ihre biologischen Konsequenzen. Kungl. Svenska Vetenskapskakademiens Handlingar. **51**(1), 1–91 (1913)
7. Bear, R.S.: The structure of the myelin sheath. Optical studies. Neurosci. Res. Program Bull. **9**(4), 507–510 (1971)
8. Quarles, R.H., Macklin, W.B., Morell, P.: Myelin formation, structure and biochemistry. In: Siegel, G., Albers, R.W., Brady, S., Price, D. (eds.) Basic Neurochemistry: Molecular, Cellular and Medical Aspects, pp. 51–71, 7th edn. Elsevier Academic Press, Burlington (2006)
9. Jones, R.C.: A new calculus for the treatment of optical systems. J. Optical Soc. Am. **31**, 488–503 (1941). doi:10.1364/JOSA.31.000488
10. Jones, R.C.: A new calculus for the treatment of optical systems. iv. J. Optical Soc. Am. **32**, 486–486 (1942). doi:10.1364/JOSA.31.000488
11. Menzel, M., Michielsen, K., De Raedt, H., Reckfort, J., Amunts, K., Axer, M.: A Jones matrix formalism for simulating three-dimensional polarized light imaging of brain tissue. J. R. Soc. Interface **12**, 20150734 (2015). doi:10.1098/rsif.2015.0734
12. Glazer, A.M., Lewis, J.G., Kaminsky, W.: An automatic optical imaging system for birefringent media. Proc. R. Soc. A **452**, 2751–2765 (1996). doi:10.1098/rspa.1996.0145

13. Menzel, M., Dohmen, M., De Raedt, H., Michielsen, K., Amunts, K., Axer, M.: Simulation-based validation of the physical model in 3D polarized light imaging. Optics and the Life Sciences, OSA Technical Digest (online), JT3A.33 (2015) doi:10.1364/BODA.2015.JT3A.33

14. Dohmen, M., Menzel, M., Wiese, H., Reckfort, J., Hanke, F., Pietrzyk, U., Zilles, K., Amunts, K., Axer, M.: Understanding fiber mixture by simulation in 3D Polarized Light Imaging. NeuroImage **111**, 464–475 (2015). doi:10.1016/j.neuroimage.2015.02.020

15. Taflove, A., Hagness, S.C.: Computational Electrodynamics: The Finite- Difference Time-Domain Method, 3rd edn. Artech House, Boston (2005)

16. Yee, K.S.: Numerical solution of initial boundary value problems involving Maxwell's equations in isotropic media. IEEE Trans. Antennas Propag. **14**, 302–307 (1966). doi:10.1109/TAP.1966.1138693

17. De Raedt, H.: Advances in unconditionally stable techniques. In: Taflove, A., Hagness, S.C. (eds.) Computational Electrodynamics: The Finite-Difference Time-Domain Method, Chap. 18, 3rd edn. Artech House, Boston (2005)

18. Stephan, M., Docter, J.: JUQUEEN: IBM Blue Gene/Q supercomputer system at the Jülich supercomputing centre. J. Large-Scale Res. Facil. **1**, A1 (2015). doi:10.17815/jlsrf-1-18

19. De Raedt, H., Michielsen, K.: Unconditionally stable perfectly matched layer boundary conditions. Physica Status Solidi (b) **244**(10), 3497–3505 (2007). doi:10.1002/pssb.200743148

Visual Processing in Cortical Architecture from Neuroscience to Neuromorphic Computing

Tobias Brosch, Stephan Tschechne, and Heiko Neumann[✉]

Neural Information Processing, Faculty of Engineering, Computer Science, and Psychology, Ulm University, Oberer Eselsberg, 89081 Ulm, Germany
{tobias.brosch,stephan.tschechne,heiko.neumann}@uni-ulm.de
http://www.uni-ulm.de/in/neuroinformatik/mitarbeiter/

Abstract. Primate cortices are organized into different layers which constitute a compartmental structure on a functional level. We show how composite structural elements form building blocks to define canonical elements for columnar computation in cortex. As a further abstraction, we define a dynamical three-stage model of a cortical column for processing that allows to investigate the dynamic response properties of cortical algorithms, e.g., feedforward signal integration as feature detection filters, lateral feature grouping, and the integration of modulatory (feedback) signals. Using such multi-stage cortical model, we investigate the detection and integration of spatio-temporal motion measured by event-based (frame-less) cameras. We demonstrate how the canonical neural circuit can improve such representations using normalization and feedback and develop key computational elements to map such a model onto neuromorphic hardware (IBM's TrueNorth chip). This makes a step towards implementing real-time and energy-efficient neuromorphic optical flow detectors based on realistic principles of computation in cortical columns.

Keywords: Canonical neural circuit · Cortical column · Motion detection · Optical flow · Feedback · Neuromorphic computing

1 Introduction and Motivation

Vision in primates needs to solve various tasks in order to steer an agent's behavioral control. For example, grouping elementary items, the segregation of a figure against the visual background, and the recognition of objects in cluttered scenes define some fundamental tasks. In order to achieve such functionality robustly and under varying conditions, the brain processes input signals along a hierarchy of different subcortical and cortical stages. Some perceptual tasks appear to be effortless and automatic while other tasks are difficult and time-consuming (see Fig. 1).

We propose a conceptual framework of how such processes are implemented in visual cortex utilizing a multi-layer hierarchy of different processing stages and representations. In accordance with this framework, some tasks like single

© Springer International Publishing AG 2016
K. Amunts et al. (Eds.): BrainComp 2015, LNCS 10087, pp. 86–100, 2016.
DOI: 10.1007/978-3-319-50862-7_7

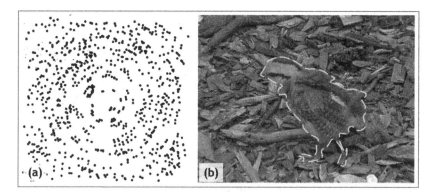

Fig. 1. Visual segmentation tasks. (a) A circular pattern is perceived from two superposed rotated copies of random dot patterns. Grouping the dots appears to be spontaneous and quick. (b) A bird with textured feather pattern appears almost indistinguishable against a textured background. Its segregation requires detailed analysis of multiple feature conjunctions for grouping discontinuities into a bounding contour with assigned border-ownership (highlighted by the dashed outline). Reprinted with permission from Nature 246 (1973) [14] (a) and Ann. Rev. Neurosci. 29 (2006) [33] (b).

object detection and recognition can be considered as mainly based on a multi-layer feedforward driven sequence of operations. For those tasks that need to evaluate several feature combinations in order to segregate parts of the visual scene a flexible more time-consuming mechanism is needed. Such mechanisms are implemented in cortical areas which are connected reciprocally so that feedforward signals are combined with feedback signals from higher-level representations reentering to augment the processing at earlier stages. Evidence suggests that cortical computation employs a set of canonical operations yielding to an abstract level description of modular computational brain function. Such components are identified, for example, for the driving feedforward signal filtering for feature detection [17], the activity gain control via reentrant signals that deliver contextual information [30], and activity normalization [8,19,20]. The signal flows along feedforward and feedback pathways define a system of counter-streams [37] which are combined at the level of individual cortical columns [21]. Different theoretical frameworks have been defined to account for the computational function of recurrent stream interaction, e.g., *predictive coding* and *biased competition.*

We show that such functional principles can be linked to patterns of cortical circuit elements that define chunks which are composed into larger simplified canonical circuits. A model scheme is derived with three hierarchically organized stages formally described by first-order dynamic equations to characterize the gradual activation dynamics over a spatially organized feature representation. This, in turn, allows to investigate the dynamics of such systems and qualitative changes of their behavior. The model framework has already been demonstrated to successfully implement models of shape processing, contour grouping and figure-ground segregation, texture boundary extraction, stereo disparity computation, motion detection and integration, as well as articulated motion detection and parallel and sequential grouping in a learning architecture.[1] Here, we will go one step further and focus on a model architecture which utilizes retina-like event-based cameras and the detection of initial motion from such input. We finally demonstrate how in such a framework computational stages can be mapped onto neuromorphic hardware.

2   Toward a Canonical Cortical Circuit Architecture

2.1   Layered Structure and Compartments

Primate cortices are organized into different layers. Six layers have been identified that differ in appearance of cell types and their densities, the pattern of lateral connectivity, and the connection of input and output from/to different areas. In addition, it has already been suggested by Lorente de No that a cortical column, or mini-column, defines a basic unitary element of organization realizing basic operations of cortical function [27].

We suggest that the layered structure can be described in terms of compartments which allows to link the collection of cells and lateral interactions with computational function for implementing (sensory) input processing and feature extraction. We distinguish the input compartment where the driving input signals from previous stages mainly terminate. The superficial and the deep level compartments build the other two substructures. Driving feedforward signals are filtered by specific filter functions, denoted by F, in the input compartment (Fig. 2A). Such filter responses generate sampled feature space representations for, e.g., orientation or movement direction, and are fed forward to the superficial compartment cell representations. There the filtered signals generate response distributions in a space-feature domain upon which cells laterally interact to link cells with similar feature selectivities [3] (Fig. 2B). Excitatory cells activate inhibitory cells in the same compartment such that the overall activation, or energy, remains balanced. Excitatory activity also feeds forward to drive other representations in different areas. Superficial compartment cells drive deep layer cells at the same location (positioned in the same column). These cells compete against cells in a larger pool that is defined over neighboring spatial locations and feature domain(s) (Fig. 2C). We suggest that this interaction scheme acts mainly in a divisive fashion upon the target cells' activation and defines the substrate of the pool normalization to account for the non-linear suppression of linear filter outputs as reported in, e.g., [8]. Cells in the deep compartment send out modulatory feedback projections to areas lower in the sensory hierarchy.

Taken together, filtering, lateral long-range integration and pool normalization may define the main functional feedforward signal pathway through a cortical column [12]. Cells in the superficial and the deep layer compartments receive modulatory input signals which are integrated from terminations in the upper

---

[1] See www.informatik.uni-ulm.de/ni/staff/HNeumann.

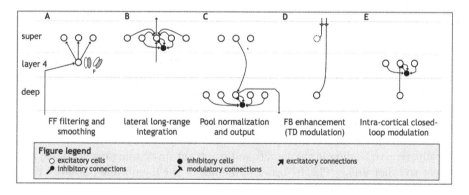

Fig. 2. Different circuit patterns. The columnar structure runs vertically and the localized lateral interactions operate orthogonal to the columns. Activations are generated by driving feedforward signals arriving at the input compartment and specialized by feature selective filtering (F;A). Activities feed forward to the superficial compartment (B) laterally linking filter responses. Superficial cell activities project to deep compartment cells at the same position to drive cells which, in turn, mutually compete against cells in a larger spatial pool of cells (C). Such cells send modulatory feedback to different areas. Cells in the superficial and deep compartments are modulated by signals that arrive in the superficial compartments (D). Deep level cells also modulate activations that arrive in the input compartment and close an intra-cortical loop of activation (E).

regions of the superficial compartment. Recipient cells reach out with their distal dendrites up to the upper section of the superficial compartment where its dendritic terminations contact the input fibers from other areas which are situated higher up in the hierarchy. These connections are mainly modulatory such that only paired signal activation from feedforward input and correlated feedback lead to a significant response amplification [21, 22] (Fig. 2D). An alternative circuitry in which excitatory axon terminals in the upper layer of the superficial compartment preferentially contact *inhibitory* cells to realize a dis-inhibition of the excitatory pyramidal cells will be discussed in Subsect. 2.3. Together with the divisive pool inhibition the modulatory feedback implements a mechanism of selective amplification while reducing activities at other locations in the space-feature domain which have not received any amplification (biased competition principle). Deep layer cells not only send modulatory feedback projections to lower sub-cortical and cortical areas but also branch to close an intra-cortical loop by amplifying the activities generated by the filtering in the input compartment [24] (Fig. 2E). In order to prevent activities to grow without bounds we suggest (in line with [28]) that inhibitory cells within these compartments balance filter activations such that the intra-cortical loop can already selectively amplify localized filter responses and at the same time suppress noisy initial responses due to clutter.

2.2   Mesoscopic Level Model of a Canonical Columnar Circuit

In the proposed abstraction the circuit patterns in Fig. 2 are combined to define a three-stage mesoscopic level model of cortical columns [13]. At the moment this leaves out the modulatory connections from deep compartments to sites in the input compartment closing the intra-cortical processing loop. Our model architecture utilizes representations consisting of two-dimensional sheets of visuotopically arranged model columns implemented as excitatory-inhibitory (E-I) pairs of single-voltage compartments (point-like) entities [18]. Model columns interact laterally, receive feeding input signals and reentrant descending connections, and project to other areas. The 1st order dynamics of the membrane potential v for such model cells is defined by

$$C_m \dot{v} = -\alpha v + (E^{ex} - v)g_{ex} + (E^{in} - v)g_{in} \, , \qquad (1)$$

where we assume resting state $E^{leak} = 0$ for the first term with leak conductance $g_{leak} = \alpha$, excitatory and inhibitory input conductances g_{ex} and g_{in} in the second and third term, respectively, and C_m the membrane capacitance.

The first stage of the columnar model cascade (Fig. 3(a) combines the circuit patterns in Fig. 2A, B with driving feedforward input signal integration and filtering F and spatial integration to form space-feature maps. The activation strengths denote the likelihood for the presence of a specific feature. Integrating, e.g., co-aligned contrast cells with similar orientation preference that mutually strengthen their activities are modelled by lateral recurrent connections [3, 25].

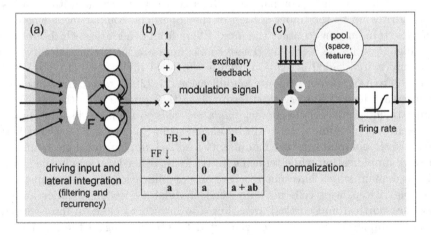

Fig. 3. Three-stage cascade. (a) Driving input signals are filtered (F) to construct (multi-dimensional) feature representations. Activations interact recurrently within the space-feature maps. (b) Activity can be amplified by modulatory feedback signals. The asymmetry in the computational role of feedforward (FF) and feedback (FB) signals is depicted in the table. (c) Down-modulation of activity through a competitive interaction with the integrated (weighted) activation of cells in a surrounding pool that is defined over the spatial and the feature domain.

The activation that is fed to the next stage of the canonical columnar circuit is calculated by

$$a_{i\theta}^{FF+lat} \propto \left(s_{i\theta}^{F} + \gamma_{lat} \cdot \left\{ \sum_{k\phi} g_r(r_{k\phi}) \cdot \Lambda_{ik,\theta\phi}^{lat+} \right\} \right), \tag{2}$$

with $i \equiv (x_i, y_i)$ and θ denoting the locations in the spatial and the feature domain, respectively; $s_{i\theta}^{F}$ defines the filter responses and $g_r(r_{k\phi})$ is the firing-rate of a lateral cell (with $g(\bullet)$ as the sigmoidal firing-rate function); the lateral connectivity is defined by a kernel $\Lambda_{ik,\theta\phi}^{lat+}$ to specify the selective weighting for grouping in the space-feature domain.

The second stage of the columnar model cascade (Fig. 3(b)) formalizes the influence of excitatory reentry signals, e.g., feedback signals from areas higher up in the processing hierarchy. Such signals enter the superficial compartment level [1] and preferentially contact the apical dendrites of pyramidal cells in layers 2/3 and 5 (c.f. Fig. 2D). In the model, where superficial compartment cells directly project to deep compartment cells in their respective column, we have lumped the excitatory influence of the reentrant signals on the feeding activity and formally represent them by a single computational stage. The influence of reentry signals is modulatory and enhances coincident feeding input [21]. In order to account for this asymmetry of bottom-up/reentrant pathways we utilize a tonic bias that is combined with the reentrant signal net^{mod}, formally denoted by

$$a_{i\theta}^{modFF} \propto a_{i\theta}^{FF+lat} \cdot (1 + \lambda \cdot net_{i\theta}^{mod}), \tag{3}$$

which yields a scheme of activity interaction depicted in the embedded contingency table Fig. 3 (b) (compare the proposal for the selective attention mechanism in [32]).

Finally, in the third stage of the columnar model cascade (Fig. 3(c)) a competitive interaction between target cells and a large spatial pool of surrounding cells is implemented. We suggest that the circuit pattern depicted in Fig. 2C implements a division of the target activations by the pool activity via shunting inhibitory interaction. This implements the nonlinear response properties of cells normalizing the local energy (over the surround pool of responses) as reported in [16]. In formal terms the generic pool integration is defined as

$$\sum_{k,\phi} g_r(r_{k,\phi}) \cdot \Lambda_{ik,\theta\phi}^{pool-}, \tag{4}$$

with the firing-rate function $g_r(\bullet)$ and Λ^{pool-} denotes a kernel of weights that considers spatial distances $(i - k)$ as well distance metrics in the feature domain $(\theta - \phi)$ allowing tuned and untuned feature selectivity for the pool integration [20].

The driving output (feeding to subsequent stages) and modulatory activations (sent back to previous stages) are generated in different compartments, as sketched in Fig. 2 [24]. The compartmentalization of the columnar circuit model allows to incorporate influences of inhibitory activity across different cortical layers, as, e.g., in the dynamic attention model of [38]. Through the integration of the components as specified in Eqs. 2, 3, and 4 we specify the dynamics of the canonical circuit model in a 1st order 2-D system

$$\tau \dot{r}_{i\theta} = -\alpha r_{i\theta} + (\beta - r_{i\theta}) \cdot P_{i\theta} - (\eta + \gamma \cdot r_{i\theta}) \cdot g_p(p_i),$$

$$\tau_p \dot{p}_{i\theta} = -\alpha_p p_i + \beta_p \cdot \left\{ \sum_{k,\phi} g_r(r_{k,\phi}) \cdot \Lambda^-_{ik,\theta\phi} \right\} + (I_c)_i, \tag{5}$$

with excitatory net input defined by the initial filtering and the lateral recurrent integration

$$P_{i\theta} = \left(s^F_{i\theta} + \gamma_{lat} \cdot \left\{ \sum_k g_r(r_k) \cdot \Lambda^{lat+}_{ik,\theta} \right\} \right) \cdot \left(1 + \lambda \cdot net^{mod}_{i\theta} \right). \tag{6}$$

The dynamic properties of this circuit model have been investigated in [4]. In order to simplify the analysis, a reduced model has been studied. In a nutshell, the stable regimes of such a network architecture can be identified and the dependencies are shown such that properties of inhibition-stabilized response properties can be generated. Regimes of dynamic instability have been characterized as well by identification of the bifurcations and the regimes as a function of the lateral activity integration were studied numerically in a recent study [23].

2.3 Mechanisms of Feedback in Cortical Columns

Larkum and coworkers showed that somatic input of pyramidal cells can be amplified by coincident signals that arrive at the distal dendrites [21]. Driving input is, however, necessary to generate an excitatory somatic output such that the presence of a distal dendritic signal alone cannot generate an activity (Fig. 4(a)).

An alternative model is suggested on the basis of inhibitory circuit motifs [29]. Excitatory input terminals at the upper levels of the superficial compartments preferentially contact with inhibitory Vasoactive intestina peptide (VIP) expressive cells. These, in turn, contact the protein parvalbumin (PV) expressing inhibitory cells which frequently occur near the soma and contact the basal dendrites of pyramidal cells. In Fig. 4(b) a schematic diagram of such a micro-circuit is shown in which the inhibitory-to-inhibitory cell interactions (exc → VIP → PV) implement a disinhibitory mechanism acting upon the excitation of pyramidal cells. In [5] we have investigated such a mechanism from its computational perspective, analyzed its stability conditions and shown that such disinhibitory micro-circuit shows similarities with the findings of [21]. In a nutshell, it was shown in [5] that at equilibrium the change in output activation, as a special case, yields the modulatory mechanism $\Delta r \propto p \cdot (1 + net^{mod})$ as specified for the excitatory gain enhancement (Eq. 5; with membrane potential p and modulatory feedback net^{mod}).

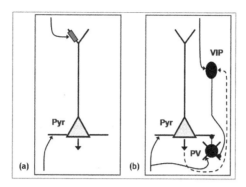

Fig. 4. Reentrant signal integration by direct excitatory modulation and disinhibition. (a) Direct excitation of driving somatic input via coincident input that arrives via the distal dendrites leads to an amplification of the gain of the somatic input. (b) Excitatory input terminals at the upper levels of the superficial compartments preferentially drive inhibitory cells which, in turn, connect to another population of inhibitory cells to disinhibit pyramidal cells (Pyr; cells with black body are inhibitory cells, with bullet-head arcs).

3 Cortical Motion Processing Using Canonical Circuits

In this section, we investigate how the canonical circuit architecture can be adopted for the detection of raw motion. Visual input is generated using a dynamic vision sensor, an event-based camera ('silicon retina'; DVS128; *iniLabs*, www.inilabs.com) which responds by emitting an event in case of above-threshold luminance change. Luminance increases and decreases are distinguished by ON and OFF events, respectively. With such a camera spike events are sent encoding a unique (x, y)-location and time stamp instead of generating full frames. We capitalize upon a novel biologically inspired motion detector which utilizes a spatio-temporal separable filter design that can be mapped to energy-efficient, real-time neuromorphic hardware [6,7].

3.1 Event-Stream Generation and Spatio-Temporal Filtering

The input data is generated by an event-driven spatial sensor that approximates a retinal image. We describe the stream of events by the function $e : \mathbb{R}^2 \times \mathbb{R} \rightarrow \{-1, 0, 1\}$ (c.f. [7]; c.f. Fig. 5(a)) which is always zero except for tuples $(x_k, y_k; t_k) = (\boldsymbol{p}_k; t_k)$ to define the location and time of an event k generated when the luminance function increases or decreases by a significant amount. The event-generation function $e(\boldsymbol{p}_k; t_k) = e_k$, generates 1 if the log-luminance level changed more than a threshold ϑ (ON), and -1 if it changed more than $-\vartheta$ (OFF). Sampling the lightfield then yields a temporal derivative representation of the luminance function $g(\cdot)$, i.e. $\frac{d}{dt} g(\boldsymbol{p}; t) \equiv g_t(\boldsymbol{p}; t) \approx \frac{\vartheta}{\Delta t} \sum_{k: t_k \in (t - \Delta t, t]} e_k$.

Investigations, e.g., by De Valois and coworkers suggest that spatio-temporally inseparable V1 receptive fields results from a combination of

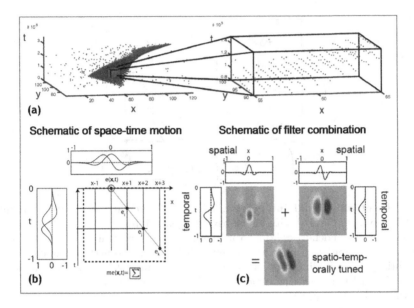

Fig. 5. Event-cloud and spatio-temporal filter. (a) Spatio-temporal event-cloud of a rotating dark bar (from [7]). (b) A regression for events generated for a moving contrast results in a tilted structure against the t-axis (tilt is proportional to the object speed). (c) Spatio-temporal filters are generated using two spatially and two temporally tuned functions derived by neurophysiological recordings [10].

separable components [10,11]. Two distinct types of V1 cells were identified, one motion-insensitive population mainly determined by a single principal component in 2D and one motion-sensitive population of cells. The receptive fields (RF) of the latter could be decomposed into *two* strong principal components in 2D (Fig. 5(b), (c)). These two principal RF components of these motion-sensitive cells were itself spatio-temporally separable with spatially out-of-phase components composed of pairs of mono- and bi-phasic distributions. In [7,35] we proposed a filter that makes use of the decomposition as illustrated in Fig. 5(b).

3.2 Motion Integration and Cortical Reentry

In the previous section we demonstrated how direction-selective neurons in model area V1 may encode spatio-temporal changes of visual patterns. Such cells respond coarsely to movements of gray-level structures given a direction ϕ orthogonal to their orientation selectivity θ and over a broad range of speeds. Such responses, denoted by $r_{\theta\phi}^{V1}(x, y, t)$, are integrated by cells in area MT which obey an increased selectivity to direction and speed [2]. We incorporated a stage of integrating early motion responses from model V1 using circular receptive field weighting functions Λ with Gaussian profile but larger spatial integration size over a neighborhood approximately 5 times the size of V1 filters. The responses are formally calculated by the following mechanism

$$\partial_t r^{MT}_{\phi,s} = -\alpha r^{MT}_{\phi,s} + \sum_{x'y',\theta} r^{V1}_{\theta\phi}(x',y') \cdot \Lambda_{xx'yy'} \Phi_s - r^{MT}_{\phi,s} \cdot q^{MT} \qquad (7)$$

(for better readability we omitted space-time locations as parameters where possible). The activations r represent membrane potentials (they are assumed here to correspond to firing rates by using a simple identity transform). In a nutshell, the mechanism integrates V1 responses over a larger spatial and temporal neighborhood to generate a velocity selectivity Φ_s. We also apply a down-sampling operator to the resulting representation of $r^{MT}_{\phi,s}(x,y,t)$ and pool normalization. The computational mechanism is formally defined by

$$\partial_t q^{MT} = -q^{MT} + \beta \sum_{x'y',(\phi,s)} r^{MT}_{\phi s}(x',y') \cdot \Lambda^{pool}_{xx'yy'}. \qquad (8)$$

This stage sums the responses over a space-velocity neighborhood and provides modulatory feedback r^{MT} to selectively amplify V1 responses that match the prediction generated by the MT feedback (see Eq. 5).

We emphasize here the impact feedback has on the response distributions generated in the representations at different cortical stages [31,34]. Figure 6 shows examples of computing V1 spatio-temporal filter responses and MT integration; Fig. 7 demonstrates how MT-V1 feedback improves the reliability and coherence of the representations generated at different model cortical stages in case of realistic articulated motions in a scene. A simple proof of concept classification architecture achieved an average performance of 91.5% recognition (see [36] for details).

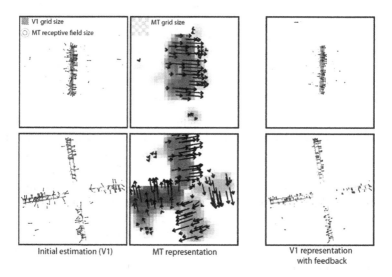

| Initial estimation (V1) | MT representation | V1 representation with feedback |

Fig. 6. Interaction of V1 and MT. Spatio-temporal filtering in model V1 and subsequent integration of activations in model MT (left and center column) for translatory motion (top row) and clockwise rotation (bottom row). V1 activities with combined feedback (right column) are less noisy and more coherent.

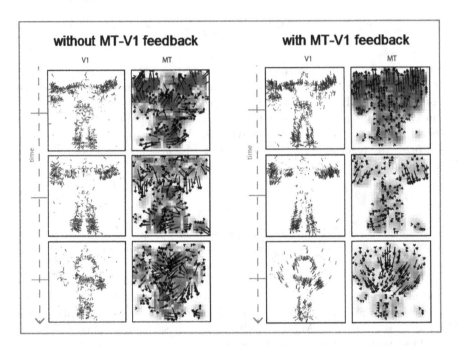

Fig. 7. Influence of MT feedback to V1 for the processing of articulated motion. Snapshots of motion responses generated for the spatio-temporal events generated by the DVS128 camera for a subject who is articulating different motions in the scene. Simulated cell responses in model V1 and MT are shown. Responses are noisy and unreliable in the case of a pure V1-MT feedforward network (left). When the MT-V1 feedback pathway is enabled only the reliable responses in model V1 survive which reliably represent the coherent motion responses. The integrated MT responses generate reliable motion representations for different articulation phases in biological motion (right).

3.3   Mapping onto a Neuromorphic Chip

As outlined above the mesoscopic level definition of the canonical circuit of an abstract cortical column serves as a framework for feature detection and filtering and the description of intra-cortical interactions as well as the modulatory reentrant interaction of feedback signals. In the specific context of event-based optical flow processing we have demonstrated that feedback and normalization can help to disambiguate responses [7]. In [6] we have sketched, how the optical flow detector as initial filtering stage can be mapped to an existing neuromorphic processor called TrueNorth [26]. Ongoing work has demonstrated that it is indeed possible to perform real time optical flow detection from event-based sensors. To realize multiplicative interactions, however, the computation of products is required as well in order to realize the canonical neural circuit model (Eq. (5)). To realize a unit to calculate the product of two input signals (also c.f. [9], their Fig. 8) one can use the relation of the joint probability of two events A and B, $P(A \cap B) = P(A) \cdot P(B)$. Let us consider a unit for which only coincident spikes can evoke a spike. The probability of coincident spikes results in just the joint probability shown above, such that the mean spike rate of the unit can be calculated by the product of the mean spike rates of its inputs. We conclude that such products can be used to calculate each of the modulation terms for the dynamic state variables, like the down-modulation $r_{i\theta} \cdot g_p(p_i)$ to realize a shunting pool inhibition (as shown in [7,35]) or the gain enhancement of $a_{i\theta}^{FF+lat} \cdot (1+\lambda \cdot net_{i\theta}^{mod})$. In turn, processing steps of feedback and normalization can also be implemented on neuromorphic hardware.

4   Summary

In this contribution we propose a scheme of modular building blocks to describe the interaction of superficial and deep level compartments characterizing the computation in cortical columns. The modular description at a mesoscopic level of detail enables the efficient and flexible usage of these building blocks. The proposed model circuit has similarities with the laminar architecture proposed in [15]. Unlike the investigations of Grossberg we emphasize different compartments instead of individual layers of cortical structure enabling a compact mathematical description of the dynamics. The columnar structure and compartmental subdivision of excitatory and inhibitory circuit components shares properties of the work of Diesmann and colleagues [38]. Here, we put a stronger emphasis on the structural connectivity and different types of interactions (driving vs modulating) in a local population of cells. In addition, the proposed focus on compartments rather than individual layers allowed us to derive an even more abstract description of the system with entities that makes its mathematical analysis more feasible. By reducing the model to an E-I circuit, we identified conditions of stability and response bifurcations, regimes of inhibition stabilized net properties and regimes of multiple stable and unstable fixed points [4,23].

We utilized the model framework of cortical columns and the layered multistage cascade to develop a biologically plausible scheme for motion detection. The initial motion processing considers the initial stages of the cortical motion processing cascade, namely areas V1 and MT consisting of an initial detection of raw flow information using spatio-temporal filtering. Input based on eventsequences from a 'silicon retina' sensor is processed and the spatio-temporal integration of activity over a pool of neighboring cells leads to activity normalization. Such outputs are fed forward and integrated by model MT cells. After normalization these activities are fed back and reenter V1 processing by enhancing the gain of V1 cell selectivities that match the MT cell feature preferences. Examples of model simulations demonstrate the capabilities to significantly reduce noise and outlier responses and to disambiguate and stabilize the motion pattern representations.

Finally, the computational circuit mechanisms and the motion detection stage have been mapped onto neuromorphic architecture. Here, we focused on one such model framework that has recently been developed, namely IBM's TrueNorth chip architecture [26]. Its computational principles are designed in the spirit of event-based processing such that the frameless sensing using a DVS neuromorphic retina can be neatlessly integrated into the architecture. We used our framework of event-based motion detection and its integration as part of the canonical circuit model of a cortical column. The space-time inseparable motion filter at the first stage of the canonical circuit can be assembled by the superposition of space-time separable filters using different 1D functions. Based on the decomposition of the circuit dynamics and the arithmetic operations being involved in their calculation, we derived a specification of the operations that can be mapped onto the neuromorphic chip architecture. The filtering, particularly the temporal filtering, as well as the multiplicative combination of different signal streams define the challenges for such an algorithm that is mapped and executed on the neuromorphic platform. Numerical simulations of a flow estimation task for detecting moving cars in a traffic scenario demonstrate that the approximate solutions of simulations using the mapped filter algorithm lead to robust results under realistic conditions.

Acknowledgments. This work has been supported in part by a grant from the Transregional Collaborative Research Center "A Companion-Technology for Cognitive Technical Systems" SFB/TRR 62 funded by the German Research Foundation (DFG). The authors also gratefully acknowledge the support via a field test agreement between Ulm University and IBM Research Almaden as well as the support of NVIDIA Corporation with the donation of the Tesla K40 GPU used for this research.

References

1. Barbas, H., Rempel-Clower, N.: Cortical structure predicts the pattern of cortico-cortical connections. Cereb. Cortex **7**(7), 635–646 (1997)
2. Born, R.T., Bradley, D.C.: Structure and function of visual area MT. Annu. Rev. Neurosci. **28**, 157–189 (2005)
3. Bosking, W.H., Zhang, Y., Schofield, B., Fitzpatrick, D.: Orientation selectivity and the arrangement of horizontal connections in tree shrew striate cortex. J. Neurosci. **17**(6), 2112–2127 (1997)
4. Brosch, T., Neumann, H.: Computing with a canonical neural circuits model with pool normalization and modulating feedback. Neural Comput. **26**(12), 2735–2789 (2014)
5. Brosch, T., Neumann, H.: Interaction of feedforward and feedback streams in visual cortex in a firing-rate model of columnar computations. Neural Networks **54**, 11–16 (2014)
6. Brosch, T., Neumann, H.: Event-based optical flow on neuromorphic hardware. In: CMVC (2015)
7. Brosch, T., Tschechne, S., Neumann, H.: On event-based optical flow detection. Front. Neurosci. **9**(137), 1–15 (2015)
8. Carandini, M., Heeger, D.J.: Normalization as a canonical neural computation. Nat. Rev. Neurosci. **13**, 51–62 (2012)
9. Cassidy, A.S., Merolla, P., Arthur, J.V., Esser, S.K., Jackson, B., Alvarez-Icaza, R., Datta, P., Sawaday, J., Wong, T.M., Feldman, V., Amir, A., Rubin, D.B.D., Akopyan, F., McQuinn, E., Risk, W.P., Modha, D.S.: Cognitive computing building block: a versatile and efficient digital neuron model for neurosynaptic cores. In: IJCNN, pp. 1–10 (2013)

10. De Valois, R.L., Cottaris, N.P., Mahon, L.E., Elfar, S.D., Wilson, J.A.: Spatial and temporal receptive fields of geniculate and cortical cells and directional selectivity. Vision Res. **40**(27), 3685–3702 (2000)
11. DeAngelis, G.C., Ohzawa, I., Freeman, R.D.: Receptive-field dynamics in the central visual pathways. TINS **18**(10), 451–458 (1995)
12. Fregnac, Y., Blatow, M., Changeux, J.P., de Felipe, J., Lansner, A., Maass, W., McCormick, D.A., Michel, C.M., Monyer, H., Szathmary, E., Yuste, R.: UPs and DOWNs in cortical computation. In: Grillner, S., Graybiel, A.M. (eds.) The Interface between Neurons and Global Brain Function, pp. 393–433. Dahlem Workshop Report 93, MIT Press (2006)
13. Frégnac, Y., Monier, C., Chavane, F., Baudot, P., Graham, L.: Shunting inhibition a silent step in visual cortical computation. J. Physiol. **97**(4–6), 441–451 (2003)
14. Glass, L., Perez, R.: Perception of random dot interference patterns. Nature **246**, 360–362 (1973)
15. Grossberg, S.: How does the cerebral cortex work? Learning, attention, and grouping by the laminar circuits of visual cortex. Spatial Vision **12**, 163–185 (1999)
16. Heeger, D.J.: Normalization of cell responses in cat striate cortex. Visual Neurosci. **9**(2), 191–197 (1992)
17. Hubel, D.H., Wiesel, T.N.: Receptive fields, binocular interaction and functional architecture in the cat's visual cortex. J. Physiol. **160**(1), 106–154 (1962)
18. Koch, C.: Biophysics of Computation: Information Processing in Single Neurons. Oxford University Press, New York (1999)
19. Kouh, M., Poggio, T.: A canonical neural circuit for cortical nonlinear operations. Neural Comput. **20**(6), 1427–1451 (2008)
20. Krause, M.R., Pack, C.C.: Contextual modulation and stimulus selectivity in extrastriate cortex. Vision Res. **104**, 36–46 (2014)
21. Larkum, M.: A cellular mechanism for cortical associations: an organizing principle for the cerebral cortex. Trends Neurosci. **36**(3), 141–151 (2013)
22. Larkum, M.E., Senn, W., Lüscher, H.R.: Top-down dendritic input increases the gain of layer 5 pyramidal neurons. Cereb. Cortex **14**(10), 1059–1070 (2004)
23. Layher, G., Brosch, T., Neumann, H.: Towards a Mesoscopic-level canonical circuit definition for visual cortical processing. In: CMVC (2015)
24. Lee, C.C., Sherman, S.M.: Modulator property of the intrinsic cortical projection from layer 6 to layer 4. Front. Syst. Neurosci. **3**(3), 1–5 (2009)
25. Li, W., Piëch, V., Gilbert, C.D.: Contour saliency in primary visual cortex. Neuron **50**(6), 951–962 (2006)
26. Merolla, P.A., Arthur, J.V., Alvarez-Icaza, R., Cassidy, A.S., Sawada, J., Akopyan, F., Jackson, B.L., Imam, N., Guo, C., Nakamura, Y., Brezzo, B., Vo, I., Esser, S.K., Appuswamy, R., Taba, B., Amir, A., Flickner, M.D., Risk, W.P., Manohar, R., Modha, D.S.: A million spiking-neuron integrated circuit with a scalable communication network and interface. Science **345**(6197), 668–673 (2014)
27. Mountcastle, V.B.: The columnar organization of the neocortex. Brain **120**(4), 701–722 (1997)
28. Packer, A.M., Yuste, R.: Dense, unspecific connectivity of neocortical parvalbumin-positive interneurons: a canonical microcircuit for inhibition? J. Neurosci. **31**(37), 13260–13271 (2011)
29. Pfeffer, C.K.: Inhibitory neurons: vip cells hit the brake on inhibition. Curr. Biol. **24**(1), R18–20 (2014)
30. Phillips, W.A., Clark, A., Silverstein, S.M.: On the functions, mechanisms, and malfunctions of intracortial contextual modulation. Neurosci. Biobehav. Rev. **52**, 1–20 (2015)

31. Raudies, F., Neumann, H.: A model of neural mechanisms in monocular transparent motion perception. J. Physiol.-Paris **104**(1–2), 7183 (2010)
32. Reynolds, J.H., Heeger, D.J.: The normalization model of attention. Neuron **61**, 168–185 (2009)
33. Roelfsema, P.R.: Cortical algorithms for perceptual grouping. Ann. Rev. Neurosci. **29**, 203–227 (2006)
34. Thielscher, A., Neumann, H.: Neural mechanisms of cortico-cortical interaction in texture boundary detection: a modeling approach. Neuroscience **122**, 921–939 (2003)
35. Tschechne, S., Brosch, T., Sailer, R., von Egloffstein, N., Abdul-Kreem, L.I., Neumann, H.: On event-based motion detection and integration. In: 8th International Conference on Bio-inspired Information and Communications Technologies, BICT, pp. 298–305 (2014)
36. Tschechne, S., Sailer, R., Neumann, H.: Bio-Inspired optic flow from event-based neuromorphic sensor input. In: Gayar, N., Schwenker, F., Suen, C. (eds.) ANNPR 2014. LNCS (LNAI), vol. 8774, pp. 171–182. Springer International Publishing, Cham (2014). doi:10.1007/978-3-319-11656-3_16
37. Ullman, S.: Sequence seeking and counter streams: a computational model for bidirectional information flow in the visual cortex. Cereb. Cortex **5**(1), 1–11 (1995)
38. Wagatsuma, N., Potjans, T.C., Diesmann, M., Fukai, T.: Layer-dependent attentional processing by top-down signals in a visual cortical microcircuit model. Front. Comput. Neurosci. **5**(31), 1–15 (2011)

Bio-Inspired Filters for Audio Analysis

Nicola Strisciuglio[1,2(✉)], Mario Vento[2], and Nicolai Petkov[1]

[1] Johann Bernoulli Institute for Mathematics and Computer Science,
University of Groningen, Groningen, The Netherlands
{n.strisciuglio,n.petkov}@rug.nl
[2] Department of Information and Electrical Engineering and Applied Mathematics,
University of Salerno, Fisciano, Italy
mvento@unisa.it

Abstract. Nowadays, much is known about the functions of the components of the human auditory system. Computational models of these components are widely accepted and recently inspired the work of researchers in pattern recognition and signal processing. In this work we present a novel filter, which we call COPE (Combination of Peaks of Energy), that is inspired by the way the sound waves are converted into neuronal firing activity on the auditory nerve. A COPE filter creates a model of the pattern of the neural activity generated by a sound of interest and is able to detect the same pattern and modified versions of it. We apply the proposed method on the task of event detection for surveillance of roads. For the experiments, we use a publicly available data set, namely the MIVIA road events data set. The results that we achieve (recognition rate equal to 94% and false positive rate lower than 4%) and the comparison with existing methods demonstrate the effectiveness of the proposed bio-inspired filters for audio analysis.

Keywords: Audio analysis · Auditory system · Bio-inspired filters · Event detection · Trainable COPE filters

1 Introduction

Hearing is one of the basic abilities of humans and it has attracted the interest of many researchers along time. They aimed at modeling the functions of the single components of the auditory system and at understanding the overall functions of hearing. Nowadays we have a great deal of information about outer, middle and inner ear as well as many evidences and facts about the functions of the components of the auditory brainstem. However, models of individual anatomically defined components alone cannot explain hearing. Lately, the interest of neuroscience researchers is devoted to model the auditory system as a whole, in order to understand how humans and animals extract useful information from the environment. In the last years, researchers in the pattern recognition community showed an increasing interest in the application of computational models of visual and auditory systems to various recognition and classification problems.

© Springer International Publishing AG 2016
K. Amunts et al. (Eds.): BrainComp 2015, LNCS 10087, pp. 101–115, 2016.
DOI: 10.1007/978-3-319-50862-7_8

For instance, models of the neurons in area V1 of the primary visual cortex have been proposed for image processing, such as the Gabor model [11] and the CORF model [1]. Other researchers, instead, recognized the importance of hierarchical organization of the visual system and applied it to computer vision [15]. In [16], the authors proposed an early model of superior olivary nucleus, which inspired the work of researchers on sound source localization [4].

In this work we present a novel filter, which we call COPE (Combination of Peaks of Energy), for audio analysis. It is inspired by how the peripheral part of the auditory system (outer, middle and inner ear) processes the incoming sound waves and converts them into firing activity on the auditory nerve.

We apply the proposed filters to the problem of audio event detection for monitoring of roads. In particular we focus on the detection of car crash and tire skidding events, which are abnormal situations that can occur on roads.

A survey on intelligent audio surveillance has been recently published [10]. The existing methods can be organized in two groups on the basis of their classification architecture and data representation. The first group is composed of methods that compute feature vectors composed of standard descriptors (time-related features, Mel-Frequency Cepstral Coefficients, Wavelet transform coefficients, energy ratio in sub-bands, etc.) and use them in combination with a classifier. Gaussian Mixture Model (GMM) based classifiers are employed to detect abnormal events [8,32] or to model the background sound [33]. Other approaches [17,28] employ one-class Support Vector Machine (oc-SVM) classifiers with novel dissimilarity measures so as to increase the robustness to background noise. In the second group, approaches with more sophisticated classification architectures or data representation are present. A classification scheme with different stages was proposed in [20], which detects abnormal sounds in a first stage and then determines the class of the events in further stages by means of specifically trained classifiers. In [9], a reject option module was proposed to refine the decision of a Learning Vector Quantization classifier. In [13], instead, the authors formulated the audio event detection problem as an object detection task in gammatonegram images and employed image-based techniques to classify the events of interest. A more complex representation of the input stream, based on a bag of features approach, was proposed in [6,14]. The authors considered the occurrence of particular units of sound, regardless of their temporal arrangement, in a certain time interval as distinctive for the presence of a particular event. In [7,25], instead, the authors proposed to take into account the sequence of particular audio units so as to improve the robustness of the detectors.

In this work, we present trainable COPE filters, which we configure on specific events of interest and use as feature extractors for an application of audio event detection. The COPE filters are trainable, that is their structure is learned during an automatic configuration process on prototype samples rather than being fixed in the implementation. Trainable filters have been previously employed in image processing and object recognition tasks [2,3].

We introduce a novel way of representing and processing the audio signals that is inspired by biological evidence of some functions of the human auditory system. We carry out an experimental analysis of the performance of the proposed approach on the publicly available MIVIA road events data set [12]. The results that we achieve, compared with the ones of existing methods, confirm the robustness and applicability of the method.

The paper is organized as follows. In Sect. 2 we explain the biological motivations that inspired the design of COPE filter. We present the details of the proposed approach in Sect. 3 and an experimental analysis in Sect. 4. After a discussion about performance and future works in Sect. 5, we draw conclusions in Sect. 6.

2   Biological Motivation

The periphery of human auditory system is composed by outer, middle and inner ear. The middle ear is composed of the *eardrum* and three ossicles that convert the sound pressure waves that hit the outer ear into waves in the fluid and membranes of the inner ear. At the end of the middle ear there is a membrane called *cochlea* that vibrates according to the frequency of the hitting waves. It is worth noting that the cochlea membrane is tono-topic, i.e. its parts are responsive for different basis frequencies. When it vibrates, it generates energy patterns according to the frequency of the incoming sound (Fig. 2). We employ the Gammatone filterbank as a model of the vibrations of the cochlea, whose output is a spectrogram-like image called auditory map [23,24]. The back of the cochlea is pervaded by neurons, called *inner hair cells (IHC)*, that fire when the energy of the vibrations is higher than a certain threshold, generating neural activity patterns on the fibers of the auditory nerve. Different types of sound generate distinctive neural activity patterns, which we consider as a description of the sounds of interest.

Given a prototype sound of interest, the COPE filter creates a model of a particular firing activity and finds the same pattern or slightly modified version of it in an audio stream. We consider the local energy maxima points in the cochlear response as the points in which the firing activity of neurons occur. This choice is motivated by the fact that the local energy maxima are robust to additive noise [34] and variations of signal to noise ratio. We consider the relative arrangement of such points as a description of the underlying neural activity.

3   Method

The proposed method is based on bio-inspired COPE filters, which are able to extract important features in audio streams. The structure of COPE filters is not determined a-priori but rather configured by an automatic process performed on prototype sounds. This trainable character introduces flexibility in the use of the filters and their adaptability to different problems.

In this work, we employ the COPE filters in two phases, which we summarize in Fig. 1. In the first phase, their structure is automatically configured on given prototype sounds (Fig. 1a). In the second phase, namely the application phase,

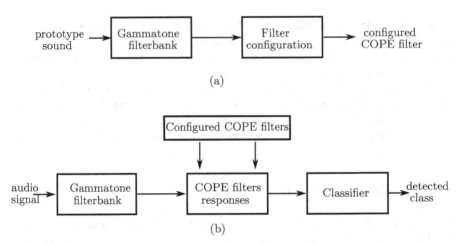

Fig. 1. Overview of the (a) configuration and (b) application phases of the proposed COPE filters.

the responses of a bank of previously configured filters are taken to form feature vectors that are used in combination with a classifier to perform the detection (Fig. 1b).

3.1 Gammatonegram

A common approach in signal processing is to visualize the time-frequency distribution of the energy of the signal. This is usually done by Short-Time Fourier Transform (STFT), also known as spectrogram. In the inner ear of the human auditory system, as mentioned above, this time frequency analysis is performed by the cochlea membrane that vibrates according to the base frequency of the input sound [23]. In this work, we use the Gammatone filterbank, which has been shown to be a model of the response of the cochlea membrane. The response of the gammatone filterbank generates and auditory image called Gammatonegram [23,24].

Although the spectrogram is the traditional and most used time-frequency representation, there are important differences with respect to the way in which the ear processes the input sounds. In the spectrogram the frequency-axis is divided into sub-bands that have the same bandwidth. In the ear, instead, the resolution in the perception of frequency differences is not constant. The same absolute difference in frequency is perceived as much stronger at lower frequency than at higher frequency. This is due to the fact that the ear processes the sounds differently according to their base frequency. Thus, the bandwidth of the band-pass filters in the Gammatone filterbank is narrower at lower frequency than at higher frequency.

The gammatonegram image is computed through a bank of gammatone filters [26]. The impulse response of a gammatone filter is the product of a gamma distribution with a sinusoidal tone. Analytically, it is expressed as:

$$g(t) = at^{n-1}e^{-2\pi bt}\cos(2\pi f_c t + \phi), t > 0 \qquad (1)$$

where f_c is the central frequency of the filter, and ϕ is the phase which is usually set to be 0. The constant a controls the gain, n is the order of the filter. Finally b is the decay factor, that determines the bandwidth of the filter and the duration of the impulse response. The center frequencies of the band-pass filters in the filterbank are distributed across the frequency axis in proportion to their bandwidth as defined my the Equivalent Rectangular Bandwidth (ERB) scale:

$$ERB = 24.7 + 0.108 f_c \qquad (2)$$

We divide the input audio signal in partially overlapped chunks (50% of their length) of T_f milliseconds, which we filter by a bank of N Gammatone filters tuned at various central frequencies. In this way, we extract short-time properties of the distribution of the energy of the sound. The result of this operation is a vector of responses that we consider as column vector and concatenate to the Gammatonegram image $X_{gt}(t, f)$. The t-th column corresponds to the response of the Gammatone filterbank at time instant t. We show the Gammatonegram images of a glass breaking and a scream in Figs. 2a and b, respectively.

3.2   COPE Filter

The COPE filter takes as input a time-frequency representation of the audio signal and is able to detect a particular pattern of energy. The structure of the filter is not fixed in the implementation but it is rather learned during an automatic configuration process that is performed on a prototype sound of interest. The COPE filter can work with any time-frequency representation (e.g. spectrogram, scalogram, etc.), but in this work we use the Gammatonegram. Our core idea is to use this filter to model the constellation of local energy maxima in the gammatonegram image of a prototype sound. It has been shown that the local energy maxima in the time-frequency domain are robust to background noise [21]. In the following, we explain in detail how a COPE filter is configured and then applied for recognition of similar pattern to the one used for the configuration.

Local Energy Maxima. Strong vibrations of the cochlea membrane activate the corresponding inner hair cells that produce a firing activity on the fibers of the auditory nerve. We consider the local energy maxima points in the gammatonegram images as the locations in which the vibrations of the cochlea membrane determine the firing of the inner hair cells.

For every point of a Gammatonegram image in Fig. 3a, we evaluate if it is a local energy maximum in a 8-connected neighborhood and we suppress non-maximum points (Fig. 3b):

$$P_{gt}(\tau, f) = \begin{cases} X_{gt}(t, f), & \text{if } X_{gt}(t, f) = \max_{\substack{t-\Delta t \leq t' \leq t+\Delta t \\ f-\Delta f \leq f' \leq f+\Delta f}} X_{gt}(t', f') \\ 0, & else \end{cases} \qquad (3)$$

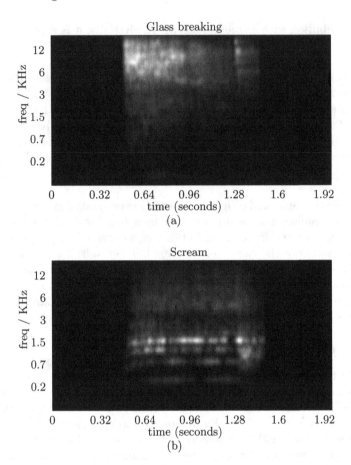

Fig. 2. Examples of gammatonegram representation of (a) glass breaking and (b) a scream. The time-frequency patterns are associated with the two events.

where Δt and Δf determine the size, in terms of time and frequency, of the neighborhood around a time-frequency point in which the local maximum intensity is evaluated. In this work, we consider 8-connected neighborhood, thus we set $\Delta t = 1$ and $\Delta f = 1$.

Filter Configuration. For a given sound pattern and point of interest (we choose the global energy maximum point), a COPE filter is automatically configured by the constellation of the local energy maxima points. In order to configure a new filter, the user has to choose only the support size of the filter, i.e. the length of a time window around the reference point, in which the energy peaks are selected as part of the model.

We describe every selected point in the filter support with a tuple of three parameters $(\Delta t_i, f_i, e_i)$: Δt_i is the offset in time of the point with respect to

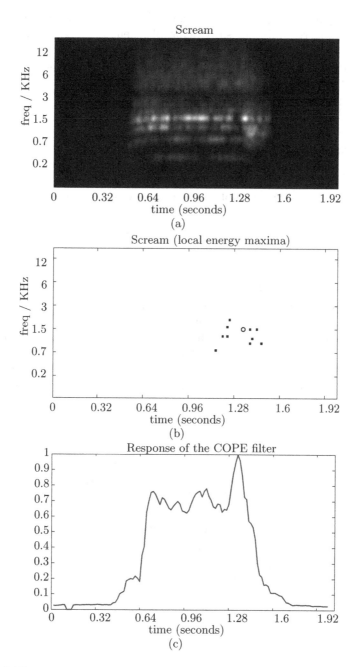

Fig. 3. (a) The gammatonegram image of a scream and (b) the local energy maxima detected around the reference point (empty circle). (c) The response $r(t)$ of the corresponding COPE filter on the scream event of interest. The highest response is 1 since the filters perfectly match the pattern used for its configuration.

the reference point, f_i represents the channel within the Gammatone filterbank and e_i is the energy value in such point. We denote by $S = \{(\Delta t_i, f_i, e_i) \mid i = 1, \ldots, P\}$ the set of 3−tuples of a COPE filter, where P is the number of considered peaks within the support of the filter. In Fig. 3b we show the detected local energy maxima points in the gammatonegram image of Fig. 3a.

We configure a set of COPE filters on L training audio samples from different classes, so as to construct a bank of filters.

Filter Response. The configuration process results in a set of tuples that describe a constellation of energy peaks in the Gammatonegram of a sound. The proposed COPE filter computes and combines the responses of its sub-components identified by the tuples in S. Formally, we define the response of the i-th tuple of the model as:

$$s_i(t) = \max_{t',f'} \{\psi(f_i, t) G_{\sigma'}(t', f')\} \tag{4}$$

$$t - \Delta t \le t' \le t + \Delta t, f_i - \Delta f \le f' \le f_i + \Delta f$$

The function $G_{\sigma'}(\cdot, \cdot)$ is a Gaussian weighting function for the local energy maxima points. It allows for some tolerance in the detection of the position of the points with respect to the model created in the configuration step. A configured COPE filter is, thus, selective for the prototype sound used for its configuration but also to modified versions of it. This choice is supported by neurophysiological evidences that the vibrations of the cochlea membrane cause the firing of specific frequency-tuned inner hair cells, but also of neighbor neurons [22]. Practically, the weighting function allows for tolerance to distortion and time-delay of the expected energy peak due to noise. The value σ' determines the size of the region of tolerance. Its general form is $\sigma' = (\sigma_0 + \alpha \rho_i)/2$, where σ_0 and α are constants, while ρ_i is the euclidean distance of the i-th point from the reference point of the filter. In the experiments, we apply the same tolerance value for the positions of all the local energy maxima, thus setting $\alpha = 0$. The term $\psi(f, t)$, instead, indicates the similarity of the concerned energy point with the one contained in the model. Here we do not consider the energy similarity, but rather only take into account the position of the energy peaks. Thus, we set $\psi(f, t) = P_{gt}(f, t)$.

The COPE filter response is computed by geometric mean of the responses of the concerned weighted local energy maxima:

$$r(t) = \left(\prod_{i=1}^{|S|} s_i(t) \right)^{1/|S|}. \tag{5}$$

In Fig. 3c, we show the response along time of the COPE filter (the considered local energy maxima are in Fig. 3b) configured on the sound in Fig. 3a. For a given interval of time $[T_1, T_2]$, we compute the response of all the configured COPE filters and construct a feature vector:

$$\mathbf{v}_{[T_1, T_2]} = \left[\hat{r}_1, \hat{r}_2, \ldots, \hat{r}_L \right] \tag{6}$$

where

$$\hat{r}_i = \max_{t \in [T_1, T_2]} r_i(t) \tag{7}$$

is the highest value of the i-th COPE filter response in the interval $[T_1, T_2]$.

3.3   Classifier

We train a multi-class Support Vector Machine (SVM) classifier with the feature vectors constructed as explained in the previous section. The SVM has the ability of finding an optimal hyperplane, that separates the samples of the classes to be recognized. It maximizes the margin between the decision boundary and the training samples, trying to avoiding over-fitting even when dealing with small-sized data sets. Since SVM is originally a binary classifier, the proposed system is designed such as to have several SVM instances operating in parallel, following a 1-vs-all training scheme.

Let M be the number of classes to be recognized. The i-th classifier (with $i = 0, ..., M$) is trained using as positive examples the samples from class C_i and as negative examples all the samples from the other classes. $M + 1$ classifiers are trained. The $(M + 1)$-th classifier is used to model the background sounds and allows to increase the robustness of the system against noise. Each classifier assigns a score z_i to the example under test: the higher the score, the more robust the decision. The final classification is performed by choosing the class that corresponds to the SVM that gives the highest score. In case all the scores are negative, the reject class C_0 (background) is chosen. The classification rule is as follows:

$$C = \begin{cases} C_0, & if \ z_i < 0 \quad \forall i = 0, \dots, M \\ \arg \max_i z_i, & otherwise. \end{cases} \tag{8}$$

4   Experiments

4.1   Data Set

For the experiments we used the MIVIA road event data set [12]. It is composed of anomalous sounds that can occur in roads, such as car crashes and tire skiddings. In order to simulate the occurrence of such sounds in real environments, they are mixed with typical road background sounds such as traffic jam, passing vehicles and crowds ranging from very quiet environments (e.g. in the country roads) to highly noisy traffic jams (e.g. in the center of a big city) and highways.

A total of 400 events (200 car crashes and 200 tire skiddings) are present in the data set and are organized in four independent folds (50 events per class per fold) for cross-validation experiments. The events of interest are distributed over 57 audio clips of about one minute each. Each audio clip simulate a particular environment, resulted from the mixing of various background sounds. The audio signals are sampled at 32 KHz with a resolution of 16 bits per PCM sample.

Table 1. Details of the MIVIA road event data set. BN refers to background noise, CC to car crash and TS to tire skidding.

MIVIA road event data set		
	#Events	Duration (s)
BN	-	2732
CC	200	326.3
TS	200	522.5

In the rest of the paper, we refer at a car crash with CC and at a tire skidding with TS, while at background noise with BN. In Table 1, we report the details of the composition of the data set. The duration of the sounds is reported in seconds.

4.2   Evaluation and Results

We evaluate the performance of the proposed method by considering the experimental protocol defined in [14]. We perform the detection of the events of interest in a time window of 3 seconds that forward shifts on the audio stream by 1 second. We consider an event as correctly detected if it is detected in at least one of the windows that overlap with it.

In the case of events detection task, it is not desirable to miss the detection of some events of interest or to detect an event when only background sound is present. In order to evaluate the performance of an event detection system, the only recognition rate and classification matrix are not complete metrics. A detection system should be robust to false and miss detection. We thus measure the performance of the proposed method by computing the following metrics: recognition rate (RR), error rate (ER), miss detection rate (MDR) and false positive rate (FPR). MDR and FPR are important metrics as they give an indication of the robustness of the detection performance of the algorithm with respect to varying background sounds.

In Table 2, we report the classification matrix achieved by the proposed method on the MIVIA road events data set. We achieved an average recognition rate of 94% with a standard deviation equal to 4.32 for 4-folds cross-validation. The high recognition rate corresponds to a reduced miss detection rate, that is equal to 4.75%. The proposed method based on bio-inspired COPE filters is robust to different background sounds. This is confirmed by the low average false positive rate ($FPR = 3.95\%$ with standard deviation equal to 1.82) achieved in the experiments.

We report in Table 3 the results achieved by the proposed method in comparison with the ones reported in [12]. In this work, the authors proposed a method based on the bag-of-features classification scheme and perform a comparative analysis of different low-level feature sets. They used such low-level features to describe short-time properties of the audio signal and then combined this infor-

Table 2. Classification results achieved on the MIVIA road events data set.

Classification matrix			
	Guessed class		
	CC	TS	Miss
True **CC**	92%	2%	6%
class **TS**	0.5%	96%	3.5%

Table 3. Comparison of the results achieved on the MIVIA roads events data set with respect to the methods proposed in [12]. RR refers to recognition rate, MDR to miss detection rate, ER to error rate and FPR to false positive rate.

Results comparison on MIVIA road events data set				
	RR	MDR	ER	FPR
Proposed method	94%	4.75%	1.25%	3.95%
σ	4.32	4.92	1.26	1.82
BoW - bark	80.25%	21.75%	3.25%	10.96%
σ	7.75	8.96	2.5	8.43
BoW - mfcc	80.25%	19%	0.75%	7.69%
σ	11.64	11.63	0.96	5.92
BoW [6]	82%	17.75%	0.25%	2.85%
σ	7.79	8.06	1	2.52

mation at a larger time-scale by computing the histogram of their occurrence. We also include in Table 3 the standard deviation of the considered performance measures. The recognition rate that is achieved by the approach proposed in the current paper (94%) is considerably higher than the ones achieved by existing methods (more than 10% higher). This, together with the low miss detection and false detection rates, confirm the effectiveness of the COPE filters used as feature extractors in the proposed approach. Bio-inspired features contribute to a considerable improvement of performance.

5   Discussion

We use the COPE filters as detectors of specific features in audio streams. One of the principal characteristics of the proposed filters is *trainability*, that is their structure is determined in an automatic configuration step rather than fixed in the implementation. The features can be determined directly from the training data and do not require a feature engineering step in which a feature set (e.g. MFCC, spectral and temporal features, Wavelets, etc.) has to be chosen or constructed to face specific problems of the audio signals. The COPE filters, instead, are flexible and can be used to detect any feature of interest in the audio signals.

It makes them suitable for other applications such as music analysis for genre recognition [31] or audio fingerprinting [5], etc.

The results that we achieved on the MIVIA road event data set are attributable to the tolerance introduced in the application phase of the filter. It is worth pointing out that COPE filters are more flexible template matching, which suffer from variations with respect to the template pattern. In the application phase, indeed, a COPE filter introduces tolerance that accounts for deformation of the prototype pattern used in the configuration process. This makes the COPE filters robust to noise and provide them with high generalization capabilities. The energy local maxima used as input for the COPE filters contribute to achieving high robustness to additive noise and varying values of the signal-to-noise ratio.

In this work we construct feature vectors by considering the response of a bank of COPE filters. We use then such feature vectors in combination with a classifier in order to perform the detection task. This learning procedure can be improved by introducing a filter selection step of the type designed in [29,30], in which machine learning techniques are used to evaluate the relevance of the filters in the filterbank and to choose an appropriate subset of filters. Such a procedure reduces the number of filters to be considered as well as the computational resources required for the processing of the filterbank.

The COPE filters are inspired by some physiological evidence of the functioning of the middle and inner ears of the human auditory systems. In particular they are inspired by the way the *cochlea* membrane vibrates when it is stimulated by incoming sound waves and how such vibrations cause a firing activity of *inner-hair cells* towards the auditory nerve fibers. As a model of the cochlea membrane vibrations we employed a bank of linear gammatone filters [24]. Other models could be used in future works, such as the model proposed in [27] that accounts for non-linear effects in the middle ear and gives more precise information about the time-frequency properties of the sound. Moreover, there is neuro-physiological evidence that the firing of IHC is subjected to an inhibition mechanism that avoids the short-time firing of the same neurons [18,19]. At a larger scale, it means that the effect of an acoustic event depends on what other acoustic events have occurred in the recent past. The investigation of such inhibition mechanism in the selection of the sub-components of COPE filters could contribute for stronger robustness to noise and higher generalization abilities. Only the significant peaks that corresponds to IHC firing activity will be thus selected in the configuration and application phases of the filter.

COPE filters are implemented in MATLAB and in sequential mode. Although they have already shown to be fast and to require small computational resources, their real-time responses can be improved by parallel implementation. Most of the computations are, indeed, independent and can be performed on different cores, such as on CUDA architecture. This will contribute to faster processing and to the possibility of building larger banks of filters.

6   Conclusions

In this paper, we presented a novel approach for audio analysis that is based on trainable COPE filters, which are inspired by some functions of the human auditory system. Specifically, the proposed filters create a model of the neural activity that is generated on the auditory nerve by incoming sound pressure waves. We demonstrated the effectiveness of the COPE filters in the task of audio events detection for monitoring of roads, by performing experiments on the MIVIA road events data set.

The COPE filter is versatile as its structure is determined by an automatic configuration process given a prototype pattern of interest. The high performance results (recognition rate equal to 94% and false positive rate equal to 3.95%) that we achieved in the experiments are mainly attributable to the flexibility of the proposed filters that are robust for deformations of the patterns of interest. This makes the COPE filters adaptable to various applications of audio analysis.

References

1. Azzopardi, G., Petkov, N.: A CORF computational model of a simple cell that relies on LGN input outperforms the Gabor function model. Biol. Cybern. **106**(3), 177–189 (2012)
2. Azzopardi, G., Petkov, N.: Trainable COSFIRE filters for keypoint detection and pattern recognition. IEEE Trans. Pattern Anal. Mach. Intell. **35**, 490–503 (2013)
3. Azzopardi, G., Strisciuglio, N., Vento, M., Petkov, N.: Trainable COSFIRE filters for vessel delineation with application to retinal images. Med. Image Anal. **19**(1), 46–57 (2015)
4. Blauert, J.: The Technology of Binaural Listening. Modern Acoustics and Signal Processing (2013)
5. Cano, P., Batlle, E., Kalker, T., Haitsma, J.: A review of audio fingerprinting. J. VLSI Sig. Process. Syst. Sig. Image Video Technol. **41**(3), 271–284 (2005)
6. Carletti, V., Foggia, P., Percannella, G., Saggese, A., Strisciuglio, N., Vento, M.: Audio surveillance using a bag of aural words classifier. In: IEEE AVSS, pp. 81–86, August 2013
7. Chin, M., Burred, J.: Audio event detection based on layered symbolic sequence representations. In: IEEE ICASSP, pp. 1953–1956 (2012)
8. Clavel, C., Ehrette, T., Richard, G.: Events detection for an audio-based surveillance system. In: ICME, pp. 1306–1309 (2005)
9. Conte, D., Foggia, P., Percannella, G., Saggese, A., Vento, M.: An ensemble of rejecting classifiers for anomaly detection of audio events. In: IEEE AVSS, pp. 76–81, September 2012
10. Crocco, M., Cristani, M., Trucco, A., Murino, V.: Audio surveillance: a systematic review. CoRR abs/1409.7787 (2014)
11. Daugman, J.G.: Uncertainty relation for resolution in space, spatial frequency, and orientation optimized by two-dimensional visual cortical filters. J. Opt. Soc. Am. A **2**(7), 1160–1169 (1985)
12. Foggia, P., Petkov, N., Saggese, A., Strisciuglio, N., Vento, M.: Audio surveillance of roads: a system for detecting anomalous sounds. IEEE Trans. Intell. Transp. Syst. **PP**(99), 1–10 (2015)

13. Foggia, P., Saggese, A., Strisciuglio, N., Vento, M.: Cascade classifiers trained on gammatonegrams for reliably detecting audio events. In: IEEE AVSS, pp. 50–55, August 2014

14. Foggia, P., Petkov, N., Saggese, A., Strisciuglio, N., Vento, M.: Reliable detection of audio events in highly noisy environments. Pattern Recogn. Lett. **65**, 22–28 (2015)

15. Geman, S., Geman, D.: Stochastic relaxation, gibbs distributions, and the bayesian restoration of images. IEEE Trans. Pattern Anal. Mach. Intell. **PAMI–6**(6), 721–741 (1984)

16. Jeffress, L.A.: A place theory of sound localization. J. Comp. Physiol. Psychol. **41**(1), 35–39 (1948)

17. Lecomte, S., Lengelle, R., Richard, C., Capman, F., Ravera, B.: Abnormal events detection using unsupervised one-class svm - application to audio surveillance and evaluation. In: IEEE AVSS, pp. 124–129, 30 2011-September 2 2011

18. Lopez-Poveda, E.A., Eustaquio-Martín, A.: A biophysical model of the inner hair cell: The contribution of potassium currents to peripheral auditory compression. J. Assoc. Res. Otolaryngol. **7**(3), 218–235 (2006). http://dx.doi.org/10.1007/s10162-006-0037-8

19. Meddis, R.: Auditory-nerve first-spike latency and auditory absolute threshold: a computer model. J. Acoust. Soc. Am. **119**(1), 406–417 (2006)

20. Ntalampiras, S., Potamitis, I., Fakotakis, N.: An adaptive framework for acoustic monitoring of potential hazards. EURASIP J. Audio Speech Music Process. **2009**, 13:1–13:15 (2009)

21. Ogle, J.P., Ellis, D.P.W.: Fingerprinting to identify repeated sound events in long-duration personal audio recordings. In: IEEE International Conference on Acoustics, Speech and Signal Processing, 2007, ICASSP 2007, vol. 1, pp. I-233–I-236, April 2007

22. Palmer, A., Russell, I.: Phase-locking in the cochlear nerve of the guinea-pig and its relation to the receptor potential of inner hair-cells. Hear. Res. **24**(1), 1–15 (1986)

23. Patterson, R.D., Moore, B.C.J.: Auditory filters and excitation patterns as representations of frequency resolution. Frequency selectivity in hearing, pp. 123–177 (1986)

24. Patterson, R.D., Robinson, K., Holdsworth, J., Mckeown, D., Zhang, C., Allerhand, M.: Complex Sounds and auditory images. In: Cazals, Y., Demany, L., Honer, K. (eds.) Auditory Physiology and Perception, Pergamon, Pergamon, Oxford, pp. 429–443 (1992)

25. Phan, H., Hertel, L., Maass, M., Mazur, R., Mertins, A.: Audio phrases for audio event recognition. In: 23nd European Signal Processing Conference, EUSIPCO 2015 (2015)

26. Pour, A.F., Asgari, M., Hasanabadi, M.R.: Gammatonegram based speaker identification. In: 2014 4th International eConference on Computer and Knowledge Engineering (ICCKE), pp. 52–55, October 2014

27. Poveda, E.A.L., Meddis, R.: A human nonlinear cochlear filterbank. J. Acoust. Soc. Am. **110**(6), 3107–18 (2001)

28. Rabaoui, A., Davy, M., Rossignol, S., Ellouze, N.: Using one-class svms and wavelets for audio surveillance. IEEE Trans. Inf. Forensics Security **3**(4), 763–775 (2008)

29. Strisciuglio, N., Azzopardi, G., Vento, M., Petkov, N.: Multiscale blood vessel delineation using *B*-COSFIRE filters. In: Azzopardi, G., Petkov, N. (eds.) CAIP 2015. LNCS, vol. 9257, pp. 300–312. Springer, Heidelberg (2015). doi:10.1007/978-3-319-23117-4_26

30. Strisciuglio, N., Azzopardi, G., Vento, M., Petkov, N.: Supervised vessel delineation in retinal fundus images with the automatic selection of B-COSFIRE filters. Mach. Vis. Appl., 1–13 (2016). doi:10.1007/s00138-016-0781-7

31. Sturm, B.L.: A survey of evaluation in music genre recognition. In: Nürnberger, A., Stober, S., Larsen, B., Detyniecki, M. (eds.) AMR 2012. LNCS, vol. 8382, pp. 29–66. Springer, Heidelberg (2014). doi:10.1007/978-3-319-12093-5_2

32. Vacher, M., Istrate, D., Besacier, L., Serignat, J.F., Castelli, E.: Sound detection and classification for medical telesurvey. In: ACTA Press (eds.) Proceedings of the 2nd ICBME, Innsbruck, Austria, pp. 395–398, February 2004

33. Valenzise, G., Gerosa, L., Tagliasacchi, M., Antonacci, F., Sarti, A.: Scream and gunshot detection and localization for audio-surveillance systems. In: IEEE AVSS, pp. 21–26 (2007)

34. Wang, A.L.-C., Th Floor Block F.: An industrial-strength audio search algorithm. In: Proceedings of the 4th International Conference on Music Information Retrieval (2003)

Sophisticated LVQ Classification Models - Beyond Accuracy Optimization

Thomas Villmann[✉]

Computational Intelligence Group, University of Applied Sciences Mittweida,
DE Technikumplatz 17, 09648 Mittweida, Germany
thomas.villmann@hs-mittweida.de

Abstract. Learning vector quantization models (LVQ) belong to
the most successful machine learning classifiers. LVQs are intuitively
designed and generally allow an easy interpretation according to the class
dependent prototype principle. Originally, LVQs try to optimize the classification accuracy during adaptation, which can be misleading in case of
imbalanced data. Further, it might be required by the application that
other statistical classification evaluation measures should be considered,
e.g. sensitivity and specificity like frequently demanded in bio-medical
applications. In this article we present recent approaches, how to modify
LVQ to integrate those sophisticated evaluation measures as objectives
to be optimized. Particularly, we show that all differentiable functions
built fro contingency tables can be incorporated into a LVQ-scheme as
well as receiver operating characteristic curve optimization.

1 Introduction

One of the most important tasks in machine learning is the automatic detection
of classification decision rules based on available training data. The mathematical
basis is the Bayesian decision theory [1]. The Bayes decision theory assumes the
knowledge of the class distributions, which have to be estimated from the data
in machine learning scenarios. Learning vector quantizers (LVQ) were developed
for classification learning of vector data [2]. The motivation for this approach
was to combine the Bayes statistical decision theory with unsupervised vector
quantization for class distribution learning [3]. The estimation of class distributions generally is a crucial step in classification learning. Unsupervised vector
quantizers, like k-means or neural gas as prototype based methods [4,5], frequently provide a robust method for data distribution learning. Particularly, the
magnification property describing the prototype distribution according to the
data density delivers the demanded class density approximation property [6,7],
as required for classification decisions.

Yet, classification learning by LVQ as well as other adaptive classifiers like
support vector machines (SVM, [8]), multi-layer perceptrons (MLP, [9]) aim to
optimize the classification accuracy. This can be misleading in case of imbalanced classes. In this case, for example, the classification accuracy might be

© Springer International Publishing AG 2016
K. Amunts et al. (Eds.): BrainComp 2015, LNCS 10087, pp. 116–130, 2016.
DOI: 10.1007/978-3-319-50862-7_9

very high just ignoring completely underrepresented classes. This problem frequently occurs in medicine, when only a few patient data are available compared to the number of data of volunteers [10,11].

For those imbalanced data, other statistical quality measures for classification might be more appropriate. Examples for the binary case are the *true positive rate (TPR)* and the *false positive rate (FPR)* or the well-known F_β-measure, balancing the geometric and the arithmetic mean of precision and recall. Particularly, for classifiers based on a continuous discriminant function, the receiver operating characteristics (ROC) analysis provides a further alternative tool for the classifier evaluation and performance comparison [12,13]. In particular, the area under the ROC-curve (AUC) allows the user to decide the trade-off between high true-positive rate and good false-positive performance [14,15].

In this contribution, we summarize and explain recent approaches, which modify the basic LVQ scheme in such manner that those non-standard classification evaluation measures can be optimized explicitly. For this purpose, we first reconsider the cost function based generalized LVQ (GLVQ, [16]), followed by a brief resume of statistical classification evaluation measures for binary problems being in the focus of many applications. Thereafter we explain, how to realize these measures as optimization goal for GLVQ.

2   Classification by Learning Vector Quantization Based on Accuracy Optimization

Learning vector quantizers (LVQ) belong to prototype-based adaptive classifiers for processing vectorial data [3]. For those classifiers, training samples are assumed to be vectors $\mathbf{v} \in V \subseteq \mathbb{R}^n$ with class labels $x_\mathbf{v} = x(\mathbf{v}) \in \mathcal{C} = \{1, \dots, C\}$. The classes should be represented by a set of prototypes $W = \{\mathbf{w}_j \in \mathbb{R}^n, j = 1 \dots M\}$ with respective labels $y_j \in \mathcal{C}$, such that each class is represented by at least one prototype. Classification decisions for unknown data samples $\tilde{\mathbf{v}}$ are usually made according to a winner take all rule, i.e.

$$x_{\tilde{\mathbf{v}}} := y_{s(\tilde{\mathbf{v}})} \text{ with } s(\tilde{\mathbf{v}}) = \texttt{argmin}_j \left(d\left(\tilde{\mathbf{v}}, \mathbf{w}_j\right) \right)$$

where $d\left(\tilde{\mathbf{v}}, \mathbf{w}_j\right)$ is a dissimilarity measure in the data space, frequently chosen as the Euclidean distance.

LVQ training distributes the prototypes in the data space according to the given training data V, such that the classification error is reduced. For this purpose, KOHONEN originally proposed several LVQ learning schemes requiring the Euclidean metric to be valid in the data space [2,17]. The simple adaption strategy is based on attraction and repulsion of prototypes depending on their distance to the presented training sample and their class coincidence [18]. Particularly, the basic LVQ learning scheme consists of the attracting vector shift

$$\Delta \mathbf{w}_{s(\mathbf{v})} \propto \varepsilon \left(\mathbf{v} - \mathbf{w}_{s(\mathbf{v})}\right) \text{ iff } x_\mathbf{v} = y_{s(\mathbf{v})} \tag{1}$$

for an already correctly evaluated training sample $\mathbf{v}$ or a respective punishing (repulsion)

$$\Delta \mathbf{w}_{s(\mathbf{v})} \propto -\varepsilon \left(\mathbf{v} - \mathbf{w}_{s(\mathbf{v})} \right) \text{ iff } x_{\mathbf{v}} \neq y_{s(\mathbf{v})} \tag{2}$$

in case of a current misclassification. The parameter $0 < \varepsilon \ll 1$ is denoted as the learning rate. Beside the robust behavior and the almost certainly good performance, this intuitive learning scheme greatly redounds to the big popularity of the LVQ classifiers. Unfortunately, this basic LVQ scheme does not correspond to any cost function to be optimized and, hence, does not minimize the (expected) classification error.

This disadvantage was overcome by SATO&YAMADA, who introduced a LVQ variant minimizing an approximation of the classification error while keeping the simple attraction and repulsing scheme of LVQ [16]. Particularly, they considered the cost function

$$E_A (W, f) = \frac{1}{2} \sum_{\mathbf{v} \in V} f (\mu (\mathbf{v})) \tag{3}$$

with

$$\mu (\mathbf{v}) = \frac{d^+ (\mathbf{v}) - d^- (\mathbf{v})}{d^+ (\mathbf{v}) + d^- (\mathbf{v})} \tag{4}$$

is the so-called classifier or discriminant function and $d^+ (\mathbf{v}) = d (\mathbf{v}, \mathbf{w}^+)$ is denoting the dissimilarity between the data vector $\mathbf{v}$ and the closest prototype $\mathbf{w}^+$ with the same class label $y_{s+} = x_{\mathbf{v}}$, while $d^- (\mathbf{v}) = d (\mathbf{v}, \mathbf{w}^-)$ is the distance from the best matching prototype $\mathbf{w}^-$ with a class label y_{s-} different from $x_{\mathbf{v}}$. The *modulation function* f in (3) is a monotonically increasing function usually chosen as a sigmoid or the identity function. A typical choice is the Fermi function

$$f_\theta (z) = \frac{1}{1 + a \cdot \exp \left(-\frac{(z - z_0)}{2\theta^2} \right)} \tag{5}$$

with $z_0 = 0$ and $a = 1$ as standard parameter values. The parameter $\theta > 0$ determines the slope of f_θ but it is frequently fixed as $\theta = 1$. We remark that $\mu (\mathbf{v}) \in [-1, 1]$ becomes negative in case of a correct classification.

As outlined in [19], the cost function (3) is an approximation of the classification error being equivalent to the accuracy. This can be stated, because for $\theta \searrow 0$ the limit $f_\theta (z) \to H (z)$ is valid, where

$$H (z) = \begin{cases} 0 \text{ if } z \leq 0 \\ 1 \text{ else} \end{cases} \tag{6}$$

is the Heaviside function. Hence, the cost function $E_A (W, f_\theta)$ just counts misclassifications in this limit and, therefore, is equivalent to the accuracy (indicated by the subscript A) in the formula. We denote this counting as *soft-counting*.

Stochastic gradient learning (SGDL, [20,21]) regarding $E (W, f_\theta)$ for GLVQ performs update steps of the form

$$\Delta \mathbf{w}^\pm \propto -\varepsilon \frac{\partial f_\theta (\mu (\mathbf{v}))}{\partial \mu (\mathbf{v})} \cdot \frac{\partial \mu (\mathbf{v})}{\partial d^\pm (\mathbf{v})} \cdot \frac{\partial d^\pm (\mathbf{v})}{\partial \mathbf{w}^\pm} \tag{7}$$

for a randomly chosen data sample $\mathbf{v} \in V$. Again, the parameter $0 < \varepsilon \ll 1$ is the learning rate. In this update rule we obtain

$$\frac{\partial d^{\pm}(\mathbf{v})}{\partial \mathbf{w}^{\pm}} = -2(\mathbf{v} - \mathbf{w})$$

in (7) if the squared Euclidean distance is used as dissimilarity measure d, such that the GLVQ prototype updates realize vector shifts corresponding to the updates (1) and (2) for the basic LVQ as proposed by KOHONEN, but here with

$$\xi^{\pm}(\mathbf{v}) = \frac{\partial f_{\theta}(\mu(\mathbf{v}))}{\partial \mu(\mathbf{v})} \cdot \frac{\partial \mu(\mathbf{v})}{\partial d^{\pm}(\mathbf{v})}$$

as the local scaling factor.

Obviously, more general differentiable dissimilarity measures than the Euclidean distance can also be applied such as scaled Euclidean distances or kernel distances, we refer to [22, 23] for details.

3 Statistical Classification Evaluation Measures and How to Integrate in GLVQ

3.1 Mathematical Investigations

In the following we consider two-class problems with a positive class A and a negative class B with N_+ and N_- samples, respectively. Correctly classified samples are denoted as *true positives* (TP) and *true negatives* (TN). Misclassifications can be distinguished into the *false positives* (FP) and *false negatives* (FN) according to the contingency table, see Table 1.

Table 1. Contingency table / Confusion matrix: TP - true positives, FP - false positives, TN - true negatives, FN - false negatives, $N_{\pm}$- number of true positive/negative data, $\widehat{N}_{\pm}$ - number of predicted positive/negative samples.

Labels	True		
	A	B	
Predicted A	TP	FP	$\widehat{N}_+$
B	FN	TN	$\widehat{N}_-$
	N_+	N_-	N

As mentioned in the introduction, simple detection of misclassifications is not always an appropriate evaluation criterion for classifier models, in particular, if the data are imbalanced [24–26]. Accordingly, optimization of a classifier regarding the avoidance of misclassifications without further differentiation.

In statistical analysis contingency table evaluations are well-known to deal with this problem more properly. Several measures were developed to judge the classification quality based on the confusion matrix emphasizing different aspects. For example, *precision* π and *recall* ρ, defined as

$$\pi = \frac{TP}{TP + FP} = \frac{TP}{\widehat{N}_+} \tag{8}$$

and

$$\rho = \frac{TP}{TP + FN} = \frac{TP}{N_+} \tag{9}$$

respectively. Here, $\widehat{N}_\pm$ denotes the number of predicted (by the classifier) positive/negative samples. In medical or life science context, the precision π is also denoted as *sensitivity*, whereas the *specificity* is defined as

$$\varsigma = \frac{TN}{TN + FP} = \frac{TN}{N_-}. \tag{10}$$

Both quantities are frequently used in test statistics for evaluation of the efficiency of therapies or drugs [27]. Additionally, the negative prediction rate

$$\xi = \frac{TN}{TN + FN} = \frac{TN}{\widehat{N}_-}$$

plays an important role in biomedical applications. These values can be combined in the *weighted accuracy*

$$wAC_\Sigma = \alpha_1 \rho + \alpha_2 \pi + \alpha_3 \varsigma + \alpha_4 \xi$$

with the signature $\Sigma = (\alpha_1, \alpha_2, \alpha_3, \alpha_4)$, which takes into account ll four quantities of the contingency table [28].

In engineering, the F_β-measure

$$F_\beta = \frac{(1 + \beta) \cdot \pi \cdot \rho}{\beta \cdot \pi + \rho} \tag{11}$$

developed by C.J. VAN RIJSBERGEN is he widely applied [29–31], where $\beta > 0$ is a parameter to be chosen. For example, $\beta = 1$ yields the ratio of the geometric and arithmetic mean with respect to the precision π and the recall ρ. The recall ρ is also denoted as *true positive rate* (TPR) whereas the quantity

$$FPR = \frac{FP}{N_-} \tag{12}$$

is called *false positive rate*.

If those statistical quantities should be optimized by a GLVQ classifier, the cost function E_A has to be adapted accordingly. For this purpose we make use of the same idea, which SATO&YAMADA applied to LVQ for obtain a valid cost function. Instead of approximating the accuracy by soft-counting of the misclassifications as they did, we will *soft-count* the quantities TP, TN, FP, FN from the contingency table. Particularly, we consider a modified *soft-classifier function* $\hat{\mu}_\theta(\mathbf{v}) = f_\theta(-\mu(\mathbf{v}))$ depending on the smoothness parameter θ according tovia the sigmoid function f_θ from (5). Thus we get $\hat{\mu}_\theta(\mathbf{v}) \approx 1$ iff the data point $\mathbf{v}$ is correctly classified and $\hat{\mu}_\theta(\mathbf{v}) \approx 0$ otherwise. Now we can approximate all quantities of the confusion matrix in terms of the new classifier function $\hat{\mu}_\theta(\mathbf{v})$:

$$\widetilde{TP} = \sum_{j=1}^{N} \delta_{A,x_{\mathbf{v}_j}} \cdot \hat{\mu}_\theta(\mathbf{v}), \quad \widetilde{FP} = \sum_{j=1}^{N} \delta_{B,x_{\mathbf{v}_j}} \cdot (1 - \hat{\mu}_\theta(\mathbf{v}))$$

$$\widetilde{FN} = \sum_{j=1}^{N} \delta_{A,x_{\mathbf{v}_j}} \cdot (1 - \hat{\mu}_\theta(\mathbf{v})) \text{ and } \widetilde{TN} = \sum_{j=1}^{N} \delta_{B,x_{\mathbf{v}_j}} \cdot \hat{\mu}_\theta(\mathbf{v})$$

with $\delta_{A,x_{\mathbf{v}_j}}$ being the Kronecker symbol and $\delta_{B,x_{\mathbf{v}_j}} = 1 - \delta_{A,x_{\mathbf{v}_j}}$, whereby the exact quantities are obtained in the limit $\theta \searrow 0$.

We remark that all these approximating quantities are differentiable with respect to the modified soft-classifier function $\hat{\mu}_\theta(\mathbf{v})$ and, hence, also with respect to the prototypes $\mathbf{w}_k$. Now, we suppose a general statistical measure $S(TP, FP, FN, TN)$ to be minimized, which is *continuous and differentiable* with respect to TP, FP, FN, and/or TN or rather their smooth approximations. It is clear that the previously discussed statistical classification evaluation measure like F_β, sensitivity π, specificity ς etc. all belong to this class of functions. According to the chain rule for differentiation, these functions are differentiable with respect to the prototypes $\mathbf{w}_k$, e.g.

$$\frac{\partial S}{\partial \mathbf{w}_k} = \frac{\partial S}{\partial \widetilde{TN}} \cdot \frac{\partial \widetilde{TN}}{\partial \mathbf{w}_k}.$$

In consequence, all these measures can serve as a cost function in a GLVQ based classifier using the SGDL adaptation scheme and, hence, the prototypes are adapted to optimize the chosen measure.

Recently, GLVQ variants were proposed, which explicitly optimize those statistical quality measures derived from the confusion matrix [28]. These measures might be preferred if the classes are imbalanced or if optimization of these measures is explicitly required like in medical application problems, where sensitivity and specificity are frequently favored over classification accuracy. Another criterion of classifier performance and comparison frequently applied in bio-medical problems is the receiver operating characteristics [14, 32–34], which will be studied in relation to GLVQ learning in the next section.

3.2   Illustrating Numerical Example

We consider an illustrating toy example of imbalanced data in $\mathbb{R}^2$, see Fig. 1. The A-class or 0-class cloud contains 200 samples, whereas the non-linear B-class or 1-class consists of 800 data points. Both classes overlap.

We trained a standard GLVQ for comparison and a F_β-GLVQ for different choices of β optimizing the respective statistical evaluation measures. Thereby,

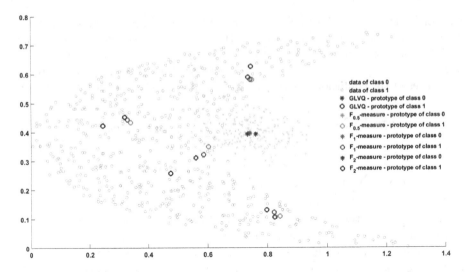

Fig. 1. Visualization of the data distribution and the prototypes for several F_β-GLVQ variants in comparison to the basic GLVQ. We observe a systematic change of the prototype locations depending on the parameter β.

all models took only one prototype for class A and four prototypes for class B to reflect the data ratio. The learning rate was constant $\varepsilon = 0.001$ and we trained the models during 1000 epochs for randomly initialized prototypes. The numerical results of the simulations are collected in Table 2.

As we can see, the F_β-GLVQ delivers the best F_β-value if the β-values coincide. Further, highest precision π is obtained for lowest β-value, whereas highest

Table 2. Classification results of several GLVQ variants for the illustrating toy data set. As expected, the F_β-measure takes the highest value for the respective variant in dependence on the β-value.

GLVQ variant	basic GLVQ		F_β-GLVQ $\beta = \frac{1}{2}$		F_β-GLVQ $\beta = 1$		F_β-GLVQ $\beta = 2$	
	true		true		true		true	
predicted	93.3%	4.1%	84.8%	0.4%	90.3%	2.2%	93.3%	3.4%
	6.8%	95.9%	15.2%	99.6%	9.7%	97.8%	6.7%	96.6%
precision π	0.882		**0.986**		0.930		0.901	
recall ρ	0.933		0.848		0.903		**0.934**	
F_β-value ($\beta = \frac{1}{2}$)	0.898		**0.935**		0.916		0.911	
F_β-value ($\beta = 1$)	0.906		0.911		**0.921**		0.916	
F_β-value ($\beta = 2$)	0.915		0.889		0.912		**0.923**	

recall ρ was delivered for the highest β-value demonstrating their different properties for classification evaluation.

Looking at Fig. 1, we observe that the prototypes locations systematically change with the β-parameter to achieve the best performance regarding the respective costs F_β.

Thus, we can conclude that the respective GLVQ variants do exactly the demanded and expected job.

4   Receiver Operation Characteristic Optimization and GLVQ

The Receiver operation characteristic (ROC) gains more and more attraction for evaluation and comparison of classifiers [34, 35]. It provides a more sophisticated tool for classifier analysis than simple accuracy comparison [12, 15, 36]. In this chapter we will concentrate how to integrate ROC-analysis into the GLVQ setting and how to modify the basic GLVQ to optimize the classifier regarding the ROC objectives.

4.1   Receiver Operation Characteristic - Mathematical Description And Basic Description

The ROC analysis considers binary classifiers. Thus we suppose two classes A and B with related data sets V_A and V_B and cardinalities $\#V_A$, $\#V_B$, respectively.

The two-dimensional ROC space is spanned along the axes TPR and FPR. Each classifier is represented by a point in this ROC-space. Exemplarily, in Fig. 2(left), a ROC graph with five classifiers A trough E is depicted. The diagonal in the ROC diagram represents the random guess line (RGL).

Following the interpretation given in [15] we can assess a classifier better the more it is positioned in the more north-west corner of the ROC diagram. Classifiers located on the left hand-side of the ROC graph are said to be conservative avoiding false positives, whereas classifiers appearing on the right hand-side may be thought of as 'liberal' preferring a high TPR-value while accepting high FPR-values. Classifiers depicted below the RGL perform worse than random guess. Thus, the ROC analysis of classifiers allows a good comparison of the classifier performance.

The ROC analysis becomes more interesting if we compare parametrized binary classifiers in dependence of their parametrization. More precisely, we assume classifiers with a rank-based discriminant function $\vartheta_\gamma(\mathbf{v})$ for a given data vector $\mathbf{v}$ in dependence on a threshold parameter γ. If $\vartheta_\gamma(\mathbf{v}) > 0$ is valid, the first class A is selected. Otherwise, the sample is assigned to the opposite class B. Thus we obtain for each threshold value γ a different classifier. If we assume a continuous dependence of the decision function $\vartheta_\gamma(\mathbf{v})$ from γ, the respective classifiers are represented as a continuous curve in the ROC space preferring either class A for low γ-values or B, see Fig. 2(right).

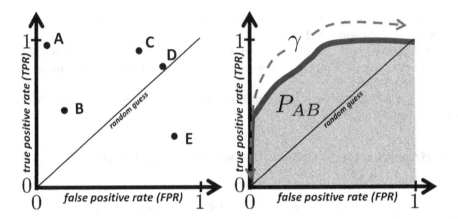

Fig. 2. Visualization of the ROC space with classifier performances (adapted from [15]). **left:** 5 classifiers are displayed according to there performances. A - nearly perfect classifier, B - 'conservative' classifier, C - 'liberal' classifier, D - random guess classifier, E - worse than random guess classifier (adapted from [15]); **right:** ROC curve for a classifier with continuous discriminant function and threshold parameter γ. Different γ-values correspond to different classifier performances generating the ROC-curve. The area under the ROC-curve (AUC) is equal to the probability P_{AB} that a classifier will rank a randomly chosen A-instance higher than a randomly chosen B-instance.

If we consider two classifiers with parametrized discriminant functions $\vartheta_\gamma(\mathbf{v})$ and $\varphi_\gamma(\mathbf{v})$, an adequate comparison is to investigate the areas under the respective ROC-curves. The higher the area under the curve (AUC), the better is the classifier assessment. Further, the comparison of the ROC-graphs allow a visual inspection of the classifiers performances and behaviors.

Yet, there is another interesting interpretation of the AUC-value: This value is equal to the probability P_{AB} that a classifier with the given discriminant function $\vartheta(\mathbf{v})$ will rank a randomly chosen A-instance $\mathbf{v}_A \in V_A$ higher than a randomly chosen B-instance $\mathbf{v}_B \in V_B$ [14,37]. Further, P_{AB} can be estimated using sampling [38]. In fact, the normalized Wilcoxon-Mann-Whitney statistics reveals the maximum likelihood of the true AUC for a given classifier [39]. For the respective sampling method we consider an *ordered pair*

$$\mathbf{v}_{AB} = (\mathbf{v}_A, \mathbf{v}_B) \tag{13}$$

of samples, where $\mathbf{v}_{AB}$ is an element of the Cartesian data space $V_{AB} = V_A \times V_B$, and a (local) ordering function

$$O(\mathbf{v}_{AB}) = H(\vartheta(\mathbf{v}_A) - \vartheta(\mathbf{v}_B)) \tag{14}$$

with H being Heaviside function from (6). Using this sampling method, we can approximate P_{AB} by

$$\hat{P}_{AB} = \frac{1}{\#V_{AB}} \sum_{\mathbf{v}_{AB} \in V_{AB}} O(\mathbf{v}_{AB}) \tag{15}$$

converging to the true value P_{AB} in the limit $\#V_{AB} \to \infty$ according to the underlying rank statistics [37,38].

4.2 GLVQ and AUC-Curves

In this section we consider how to integrate the ROC-analysis into the GLVQ framework.

Basic GLVQ and AUC-Curves. Obviously, we can introduce for a given binary GLVQ model a parametrized decision function

$$\mu_\gamma (\mathbf{v}) = \mu (\mathbf{v}) - \gamma \tag{16}$$

with $\gamma \in [-1,1]$ according to the GLVQ discriminant function $\mu(\mathbf{v})$ from (4). Hence, a given GLVQ model refers to a certain ROC-curve and the user can decide, which threshold parameter should be applied during the recall phase either to prefer the A-class or the B-class for this model. Accordingly, different GLVQ models deliver different curves. Comparing their AUC-values would determine the best model.

Thus the question arises, whether a GLVQ-like model would be able to adapt the prototypes in such a manner that the AUC value is maximized.

A GLVQ-Variant Optimizing the AUC-Value. The last thoughts in the previous sub-section lead to the question, whether the AUC-value could serve as a cost to be maximized by a GLVQ-like model, such that the attraction and repulsing scheme of GLVQ is kept. For this purpose, the GLVQ discriminant function $\mu(\mathbf{v})$ from (4) has to be adapted such that the ordering function $O(\mathbf{v}_{AB})$ from (14) can be modeled.

Accordingly, the prototype based discriminant function

$$\mu_{AB} (\mathbf{v}, \gamma) = \frac{d^B (\mathbf{v}) - d^A (\mathbf{v})}{d^A (\mathbf{v}) + d^B (\mathbf{v})} - \gamma \tag{17}$$

is considered, with $d^A (\mathbf{v}) = d^A (\mathbf{v}, \mathbf{w}_A^* (\mathbf{v}))$ where $\mathbf{w}_A^* (\mathbf{v})$ is the closest prototype to $\mathbf{v}$ responsible for class A and, analogously, $\mathbf{w}_B^*$ and $d^B (\mathbf{v})$ are defined in the same manner [40]. Again, the parameter γ plays the role of the threshold of this discriminant function preferring either class A or B as demanded for AUC analysis. Further, we approximated the Heaviside function in the local ordering function $O(\mathbf{v}_{AB})$ by sigmoid function f_θ from (5) and obtain

$$O_\theta^{\mu_{AB}} (\mathbf{v}_{AB}, W) = f_\theta (\mu_{AB} (\mathbf{v}_A, \gamma) - \mu_{AB} (\mathbf{v}_B, \gamma)) \tag{18}$$

as a soft approximation $O(\mathbf{v}_{AB})$ with GLVQ-inspired discriminant function depending on the prototypes W, which depends on the ordered pair vector $\mathbf{v}_{AB}$

already introduced in (13) and now interpreted as a *structured input*. Then the cost function to be *maximized* becomes

$$E_{ROC-GLVQ}(\theta, V_{AB}, W) = \frac{1}{\#V_{AB}} \sum_{\mathbf{v}_{AB} \in V_{AB}} O_\theta^{\mu_{AB}}(\mathbf{v}_{AB}, W) \qquad (19)$$

which is a smooth approximation of the probability P_{AB}, whereby the sigmoid function f_θ controls the smoothness by the slope parameter θ and

$$E_{ROC-GLVQ}(\theta, V_{AB}, W) \xrightarrow{\theta \searrow 0} P_{AB} \qquad (20)$$

is valid.

Stochastic gradient ascent learning (SGAL) for this cost function requires the derivatives

$$\frac{\partial \mu_{AB}(\mathbf{v}, \gamma)}{\partial \mathbf{w}_A^*(\mathbf{v})} = \frac{2 \cdot d^B(\mathbf{v})}{(d^A(\mathbf{v}) + d^B(\mathbf{v}))^2} \cdot \frac{\partial d^A(\mathbf{v})}{\partial \mathbf{w}_A^*(\mathbf{v})} \qquad (21)$$

and

$$\frac{\partial \mu_{AB}(\mathbf{v}, \gamma)}{\partial \mathbf{w}_B^*(\mathbf{v})} = -\frac{2 \cdot d^A(\mathbf{v})}{(d^A(\mathbf{v}) + d^B(\mathbf{v}))^2} \cdot \frac{\partial d^B(\mathbf{v})}{\partial \mathbf{w}_B^*(\mathbf{v})} \qquad (22)$$

as well as the local gradients of the GLVQ-adapted ordering function $O_\theta^{\mu_{AB}}(\mathbf{v}_{AB}, W)$ regarding to both $\mathbf{v}_A$ and $\mathbf{v}_B$, respectively:

$$\frac{\partial O_\theta^{\mu_{AB}}(\mathbf{v}_{AB}, W)}{\partial \mathbf{w}_A^*(\mathbf{v}_A)} = \left.\frac{\partial f_\theta}{\partial z}\right|_z \cdot \left(\frac{\partial \mu_{AB}(\mathbf{v}_A, \gamma)}{\partial \mathbf{w}_A^*(\mathbf{v}_A)} - \frac{\partial \mu_{AB}(\mathbf{v}_B, \gamma)}{\partial \mathbf{w}_A^*(\mathbf{v}_A)}\right) \qquad (23)$$

$$\frac{\partial O_\theta^{\mu_{AB}}(\mathbf{v}_{AB}, W)}{\partial \mathbf{w}_A^*(\mathbf{v}_B)} = \left.\frac{\partial f_\theta}{\partial z}\right|_z \cdot \left(\frac{\partial \mu_{AB}(\mathbf{v}_A, \gamma)}{\partial \mathbf{w}_A^*(\mathbf{v}_B)} - \frac{\partial \mu_{AB}(\mathbf{v}_B, \gamma)}{\partial \mathbf{w}_A^*(\mathbf{v}_B)}\right) \qquad (24)$$

$$\frac{\partial O_\theta^{\mu_{AB}}(\mathbf{v}_{AB}, W)}{\partial \mathbf{w}_B^*(\mathbf{v}_A)} = \left.\frac{\partial f_\theta}{\partial z}\right|_z \cdot \left(\frac{\partial \mu_{AB}(\mathbf{v}_A, \gamma)}{\partial \mathbf{w}_B^*(\mathbf{v}_A)} - \frac{\partial \mu_{AB}(\mathbf{v}_B, \gamma)}{\partial \mathbf{w}_B^*(\mathbf{v}_A)}\right) \qquad (25)$$

$$\frac{\partial O_\theta^{\mu_{AB}}(\mathbf{v}_{AB}, W)}{\partial \mathbf{w}_B^*(\mathbf{v}_B)} = \left.\frac{\partial f_\theta}{\partial z}\right|_z \cdot \left(\frac{\partial \mu_{AB}(\mathbf{v}_A, \gamma)}{\partial \mathbf{w}_B^*(\mathbf{v}_B)} - \frac{\partial \mu_{AB}(\mathbf{v}_B, \gamma)}{\partial \mathbf{w}_B^*(\mathbf{v}_B)}\right) \qquad (26)$$

with $z = \mu_{AB}(\mathbf{v}_A, \gamma) - \mu_{AB}(\mathbf{v}_B, \gamma)$. Using these derivatives, we are able to realize a SGAL for the cost function $E_{ROC-GLVQ}$ in dependence from a given *structured input* $\mathbf{v}_{AB} = (\mathbf{v}_A, \mathbf{v}_B)$. However, in difference to standard GLVQ, the SGAL for structured inputs involves all four quantities $\mathbf{w}_A^*(\mathbf{v}_A)$, $\mathbf{w}_A^*(\mathbf{v}_B)$, $\mathbf{w}_B^*(\mathbf{v}_A)$, and $\mathbf{w}_B^*(\mathbf{v}_B)$ using the derivatives (23)–(26). We finally get

$$\Delta \mathbf{w}_X^*(\mathbf{v}_Y) = \varepsilon \cdot \frac{\partial O_\theta^{\mu_{AB}}(\mathbf{v}_{AB}, W)}{\partial \mathbf{w}_X^*(\mathbf{v}_Y)} \qquad (27)$$

as the respective prototype updates with the specifications A and B for X and Y, accordingly.

We denote this algorithm as ROC-GLVQ.

4.3   Illustrating Numerical Example

For numerical simulations we used the same data set as before in Sect. 3. We trained standard GLVQ and ROC-GLVQ with 3 and 6 prototypes per class reflecting the different class distributions.

Table 3. AUC-values and classification accuracies. The accuracies reported here are obtained for $\gamma = 0$ in (16) and (17).

Data set	GLVQ	ROC-GLVQ
Accuracy	97.39 %	96.28 %
AUC	0.9922	0.9957

As before, the learning rate was chosen to be constant $\varepsilon = 0.001$ and we trained the models during 1000 epochs for randomly initialized prototypes. The numerical results of the simulations are depicted in Table 3. We detect a decreased accuracy of ROC-GLVQ compared to GLVQ for $\gamma = 0$ in (17) and (16), respectively. Variation of the γ-parameter in both models yields the ROC-curves with increased AUC-value for ROC-GLVQ, as expected according to the theory. In Fig. 3 a visualization of the simulation results is depicted. The positions of the prototypes for GLVQ and ROC-GLVQ differ significantly, Fig. 3(left), whereas the ROC-curve for ROC-GLVQ is almost everywhere above the ROC-curve from basic GLVQ.

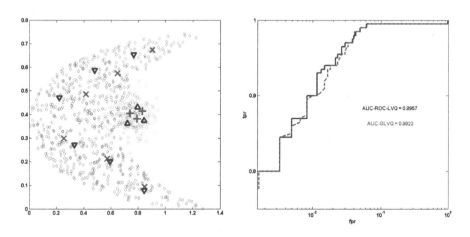

Fig. 3. Visualization ROC-GLVQ simulation results for the artificial data set from Sect. 3. **left**: Distribution of the two classes (green 'o' and magenta '◇') together with the respective prototypes obtained from GLVQ (red '+' and '×') and ROC-LVQ (blue '△' and '▽'). **right**: ROC-curves obtained from GLVQ (red dashed line) and ROC-GLVQ (blue solid line) - logarithmic *fpr*-axis. (Color figure online)

5   Conclusion and Remarks

We present in this article the mathematical framework for learning of prototype-based LVQ-classifiers to optimize statistical classification evaluation measures beyond the standard classification accuracy. In particular, we considered binary classification problems such that those statistical measures are calculated based on the entries of the contingency table. Applying the soft-counting principle for the classifier function of GLVQ or respective modifications, all entries of this table as well as differentiable functions thereof can serve as a cost function in a corresponding GLVQ variant. These modifications include sensitivity and specificity but also the F_β-measure.

Further, a GLVQ variant for AUC-maximization related to ROC-analysis was presented taking advantage of the continuous discriminant function of GLVQ. For training of this model structured inputs are required during learning, each consisting of a pairs of data vectors and the pair pieces belong different classes.

Obviously, the presented GLVQ variants can be easily combined with other advanced GLVQ-techniques like relevance and matrix learning for task dependent dissimilarity adaptation or kernelized variants [22,40–42] or reject option including GLVQ for secure classification [43].

Acknowledgement. The author thanks Marika Kaden (University of Applied Sciences Mittweida) for the numerical simulations and helpful discussions as well as Michael Biehl (University Groningen) for stimulating discussions regarding the ROC- and AUC-interpretation of classifiers with continuous discriminant functions for machine learning approaches.

References

1. Berger, J.O.: Statistical Decision Theory and Bayesian Analysis. Springer Series in Statistics, 3rd edn. Springer, New York (1993)
2. Kohonen, T.: Learning vector quantization for pattern recognition. Report TKK-F-A601, Helsinki University of Technology, Espoo, Finland (1986)
3. Kohonen, T.: Self-organizing Maps. Springer Series in Information Sciences, vol. 30. Springer, Heidelberg (1995). (Second Extended Edition 1997)
4. Linde, Y., Buzo, A., Gray, R.M.: An algorithm for vector quantizer design. IEEE Trans. Commun. **28**, 84–95 (1980)
5. Martinetz, T.M., Berkovich, S.G., Schulten, K.J.: 'Neural-gas' network for vector quantization and its application to time-series prediction. IEEE Trans. Neural Netw. **4**(4), 558–569 (1993)
6. Zador, P.L.: Asymptotic quantization error of continuous signals and the quantization dimension. IEEE Trans. Inf. Theor. **IT−28**, 149–159 (1982)
7. Villmann, T., Claussen, J.-C.: Magnification control in self-organizing maps and neural gas. Neural Comput. **18**(2), 446–469 (2006)
8. Schölkopf, B., Smola, A.: Learning with Kernels. MIT Press, Cambridge (2002)
9. Haykin, S.: Neural Networks. A Comprehensive Foundation. Macmillan, New York (1994)

10. Hermann, W., Barthel, H., Hesse, S., Grahmann, F., Kühn, H.-J., Wagner, A., Vill-mann, T.: Comparison of clinical types of Wilson's disease and glucose metabolism in extrapyramidal motor brain regions. J. Neurol. **249**(7), 896–901 (2002)

11. Villmann, T., Blaser, G., Körner, A., Albani, C.: Relevanzlernen und statistische Diskriminanzverfahren zur ICD-10 Klassizierung von SCL90-Patienten–Prolen bei Therapiebeginn. In: Plöttner, G. (ed.) Aktuelle Entwicklungen in der Psychother-apieforschung, pp. 99–118. Leipziger Universitätsverlag, Leipzig, Germany (2004)

12. Bradley, A.P.: The use of the area under the ROC curve in the evaluation of machine learning algorithms. Pattern Recogn. **30**(7), 1149–1155 (1997)

13. Huang, J., Ling, C.X.: Using AUC and accuracy in evaluating learning algorithms. IEEE Trans. Knowl. Data Eng. **17**(3), 299–310 (2005)

14. Hanley, J.A., McNeil, B.J.: The meaning and use of the area under a receiver operating characteristic. Radiology **143**, 29–36 (1982)

15. Fawcett, T.: An introduction to ROC analysis. Pattern Recogn. Lett. **27**, 861–874 (2006)

16. Sato, A., Yamada, K.: Generalized learning vector quantization. In: Touretzky, D.S., Mozer, M.C., Hasselmo, M.E. (eds.) Advances in Neural Information Process-ing Systems 8, Proceedings of the 1995 Conference, pp. 423–429. MIT Press, Cam-bridge, MA, USA (1996)

17. Kohonen, T.: Learning vector quantization. Neural Netw. **1**(Supplement 1), 303 (1988)

18. Kohonen, T.: Improved versions of learning vector quantization. In: Proceedings of IJCNN-90, International Joint Conference on Neural Networks, San Diego, Pis-cataway, vol. I, pp. 545–550. IEEE Service Center (1990)

19. Kaden, M., Riedel, M., Hermann, W., Villmann, T.: Border-sensitive learning in generalized learning vector quantization: an alternative to support vector machines. Soft Comput. **19**(9), 2423–2434 (2015)

20. Graf, S., Lushgy, H.: Foundations of quantization for random vectors. LNM-1730. Springer, Berlin (2000)

21. Robbins, H., Monro, S.: A stochastic approximation method. Ann. Math. Stat. **22**, 400–407 (1951)

22. Hammer, B., Villmann, T.: Generalized relevance learning vector quantization. Neural Netw. **15**(8–9), 1059–1068 (2002)

23. Villmann, T., Haase, S., Kaden, M.: Kernelized vector quantization in gradient-descent learning. Neurocomputing **147**, 83–95 (2015)

24. Japkowicz, N., Stephen, S.: The class imbalance problem: a systematic study. Intell. Data Anal. **6**(5), 429–449 (2002)

25. Lin, W.-J., Chen, J.J.: Class-imbalanced classifiers for high-dimensional data. Briefings Bioinform. **14**(1), 13–26 (2013)

26. Sachs, L.: Angewandte Statistik, 7th edn. Springer, Heidelberg (1992)

27. Mould, R.F.: Introductory Medical Statistics, 3rd edn. Institute of Physics Pub-lishing, London (1998)

28. Kaden, M., Hermann, W., Villmann, T.: Optimization of general statistical accu-racy measures for classification based on learning vector quantization. In: Verley-sen, M. (ed.) Proceedings of European Symposium on Artificial Neural Networks, Computational Intelligence and Machine Learning (ESANN), pp. 47–52, Louvain-La-Neuve, Belgium (2014). i6doc.com

29. Rijsbergen, C.J.: Information Retrieval, 2nd edn. Butterworths, London (1979)

30. Knauer, U., Backhaus, A., Seiffert, U.: Beyond standard metrics - on the selection and combination of distance metrics for an improved classification of hyperspectral data. In: Villmann, T., Schleif, F.-M., Kaden, M., Lange, M. (eds.) Advances in Self-organizing Maps and Learning Vector Quantization: Proceedings of 10th International Workshop WSOM 2014, Mittweida. Advances in Intelligent Systems and Computing, vol. 295, pp. 167–177. Springer, Berlin (2014)

31. Pastor-Pellicer, J., Zamora-Martínez, F., España-Boquera, S., Castro-Bleda, M.J.: F-measure as the error function to train neural networks. In: Rojas, I., Joya, G., Gabestany, J. (eds.) IWANN 2013. LNCS, vol. 7902, pp. 376–384. Springer, Heidelberg (2013). doi:10.1007/978-3-642-38679-4_37

32. Hanley, J.A., McNeil, B.J.: A method of comparing the area under receiver operating characteristic curves derived from the same case. Radiology **148**(3), 839–843 (1983)

33. Keilwagen, J., Grosse, I., Grau, J.: Area under precision-recall curves for weighted and unweighted data. PLOSONE **9**(3/e92209), 1–13 (2014)

34. Lasko, T.A., Bhagwat, J.G., Zou, K.H., Ohno-Machado, L.: The use of receiver operating characteristic curves in biomedical informatics. J. Biomed. Inform. **38**, 404–415 (2005)

35. Vanderlooy, S., Hüllermeier, E.: A critical analysis of variants of the AUC. Mach. Learn. **72**, 247–262 (2008)

36. Boyd, K., Eng, K.H., Page, C.D.: Erratum: area under the precision-recall curve: point estimates and confidence intervals. In: Blockeel, H., Kersting, K., Nijssen, S., Železný, F. (eds.) ECML PKDD 2013. LNCS, vol. 8190, pp. E1–E1. Springer, Heidelberg (2013). doi:10.1007/978-3-642-40994-3_55

37. Wilcoxon, F.: Andividual comparisons by ranking methods. Biometrics **1**, 80–83 (1945)

38. Mann, H.B., Whitney, D.R.: On a test whether one of two random variables is stochastically larger than the other. Ann. Math. Stat. **18**, 50–60 (1947)

39. Yan, L., Dodier, R., Mozer, M.C., Wolniewicz, R.: Optimizing classifier performance via approximation to the Wilcoxon-Mann-Witney statistics. In: Proceedings of the 20th International Conference on Machine Learning, Menlo Park, pp. 848–855. AAAI Press (2003)

40. Kaden, M., Lange, M., Nebel, D., Riedel, M., Geweniger, T., Villmann, T.: Aspects in classification learning - review of recent developments in Learning Vector Quantization. Found. Comput. Decis. Sci. **39**(2), 79–105 (2014)

41. Schneider, P., Hammer, B., Biehl, M.: Adaptive relevance matrices in learning vector quantization. Neural Comput. **21**, 3532–3561 (2009)

42. Villmann, T., Schleif, F.-M., Kaden, M., Lange, M. (eds.) Advances in Self-organizing Maps and Learning Vector Quantization - Proceedings of the 10th International Workshop, WSOM, Mittweida, Germany. Advances in Intelligent Systems and Computing, vol. 295. Springer, Heidelberg (2014)

43. Villmann, T., Kaden, M., Bohnsack, A., Saralajew, S., Villmann, J.-M., Drogies, T., Hammer, B.: Self-adjusting reject options in prototype based classification. In: Advances in Self-Organizing Maps and Learning Vector Quantization: Proceedings of 11th International Workshop WSOM 2016. Advances in Intelligent Systems and Computing, vol. 428, pp. 269–279. Springer, Berlin-Heidelberg (2016)

Classification of FDG-PET Brain Data by Generalized Matrix Relevance LVQ

M. Biehl[1(✉)], D. Mudali[1], K.L. Leenders[2], and J.B.T.M. Roerdink[1,3]

[1] Johann Bernoulli Institute for Mathematics and Computer Science,
University of Groningen, Groningen, The Netherlands
m.biehl@rug.nl
[2] Department of Neurology, University Medical Center Groningen,
Groningen, The Netherlands
[3] Neuroimaging Center, University Medical Center Groningen,
Groningen, The Netherlands

Abstract. We apply Generalized Matrix Learning Vector Quantization (GMLVQ) to the classification of Fluorodeoxyglucose Positron Emission Tomography (FDG-PET) brain data. The aim is to achieve accurate detection and discrimination of neurodegenerative syndromes such as Parkinson's Disease, Multiple System Atrophy and Progressive Supranuclear Palsy. Image data are pre-processed and analysed in terms of low-dimensional representations obtained by Principal Component Analysis in the Scaled Subprofile Model approach. The performance of the GMLVQ classifiers is evaluated in a Leave-One-Out framework. Comparison with earlier results shows that GMLVQ and Support Vector Machine with linear kernel achieve comparable performance while both outperform a C4-5 Decision Tree classifier.

1 Introduction

The accurate diagnosis of neurodegenerative disorders is instrumental for the choice of appropriate therapies, and it is particularly desirable at early stages of the diseases [1–3]. Techniques for functional brain imaging such as fluorodeoxyglucose positron emission tomography (FDG-PET) can play an important role in the detection and discrimination of syndromes like Parkinson's Disease, Multiple System Atrophy and Progressive Supranuclear Palsy [4]. FDG-PET is sensitive to local glucose intake and therefore the resulting three-dimensional images represent brain activity.

The application of trainable classifiers such as Decision Trees (DT) [5,6], Support Vector Machines (SVM) [6–9] and Learning Vector Quantization (LVQ) [10–12] to suitably pre-processed FDG-PET data has shown promising performances with respect to the discrimination of PSP, MSA, and PD patients from Healthy Controls (HC), see [13,14] for recent results in this application domain. Here we review and discuss in greater detail the application of Generalized Relevance Matrix LVQ (GMLVQ) to FDG-PET data, previously presented in [14].

© Springer International Publishing AG 2016
K. Amunts et al. (Eds.): BrainComp 2015, LNCS 10087, pp. 131–141, 2016.
DOI: 10.1007/978-3-319-50862-7_10

This approach combines prototype-based LVQ with the concept of relevance learning, i.e. the use of adaptive distance measures [12,15,16].

In the following section we briefly present the structure of the considered FDG-PET datasets. We also discuss the basic set-up of the computer experiments for the training and validation of the considered classifiers. The GMLVQ approach is presented in greater detail while alternatives (DT, SVM) are discussed only briefly.

In Sect. 3, the performance of the GMLVQ approach is presented in terms of disease specific accuracies and Receiver Operating Characteristics in the case of binary classification problems. In addition, the corresponding results are compared with those of the previously studied alternative methods. Our findings are summarised in the last Sect. 4, where we also give an outlook on future work and extensions.

2   Methods and Data

Here we first describe briefly the acquisition and pre-processing of the datasets. The basic idea and specific implementation of the GMLVQ classifier is presented in Sect. 2.2. Finally, we describe the set-up of the computer experiments and validation procedure.

2.1   FDG-PET Data and Subject Scores

We study sets of FDG-PET brain images, which were obtained from 18 Healthy Controls (HC), 20 subjects suffering from Parkinson's Disease (PD), 17 patients with Progressive Supranuclear Palsy (PSP) and 21 cases of Multi-System Atrophy (MSA). For a detailed description of the patient cohorts, the data acquisition, and pre-processing we refer the reader to [17].

Three-dimensional brain images, typically comprising on the order of 10^5 voxels each, were represented in terms of so-called subject scores. The latter were obtained following an approach termed the Scaled Subprofile Model with Principal Component Analysis (SSM/PCA), see [17–21]. SSM/PCA extracts metabolic brain patterns from a given set of FDG-PET scans in terms of principal components (PC), which are referred to as group invariant subprofiles (GIS).

In this framework, the obtained subject scores obviously depend on the dataset at hand. This particularity has to be taken into account in the design, application and validation of the classification schemes. The maximum number of PC and, therefore, the dimensionality of the subject scores are given directly by the number of subjects in the considered (sub-) set of data.

Specifically, we studied the discrimination of individual disorders (PD, PSP, MSA) vs. healthy controls (HC) as three distinct binary classification problems. In addition, we considered the four-class problems with respect to all subject groups (HC, PD, PSP, MSA) and the three-class discrimination of the disease conditions only (PD, PSP, MSA), see also [13,14].

2.2   Generalized Matrix Relevance Learning Vector Quantization

Learning Vector Quantization constitutes a successful family of classification schemes, which are based on the identification of class-specific representatives of the given data [10,11,15,16]. These so-called prototypes are defined in the same space as the feature vectors, which facilitates direct interpretation of the classifiers, for instance in discussions with the domain experts.

In a given problem with, say, C different classes, a training set

$$D = \{\mathbf{x}^{\mu}, y^{\mu}\}_{\mu=1}^{P} \tag{1}$$

contains a number P of N-dimensional feature vectors $\mathbf{x} \in \mathbb{R}^{N}$ together with the labels $y^{\mu} \in \{1, 2, \ldots C\}$ representing the class memberships. In the context of the FDG-PET data, the $\mathbf{x}^{\mu}$ correspond to N-dimensional vectors of subject scores, see Sect. 2.1. Hence, their dimension N depends on the number of samples available in the specific dataset.

After training, a set of M prototypes

$$\mathbf{w}^{j} \in \mathbb{R}^{N} \text{ carrying class labels } c^{j}, \quad j = 1, 2, \ldots M, \tag{2}$$

together with an appropriate distance measure $d(\mathbf{w}, \mathbf{x})$, parameterizes a Nearest Prototype Classifier (NPC): An arbitrary feature vector $\mathbf{x}$ is assigned to the class $y(\mathbf{x}) = c^{L}$ of the closest prototype $\mathbf{w}^{L}$ if

$$d(\mathbf{w}^{L}, \mathbf{x}) \leq d(\mathbf{w}^{j}, \mathbf{x}) \text{ for all } j \neq L.$$

Obviously, each class has to be represented by at least one prototype vector. Motivated by the relatively small number of available samples we restricted ourselves to this minimal setting which, as shown below, yields good performance already.

Here, we applied NPC schemes in all of the binary and multi-class problems. In addition, for binary classification, a *bias* was introduced by assigning a feature vector $\mathbf{x}$ to class 1 if $d(\mathbf{w}^{1}, \mathbf{x}) \leq d(\mathbf{w}^{2}, \mathbf{x}) - \theta$ and to class 2 else. By varying θ from $-\infty$ to $+\infty$, the working point of the classifier can be shifted with respect to the class-specific error rates, controlling the balance between sensitivity and specificity. Thus, the full Receiver Operator Characteristics (ROC) [22] with respect to a set of test samples can be determined, see [23–25] for applications of this concept in the bio-medical context.

A key step in the design of an LVQ system is the choice of an appropriate distance measure. Most frequently, the simple (squared) Euclidean distance

$$d_{Eu}(\mathbf{w}, \mathbf{x}) = (\mathbf{w} - \mathbf{x})^{2} = \sum_{n=1}^{N}(w_{n} - x_{n})^{2} \tag{3}$$

is employed for the comparison of feature vectors and prototypes, without further justification. While this choice appears to be natural, one has to be aware of the fact that it relates to several implicit assumptions: Features should display similar magnitude in the dataset and they should be of comparable importance for the classification. The usefulness of the measure (3) can be reduced drastically in the presence of many noisy features with little or no discriminative power. The same holds true if several features are strongly correlated and therefore dominate the distance measure.

In General Matrix Relevance LVQ, this difficulty is addressed by employing a more flexible generalized Euclidean measure of the form

$$d_\Lambda(\mathbf{w}, \mathbf{x}) = (\mathbf{w} - \mathbf{x})^\top \Lambda(\mathbf{w} - \mathbf{x}) = \sum_{m,n=1}^{N} (w_m - x_m)\,\Lambda_{mn}(w_n - x_n) \text{ with } \Lambda \in I\!R^{N \times N}. \quad (4)$$

Here, the so-called relevance matrix Λ weights individual features and pairs of features. In order to guarantee that distances are non-negative, it is re-parameterized as $\Lambda = \Omega^\top \Omega$ with $\Omega \in R^{N \times N}$. This facilitates also an alternative interpretation of the distance: Re-writing Eq. (4) as

$$d_\Lambda(\mathbf{w}, \mathbf{x}) = [\Omega\,(\mathbf{w} - \mathbf{x})]^2 \quad (5)$$

shows that Ω parameterizes a linear mapping of all data and prototypes to a transformed space in which standard Euclidean distance is applied.

Modifications of the formalism have been introduced in which a rectangular matrix $\Omega \in I\!R^{\hat{N} \times N}$ with $\hat{N} < N$ defines an implicit, low-dimensional representation of the feature space [26]. Moreover, the concept can be extended to local distance measures where an individual relevance matrix is considered for each prototype or each class, for instance [12]. Here we restrict ourselves to the simplest setting with one global measure defined by an unrestricted quadratic matrix Ω.

The measure (4) is formally reminiscent of the pair-wise version of the well-known Mahalanobis distance [27], which is computed directly from the feature vectors in the training set. In relevance learning, however, the elements of Ω and Λ are treated as adaptive parameters which emerge from the data driven training process [12,15,16,26].

In GMLVQ, prototypes and relevance matrix are optimized in one and the same training process. For a given set of training data (1), it is guided by an objective function which was first introduced in [11]:

$$H\left(\{\mathbf{w}^j\}_{j=1}^M, \Omega\right) = \sum_{\mu=1}^{P} \Phi\left[\frac{d(\mathbf{w}_\mu^J, \mathbf{x}^\mu) - d(\mathbf{w}_\mu^K, \mathbf{x}^\mu)}{d(\mathbf{w}_\mu^J, \mathbf{x}^\mu) + d(\mathbf{w}_\mu^K, \mathbf{x}^\mu)}\right]. \quad (6)$$

For a given feature vector $\mathbf{x}^\mu$ with class label y^μ, we denote by $\mathbf{w}_\mu^J$ the *closest correct* prototype, while $\mathbf{w}_\mu^K$ is the *closest incorrect* protoype:

$$\mathbf{w}_\mu^J = \underset{\mathbf{w}^j}{\operatorname{argmin}} \left\{d(\mathbf{w}^j, \mathbf{x}^\mu) \mid c^j = y^\mu\right\}_{j=1}^M$$

$$\mathbf{w}_\mu^K = \underset{\mathbf{w}^j}{\operatorname{argmin}} \left\{d(\mathbf{w}^j, \mathbf{x}^\mu) \mid c^j \neq y^\mu\right\}_{j=1}^M. \quad (7)$$

Note that the cost function depends on all prototype positions and on Ω via the distance measure, cf. Eq. (4). The monotonically increasing function Φ is frequently chosen to be a sigmoidal [11]. For simplicity, we employ here the identity $\Phi(z) = z$, a choice that has yielded good classification performance in several practical applications of GMLVQ [23–25].

In all cases discussed here, the relevance matrix was normalized such that

$$\mathrm{Tr}(\Lambda) = \sum_{m=1}^{N} \Lambda_{mm} = \sum_{m,n=1}^{N} \Omega_{mn}^2 = 1. \tag{8}$$

Note that this normalization does not impose a restriction on the classifier as it rescales all distances in the same manner. Moreover, the cost function (6) is invariant with respect to the normalization constant.

In the present study we employed gradient-based minimization of the cost function (6). Initially, prototype vectors were set equal to the class-conditional mean of the training set feature vectors; the matrix Ω was initialized as the N-dimensional identity. We resorted to the GMLVQ Matlab (TM) toolbox as provided at [28], see the documentation for details. The code implements batch gradient descent optimization of the cost function with heuristic, automated step size control along the lines of [29]. All results presented in the following were obtained using default parameter settings suggested in [28]. In all considered classification problems, the objective function and training errors appeared to have converged after 100 batch gradient steps.

Figure 1 illustrates the results of single GMLVQ training processes applied to the complete data sets of two example classification problems. The graphs show

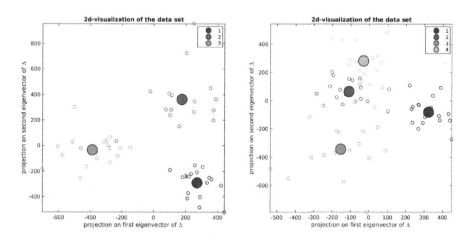

Fig. 1. Visualization of datasets and prototypes with respect to their projections on the two leading eigenvectors of the relevance matrix Λ after training. The left panel shows results corresponding to observations in a single run of GMLVQ training for the subjects representing the three classes PD (1), PSP (2), and MSA (3). The right panel displays the configuration obtained for four classes: HC (1), PD (2), PSP (3), and MSA (4).

the projections of prototypes and feature vectors onto the two leading eigenvectors of the emerging relevance matrix $\Lambda = \Omega^\top \Omega$ after training. This visualization is meaningful because LVQ relevance matrices typically display a tendency to become strongly singular in the course of training, generically Λ is dominated by a single or very few leading eigenvectors after training. A theoretical analysis of this property is provided, together with illustrative examples, in [30]. Panel (a) of Fig. 1 displays all samples and prototypes in the three-class problem of discriminating subjects with PD, PSP, and MSA. Panel (b) corresponds to the four-class problem where HC subjects are also included. While the discrimination appears nearly perfect, it is important to note that it corresponds to the classification of training data only. The quality of the classifier with respect to novel data has to be evaluated more carefully. We describe the applied validation scheme in the following subsection.

2.3   Validation Scheme and Comparison of Classifiers

The performance of the GMLVQ classifier was assessed in terms of leave-one-out cross validation (LOOCV) schemes [6]. In each run, a single subject was left out from the given dataset, while the remaining samples served as the training data. Note that the pre-processing in terms of the SSM/PCA method was performed only on the training set. Subsequently, the resulting transformation, a map from high-dimensional image data to low- dimensional subject scores, was also applied to the left-out sample.

In the actual training processes, classifiers were obtained from the subject scores of the training set only and then applied to the left-out sample for evaluation. Class-specific error rates or accuracies were obtained on average over the individual LOOCV runs. In the multi-class problems, the corresponding confusion matrices were obtained in order to gain deeper insight. In the considered two-class problems (specific disorder vs. HC) the ROC and the corresponding area under the curve (AUC) was obtained, in addition. The AUC of the ROC can serve as a heuristic criterion for the comparison of classifiers, for an explicit statistical interpretation of the AUC see [22].

For comparison, we also trained a Support Vector Machine (SVM) with linear kernel, corresponding to large margin separation of samples in the original feature space [7–9,31]. For binary classification problems we used the Matlab (TM), version R2014a, functions `fitcsvm` and `predict` with default parameters and a linear kernel, representing a large margin linear separation in the original feature space. Also, all features were scaled to zero mean and unit variance in the training set. The function `fitcsvm` returns class membership likelihoods which can be thresholded to obtain the full ROC. Multi-class classification schemes were addressed using the LIBSVM library [33] in a one-against-one approach [32].

In addition we compared the performance of GMLVQ and SVM based classification with earlier results employing the C4-5 Decision Tree (DT) method; we refer the reader to [13] for details.

3   Results

The above described LOOCV scheme was applied to the GMLVQ classifier. In addition, we report the corresponding results for the SVM with linear kernel and the C4-5 DT classifier (where available) as reported in [13,14], respectively

3.1   Parkinsonian Syndromes vs. Healthy Controls

The performances in the three considered binary classification problems, HC vs. PD, HC vs. MSA, and HC vs. PSP are summarized in Table 1. We observed that GMLVQ and SVM perform comparably well with respect to all performance measures. In particular the AUC of the ROC provides evidence for the good classification quality of the GMLVQ scheme.

Both, GMLVQ and SVM, clearly outperform the DT classifier in all three binary classification problems. Note that the high sensitivityt of the DT with respect to the detection of PD is achieved at the cost of very poor specificity only.

Table 1. Classification performance in LOOCV for the three different binary classification problems: HC vs. PD, HC vs. MSA, and HC vs. PSP. The number of available samples is given in the second column. Next, overall accuracy, sensitivity and specificity with respect to the detection of the disease are given. For GMLVQ these results correspond to the Nearest Prototype Classifier (NPC) performance, while the rightmost column provides the area under the curve (AUC) of the full ROC. Corresponding performances of the SVM with linear kernel and DT (C4-5) are shown where available. For each measure, the respective best performance is given in bold.

HC vs. ...	samples	acc. (%)	sens. (%)	spec. (%)	AUC	method
PD	38	**81.6**	75.0	**88.9**	**0.84**	GMLVQ
		76.3	75.0	77.8	**0.84**	SVM
		63.2	**100**	22.2		DT
MSA	39	92.3	**90.5**	94.4	**0.99**	GMLVQ
		94.9	**90.5**	100	0.97	SVM
		74.3	83.3	76.2		DT
PSP	35	88.6	82.4	**94.4**	**0.97**	GMLVQ
		91.4	**88.2**	**94.4**	0.92	SVM
		80	70.6	88.9		DT

3.2   Multi-class Discrimination of Parkinsonian Syndromes

The differentiation of different neurodegenerative disorder is a challenge of particular importance [3]. Table 2 summarizes the performance of the GMLVQ Nearest Prototype Classifier in terms of the confusion matrix obtained in the LOOCV

Table 2. Three-class problem confusion matrix: Differentiation of the disorders (PD,PSP,MSA). The table displays the number of subjects correctly classified for each class in bold and the class-wise accuracies (%). The overall accuracy of GMLVQ was 81.0% vs. 74.1% for the SVM. The total number of samples in the disease groups were 20 (PD), 17 (PSP), and 21 (MSA), respectively.

GMLVQ	true:	PD	PSP	MSA
PD		**19**	0	1
PSP		2	**12**	3
MSA		2	3	**16**
class acc.		95.0	70.6	76.2

SVM	true:	PD	PSP	MSA
PD		**17**	1	2
PSP		2	**10**	5
MSA		3	2	**16**
class acc.		85.0	58.8	76.2

Table 3. Four-class problem confusion matrix: Differentiation of all considered groups (HC,PSP,MSA). The table displays the number of subjects correctly classified for each class in bold and the class-wise accuracies (%). The overall accuracy of GMLVQ was 71.1% vs. 65.8% for the SVM. The total number of samples in the patient groups were 2 18 (HC), 20 (PD), 17 (PSP), and 21 (MSA), respectively.

GMLVQ	true:	HC	PD	PSP	MSA
HC		**14**	3	1	0
PD		5	**13**	1	1
PSP		2	2	**11**	2
MSA		0	1	4	**16**
class acc.		77.8	65	64.7	76.2

SVM	true:	HC	PD	PSP	MSA
HC		**12**	3	2	0
PD		4	**12**	1	3
PSP		1	2	**9**	5
MSA		0	2	2	**17**
class acc.		66.7	60.0	52.9	81.0

procedure and also displays the corresponding results obtained for the SVM with linear kernel [14] for comparision.

In particular the GMLVQ performance shows that the PD group is well separable from the other two disorders. PSP and MSA cohorts seem to overlap more significantly as indicated by a larger number of mutual misclassifications. This difficulty is also evident from the illustrative visualizations, cf. Fig. 1.

The multi-class analysis was repeated taking all four patient groups (HC, PD, PSP, MSA) into account. Table 3 displays the obtained confusion matrices for GMLVQ and SVM, respectively.

4   Discussion and Outlook

Our work demonstrates that the GMLVQ classifier achieves good performance in the classification of appropriately pre-proprocessed FDG-PET brain data. Within the limitations of the given study, in particular the relatively small number of available samples, our results show that reliable detection and discrimination of several Parkinsonian disorders is indeed possible by combining the SSM/PCA approach with a suitable trainable classifier.

GMLVQ and SVM with linear kernel were found to yield comparable performance in the binary and multi-class problems. Both clearly outperform the previously studied use of Decision Trees in the same settings. GMLVQ relevance matrix, which makes use of an adaptive weighting of features according to their discriminative power, displayed overall superior classification performance in terms of the AUC of ROC in binary classifications, cf. Table 1.

While the performance of GMLVQ and SVM appear to be comparable, matrix relevance learning offers several features which have not yet been taken advantage of to full extent: The analysis of the resulting relevance matrix allows for the identification of particularly relevant subject scores and combinations of thereof. Exploiting the linearity of PCA and of the intrinsic transformation defining the GMLVQ distance measure (5) allows to further interpret our results in terms of the original data domain. This strategy was successfully applied in [25] in a different medical context. Future studies along these lines should provide interesting insights from the clinical perspective.

The number of available example data is still fairly small and, consequently, our findings could be partly skewed. Validation in terms of leave-one-out schemes are known to bear the risk of over-estimating performances [6]. One might also expect that the prediction accuracy of DT classifiers improve significantly for larger data sets. Moreover, more sophisticated versions of the considered classifiers could be considered, or local distance measures in GMLVQ.

In future projects, we will intensify our studies in the above mentioned directions as more data become available.

References

1. Appel, L., Jonasson, M., Danfors, T., Nyholm, D., Askmark, H., Lubberink, M., Sörensen, J.: Use of 11C-PE2I PET in differential diagnosis of parkinsonian disorders. J. Nucl. Med. **56**(2), 234–242 (2015)
2. Silverman, D.H.: Brain 18F-FDG PET in the diagnosis of neurodegenerative dementias: comparison with perfusion SPECT and with clinical evaluations lacking nuclear imaging. J. Nucl. Med. **45**(4), 594–607 (2004)
3. Eckert, T., Sailer, M., Kaufmann, J., Schrader, C., Peschel, T., Bodammer, N., Heinze, H.J., Schoenfeld, M.A.: Differentiation of idiopathic Parkinson's disease, multiple system atrophy, progressive supranuclear palsy, and healthy controls using magnetization transfer imaging. Neuroimage **21**(1), 229–235 (2004)
4. van Laere, K., Casteels, C., de Ceuninck, L., Vanbilloen, B., Maes, A., Mortelmans, L., Vandenberghe, W., Verbruggen, A., Dom, R.: Dual-tracer dopamine transporter and perfusion SPECT in differential diagnosis of parkinsonism using template-based discriminant analysis. J. Nucl. Med. **47**(3), 384–392 (2006)
5. Duda, R.O., Hart, P.E., Storck, D.G.: Pattern Classification, 2nd edn. Wiley, New York (2001)
6. Hastie, T., Tibshirani, R., Friedman, J.: The Elements of Statistical Learning: Data Mining, Inference, and Prediction, 2nd edn. Springer, New York (2009)
7. Shawe-Taylor, J., Christianini, N.: Kernel Methods for Pattern Analysis. Cambridge University Press, Cambridge (2004)

8. Cristianini, N., Shawe-Taylor, J.: An Introduction to Support Vector Machines and Other Kernel-Based Learning Methods. Cambridge University Press, Cambridge (2000)
9. Cortes, C., Vapnik, V.: Support-vector networks. Mach. Learn. **20**(3), 273–297 (1995)
10. Kohonen, T.: Self-organizing Maps. Springer, Heidelberg (1995)
11. Sato, A., Yamada, K. Generalized learning vector quantization. In: Advances in Neural Information Processing Systems, pp. 423–429 (1996)
12. Schneider, P., Biehl, M., Hammer, B.: Adaptive relevance matrices in learning vector quantization. Neural Comput. **21**(12), 3532–3561 (2009)
13. Mudali, D., Teune, L.K., Renken, R.J., Leenders, K.L., Roerdink, J.: Classification of Parkinsonian syndromes from FDG-PET brain data using decision trees with SSM, PCA features. Computational, Mathematical Methods in Medicine: Article ID 136921 (2015)
14. Mudali, D., Biehl, M., Leenders, K.L., Roerdink, J.B.T.M.: LVQ and SVM classification of FDG-PET brain data. In: Merényi, E., Mendenhall, M.J., O'Driscoll, P. (eds.) Advances in Self-Organizing Maps and Learning Vector Quantization. AISC, vol. 428, pp. 205–215. Springer, Heidelberg (2016). doi:10.1007/978-3-319-28518-4_18
15. Biehl, M., Hammer, B., Villmann, T.: Distance measures for prototype based classification. In: Grandinetti, L., Lippert, T., Petkov, N. (eds.) BrainComp 2013. LNCS, vol. 8603, pp. 100–116. Springer, Heidelberg (2014). doi:10.1007/978-3-319-12084-3_9
16. Biehl, M., Hammer, B., Villmann, T.: Prototype-based models in machine learning. Wileys Interdisciplinary Reviews (WIRES). Cogn. Sci. **7**(2), 92–111 (2016)
17. Teune, L.K., Bartels, A.L., de Jong, B.M., Willemsen, A.T., Eshuis, S.A., de Vries, J.J., van Oostrom, J.C., Leenders, K.L.: Typical cerebral metabolic patterns in neurodegenerative brain diseases. Mov. Disord. **25**(14), 2395–2404 (2010)
18. Moeller, J.R., Strother, S.C., Sidtis, J.J., Rottenberg, D.A.: Scaled subprofile model: a statistical approach to the analysis of functional patterns in positron emission tomographic data. J. Cereb. Blood Flow Metab. **7**(5), 649–658 (1987)
19. Moeller, J.R., Strother, S.C.: A regional covariance approach to the analysis of functional patterns in positron emission tomographic data. J. Cereb. Blood Flow Metab. **11**(2), A121–135 (1991)
20. Spetsieris, P.G., Eidelberg, D.: Scaled subprofile modeling of resting state imaging data in Parkinson's disease: Methodological issues. NeuroImage **54**(4), 2899–2914 (2011)
21. Spetsieris, P.G., Ma, Y., Dhawan, V., Eidelberg, D.: Differential diagnosis of parkinsonian syndromes using PCA-based functional imaging features. NeuroImage **45**(4), 1241–1252 (2009)
22. Fawcett, T.: An introduction to ROC analysis. Pattern Recogn. Lett. **27**, 861–874 (2006)
23. Arlt, W., Biehl, M., Taylor, A.E., et al.: Urine steroid metabolomics as a biomarker tool for detecting malignancy in adrenal tumors. J. Clin. Endocrinol. Metab. **96**, 3775–3784 (2011)
24. Biehl, M., Bunte, K., Schneider, P.: Analysis of flow cytometry data by matrix relevance learning vector quantization. PLoS ONE **8**(3), e59401 (2013)
25. Leo, Y., Adlard, N., Biehl, M., Juarez, M., Smallie, T., Snow, M., Buckley, C.D., Raza, K., Filer, A., Scheel-Toellner, D.: Expression of chemokines CXCL4 and CXCL7 by synovial macrophages defines early stages of rheumatoid arthritis. Ann. Rheum. Dis. **75**, 763–771 (2016)

26. Bunte, K., Schneider, P., Hammer, B., Schleif, F.-M., Villmann, T., Biehl, M.: Limited rank matrix learning, discriminative dimension reduction and visualization. Neural Netw. **26**, 159–173 (2012)
27. Mahalanobis, P.C.: On the generalized distance in statistics. Proc. Natl. Instit. Sci. India **2**, 49–55 (1936)
28. Biehl, M.: A no-nonsense Matlab (TM) toolbox for GMLVQ (2015). http://www.cs.rug.nl/biehl/gmlvq.html. Accessed 16 Mar 2016
29. Papari, G., Bunte, K., Biehl, M.: Waypoint Averaging and step size control in learning by gradient descent. Machine Learning Reports MLR-2011-06, pp. 16–26 (2011)
30. Biehl, M., Hammer, B., Schleif, F.-M., Schneider, P., Villmann, T.: Stationarity of Matrix Relevance LVQ. In: Proceedings of the IEEE International Joint Conference on Neural Networks (IJCNN 2015), 8 p. IEEE (2015)
31. Burges, C.J.: A tutorial on support vector machines for pattern recognition. Data Mining Knowl. Discov. **2**(2), 121–167 (1998)
32. Hsu, C.W., Lin, C.J.: A comparison of methods for multiclass support vector machines. IEEE Trans. Neural Netw. **13**(2), 415–425 (2002)
33. Chang, C.C., Lin, C.J.: LIBSVM: A library for support vector machines. ACM Trans. Intell. Syst. Technol. **2**, 27:1–27:27 (2011). software available at http://www.csie.ntu.edu.tw/~cjlin/libsvm

A Cephalomorph Real-Time Computer

Wolfgang A. Halang[(✉)]

Chair of Computer Engineering, Fernuniversität in Hagen, 58084 Hagen, Germany
wolfgang.halang@fernuni-hagen.de

Abstract. Although the domain of hard real-time systems has thoroughly been elaborated in academia, architectural issues did not receive the attention they deserve, and in most cases just off-the-shelf computer systems are used as execution platforms — with no guarantee that they are able to meet the temporal requirements specified. Therefore, a novel asymmetrical multiprocessor architecture for embedded control systems is presented. Resembling the structure of the human brain, it inherently supports temporal determinism.

1 Introduction

Embedded computer control systems are increasingly used for a large variety of purposes and, accordingly, draw great attention of engineering science. By definition they operate in the hard real-time domain. "Real-time operation is the operating mode of a computer system in which programs for the processing of data arriving from the outside are permanently ready, so that their results will be available within predetermined periods of time. The arrival times of the data can be randomly distributed, or already be determined a priori depending on different applications" [2]. Although functionally correct, results produced beyond predetermined time frames are wrong.

Apparently the most characteristic misconception on the domain of hard real-time systems [6] was to consider real-time computing just as fast computing. It is obvious that computer speed itself cannot guarantee specified timing requirements to be met. Thus, guidelines for their design have changed from fast to fast enough: it is of utmost importance that systems meet their preset deadlines. To achieve this, determinism and predictability of the computing processes' temporal behaviour is necessary: these properties essentially imply all other requirements. Being able to assure that a process will be serviced within a predefined time frame in a multiprogramming environment can be expressed as schedulability: the ability to find, a priori, a schedule such that each task will meet its deadline. For schedulability analysis, the execution times of those hard real-time tasks must be known in advance, whose deadlines must be met in order to preserve a system's integrity. These can only be determined, however, if the system functions deterministically and predictably in time.

In the early days, the fundamental requirement of timeliness was realised in the application software by explicit synchronisation of the various tasks' execution schedules with a basic clock cycle. To this end, usually specific organisation

© Springer International Publishing AG 2016
K. Amunts et al. (Eds.): BrainComp 2015, LNCS 10087, pp. 142–156, 2016.
DOI: 10.1007/978-3-319-50862-7_11

programs were written, so-called "cyclic executives". Thus, predictable software behaviour was realised and the observation of the time conditions was guaranteed. Later, this method of cycle-synchronised programming was replaced by the more flexible approach of asynchronous multiprogramming as based on the task concept. Tasks can be activated and run at any time, asynchronously to a basic cycle. The method's flexibility and conceptual elegance was generally gained at the expense of renouncing predictability and guaranteed time conditions.

The feasible internal organisation of real-time computers has not satisfactorily been addressed with so far. Rather, conventional von Neumann computers were employed which are, however, optimised for average performance, whereas it is necessary to consider worst-case behaviour when meeting deadlines needs to be guaranteed. For process control applications conventional computers were adapted by just adding process peripherals and externally available interrupt lines. All other real-time requirements were met by software, viz. by operating systems, and by careful application programming. The problems identified in real-time systems design, however, could generally not be solved in this way.

Designed to realise predictably behaving real-time systems even in the presence of asynchronous multitasking, an asymmetrical multiprocessor architecture consisting of conventional general processors and an operating system co-processor is presented in the sequel. To motivate the concept pursued, analogies from everyday life and anatomy are analysed. Then, close attention is devoted to the earliest-deadline-first task scheduling policy, which has many advantageous properties and is, hence, employed in the system. Also with respect to the layered structure of typical real-time operating systems, we conclude that a real-time computer is organised best in form of a general-purpose processor co-operating with a co-processor dedicated to the operating system kernel.

2 Architectural Implications of Control Environments

As common in engineering, there are always many possible designs fulfilling a given set of demands — provided the problem is solvable with available technology. To derive an architecture appropriate for real-time control systems, we start off by considering analogies from other fields, where systems coping with real-time conditions have long been developed and used.

A manager and a secretary serve as first example. The secretaries' duties are receiving mail and telephone calls, eliminating unimportant chores, and minimising interruptions to the manager's work by visitors and callers. Furthermore, the secretary schedules the manager's work by arranging files in an appropriate sequence and by administrating meeting appointments. Thus, the manager's work becomes less hectic — i.e. the work's "real-time conditions" are eased — and more productive, because the tasks can be carried out with less frequent interruptions in a more sequential and organised manner.

As another analogy we consider the human brain, consisting of cerebrum, midbrain, diencephalon, cerebellum and extended spinal cord. The signals to and from various parts of the body are transmitted via the spinal marrow, which has some similarities with a computer bus. The nerves of the spinal marrow end at the brain's side in the extended spinal cord, which is closely connected to the midbrain, the diencephalon and the cerebellum. The last four organs have non-arbitrary and routine reflex functions. Specifically, they control the metabolism, the bodies' position, heat and water content, and regulate respiration and blood circulation. These organs are an important switching site between the nerves of the body and those of the brain. Furthermore, the immediate reflex centre is located here. In contrast to this, the other information processing functions of higher complexity, such as evaluation of sensual impressions, control of arbitrary actions and all intellectual tasks, are performed by the cerebrum.

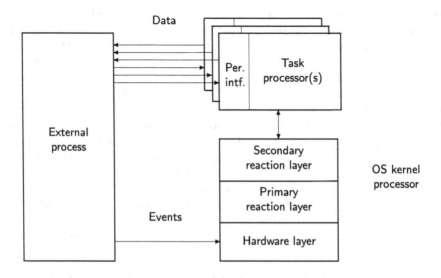

Fig. 1. Basic architecture of cephalomorph real-time computers

Taking pattern from these models, we now design the overall structure of a computer targeting to meet the specific requirements of real-time operation. The concept depicted in Fig. 1 provides for an asymmetrical system consisting of two dissimilar processors, a task processor and an operating system kernel processor. The task processor may be a classical von Neumann processor. It executes application tasks and the operating system tasks interfacing to them. Specifically, the operating system tasks allocated to this processor are mainly outer supervisor shell services, such as data exchange with peripherals and file management, provided in the form of independent tasks or subroutines called by the application tasks. Being the creative part, the task processor corresponds to the manager and to the cerebrum in the above analogies.

The operating system kernel is clearly and physically separated from the outer-layer tasks. It runs on the second dedicated processor, which houses the functions event, time and task management as well as communication and synchronisation. Although important and actually controlling the operation of the task processor, these functions are routine and would impose unnecessary burden to the latter. Thus, the kernel processor corresponds to the manager's secretary and to the brain's reflex centre, respectively. This concept can easily be extended to multiple task processors, each one executing its own task set, being controlled by a single operating system kernel co-processor.

3   Implications of Earliest-Deadline-First Scheduling

The fundamental requirement expected to be fulfilled by a process control computer employed in a hard real-time environment is to carry out all tasks within predefined time frames — assuming this is actually possible. Algorithms generating appropriate schedules for all possible task sets, such that each task concludes its execution before its given deadline, are referred to as feasible. A number of such algorithms has been identified in the literature [4, 5]. On the other hand, neither of the two scheduling policies most frequently supported by contemporary programming languages and real-time operating systems, namely the first-come-first-served and the fixed-priority algorithm, is feasible.

It is well established that the earliest-deadline-first algorithm is feasible for scheduling independent tasks on a single processor [5]. According to it, the task with the closest deadline among all ones waiting for execution is scheduled. Another algorithm feasible for both single and multiprocessor systems is the least-laxity-first scheme [4]. Unfortunately, it is only of theoretical interest, as it is pre-emptive and requires processor sharing when several tasks assume the same laxity. That, in turn, calls for counter-productive context-switching overhead. In contrast to least-laxity-first, the earliest-deadline-first algorithm does not require pre-emptive context-switches as long as no new task with an earlier deadline arrives. In fact, if the number of pre-emptions enforced by a scheduling procedure is considered as selection criterion, the earliest-deadline-first algorithm is optimal [4]. Even when tasks arrive dynamically, this policy maintains its properties and, then, generates optimal pre-emptive schedules [4].

When applied to multiprocessors, however, the earliest-deadline-first scheme ceases to be feasible. An extension of the policy re-establishing feasibility is the throw-forward algorithm [5]. It leads, however, to more pre-emptions and is more complex. This fact suggests an argument against using symmetric multiprocessors. To develop the argument further, consider the following example.

Let the set $\mathcal{T} = \{T_1 = (5,4),\ T_2 = (6,3),\ T_3 = (7,4),\ T_4 = (12,8),\ T_5 = (13,8),\ T_6 = (15,12)\}$ of six tasks be given at time $t = 0$ with each task being characterised by the tuple (Deadline, Required Execution Time), and let the tasks be processed on a homogeneous triple-processor system. The schedule provided by the throw-forward strategy[1] is displayed in Fig. 2 in form of a Gantt diagram. The example schedule requires five pre-emptions and corresponding context-switches. The latter may additionally result in repeated program loading, if the different processors do not share memory. The diagram also shows

---

[1] Note that feasible schedules with fewer pre-emptions may exist. There is, however, no algorithm (yet) to generate such schedules.

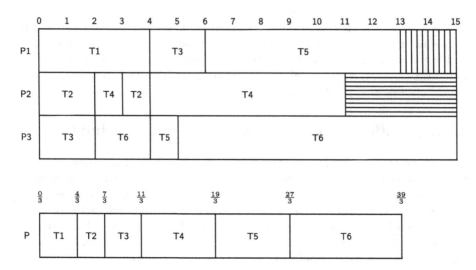

Fig. 2. Gantt diagram of a feasible schedule for a symmetric triple-processor system (top) and of a feasible schedule for a single processor system (bottom)

that two processors are idle for six time units before the task set is completely executed. Since several processors cannot simultaneously work on one task, it is impossible to balance the load and to reduce the task set's overall response time. On the other hand, if the same task set is scheduled earliest-deadline-first on a single processor assumed to be three times faster than each of the three original processors, the second Gantt diagram shown in Fig. 2 results. There, one task is executed after the other with no interruption, and there is no idling. Thus, time-consuming context-switches are prevented and, at any point in time, there needs to be only one program in main storage. Furthermore, the entire task set is processed earlier than in the triple-processor case. Since theoretical considerations usually — but unrealistically — neglect the overhead, the overall execution time proportion is further shifted in favour of the single processor structure. Hence, the factor for speeding up a single processor to reach the performance of an m-processor will generally be considerably less than m. Moreover, strictly sequential task execution eliminates synchronisation conflicts, which may give rise to waiting and processor idling in multiprocessors.

When deadlines and processor requirements of tasks are available a priori, the following necessary and sufficient condition [5] determines whether a task set given at a certain instant can be executed within its specified deadlines.

If any task's response time (until its deadline) is greater then, or equal to, the sum of its (residual) execution time and the execution times of all tasks scheduled to be run before it, then the schedule is feasible.

The complexity of schedulability analysis related to the throw-forward algorithm [5] is by far higher for the multiprocessor case than for single processors. The like holds with regard to the actual processor assignment scheme, too, since always the task with the shortest response time is executed in the single processor case. In contrast to this, the relations of task laxities to the response times of other tasks already assigned to processors need to be observed, and the algorithm also has to be invoked when a non-running task loses its slack time. Hence, the scheme must keep track of the instants when the laxities of non-assigned tasks vanish, or when a task's slack time becomes equal to the response time of another executing task. This feature adds considerably to the throw-forward algorithm's already high complexity.

In the ideal case, the earliest-deadline-first method guarantees one-at-a-time scheduling of tasks, modulo new task arrivals. Unproductive context-switches are thus eliminated. Furthermore, and even more importantly, resource access conflicts and many concurrency problems, such as deadlocks, do not occur and, hence, do not need to be handled.

The above discussion suggests to structure real-time computers as single processor systems. The idea can be extended to distributed systems by structuring them as sets of interconnected uniprocessors, each one dedicated to control a certain part of an external environment. Independent of considerations of overall system load, earliest-deadline-first scheduling is to be applied on each node in a distributed system. This scheme's implementation is facilitated by the fact that, typically, industrial process control systems are already designed in form of co-operating, possibly heterogeneous, single processor systems, even though the processors' operating systems do not yet schedule by deadlines.

This scheduling strategy establishes a guideline to be followed in designing a suitable architecture. The objective ought to be to maintain, as far as possible, strictly sequential execution of task sets. The sequential program flow in the processor(s) need(s) to be relieved of frequent interruptions caused by external and internal events. Such interruptions are counter-productive in the sense that they seldom result in immediate (re-) activations of associated tasks.

· To summarise, earliest-deadline-first task scheduling on single processors has the following advantages:

- Scheduling on the basis of task deadlines is feasible and problem-oriented.
- It allows to formulate tasks, and to extend and modify existing software without knowing the global task system.
- All tasks can be treated by a common scheduling policy, regardless of being activated sporadically or periodically, or possessing precedence relations.
- Upon a dynamic arrival of a ready task, the task's response time can be guaranteed — or a future overload detected.
- The cost of running the algorithm is almost negligible as its complexity is linear in the number of ready tasks.
- The cost of checking a task set's feasible schedulability is almost negligible as it grows linearly with the number of ready tasks and the check is trivial, i.e. the operating system is enabled to supervise if tasks are executed timely.
- Early overload detection and handling by dynamic load adaptation is facilitated, thus allowing system performance to degrade gracefully.
- The task pre-emptions required for feasible schedulability is minimised.

- Processor utilisation is maximised under the constraint that a task set's feasible schedulability is maintained.
- Schedules are essentially non-pre-emptive, i.e. task pre-emptions may only be caused when dormant tasks are activated or suspended ones are resumed.
- The sequence of task executions is determined at the instants of task (re-) activations, i.e. when a task turns ready, and remains constant afterwards; the order among the other ready tasks remains unchanged.
- The order of task processing is essentially sequential.
- Resource access conflicts and deadlocks are inherently prevented.
- Unproductive overhead is inherently minimised.
- The widely addressed priority inversion problem does not arise at all.
- Pre-emptable or not, tasks can be scheduled in a common way.

4   Architectural Concept

The asymmetric multiprocessor architecture as shown in Fig. 1 can be employed either as stand-alone device or as node in a distributed system. Each node consists of one co-processor and of one or more general task processors. The latter cannot be interchanged, because process control computers are typically hardwired to specific parts of technical processes. Hence, the functions of the general processors are determined by their respective subprocesses and cannot be migrated. Thus, the tasks assigned to each general processor can be scheduled independently of the tasks on other general processors. The data transmission lines to and from all input/output devices in the system are connected to the general processors, whereas all interrupt lines are wired to the co-processor.

Real-time computers are expected to recognise and to react to occurring events within a predefined time frame, or best instantaneously. With conventional hardware, prompt recognition and reaction are accomplished by interrupting the running task, determining the event's source, and switching to an appropriate interrupt handling task. The running task is thus pre-empted, even though it is likely to be unrelated to the interrupt. Furthermore, the task handling the newly arrived interrupt will not necessarily be executed before the pre-empted one, once the interrupt has been identified and acknowledged.

Owing to this inherent independence, the possibility to apply parallel processing — task execution as well as event recognition and administration — is given here. In order to preserve data integrity in the conventional architecture, tasks may inhibit to be interrupted during the execution of critical regions. Hence, there may be a considerable delay between the occurrence of an event and its recognition, for which no upper bound can be guaranteed. This situation is further impaired when several events occur (almost) simultaneously, thus resulting in both continuous pre-emptions of their corresponding handler tasks, and in postponement of some lower-priority reactions.

Addressing these problems, the co-processor proposed comprises a separate, independently working event recognition mechanism capable of commencing primary event reactions within predefined, guaranteed and short time frames. To

Table 1. Function assignment in the co-processor

Hardware layer	Accurate management of real time based on a high resolution clock
	Exact timing of operations (optional)
	Separate programmable interrupt generator for software simulation
	Event representation by storage element, latch for time of occurrence and counter of over-run event arrivals
	Synchroniser representation
	Shared variable representation
Primary reaction layer	Recognition of events, i.e. interrupts, signals, time events, status transfers of synchronisers and value changes of shared variables
	Commencement of secondary reactions
	Recording of events for error tracking
	Management of temporal schedules and critical instants
Secondary reaction layer	Deadline-driven processor scheduling with overload handling
	Task-oriented hierarchical storage administration
	Execution of (secondary) event reactions, esp. tasking operations
	Synchroniser administration
	Shared variable administration
	Acceptance of requests
	Initiation of processor activities

provide this capability, the co-processor is structured into three layers, whose functions are compiled in Table 1. In short, the co-processor executes the kernel of an operating system developed according to the needs of real-time application software. It maintains a real-time clock, and observes and handles all events related to this clock, to the external signals and to the accesses to common variables and synchronisers. Each of these conditions invokes assigned tasks into the ready state, which are then scheduled earliest deadline first.

The external process is controlled by tasks running on the general processors without being interrupted by the operating system. After re-scheduling caused by tasks newly invoked in response to events occurred, a running task is only pre-empted if this is unavoidable to ensure that all tasks will meet their deadlines.

Although only the co-processor (and optionally peripheral controllers for exactly timed and jitter-free I/O operations as described in [3]) really needs to know the absolute time, relative time may be available throughout a system: in any interested unit it can be implemented as a counter of time ticks generated by the co-processor and beginning at system initialisation. From the latter's recorded instant and the counter value absolute time is easily derivable.

The presented concept prevents non-deterministic interruptions from the environment to reach the general processors by (1) carefully preventing sources of unpredictable processor and system behaviour, (2) by loose coupling of task processors and (3) by synchronous operation of the co-processor. The predictability of a system's temporal execution behaviour achieved by this concept is sufficient to provide the necessary basis for the higher levels of system design.

5 Co-processor for the Operating System Kernel

To support determinism and for better performance, the operating system kernel co-processor is divided into two layers, a higher-level part called *secondary reaction layer (SRL)*, and a lower-level part or *primary reaction layer (PRL)*, see Fig. 1. Since their functions are tightly coupled, the processors implementing the two layers may communicate via a dual-port memory, where their interfaces reside in form of operating system data structures, and the real-time clock storage element. Conflicts of simultaneous access can be prevented by performing accesses exclusively in carefully defined time slots. In short, PRL performs elementary hardware functions like external event recognition, clock and time event administration etc., while SRL serves as interface to the task processors, manages their operating system service requests and carries out actual task scheduling on the basis of information on events provided by PRL.

There are several reasons for structuring the operating system kernel co-processor into two parts. An important one is the natural parallelism between the lower-level (signal sensing, administration of real-time clock, temporal schedules etc.) and the higher-level functions (scheduling, operating system routines). Exploiting this inherent parallelism improves the co-processor's performance and, hence, shortens its response times. Further, the primary reaction layer is intended to be implemented in hardware or in form of programmable logic.

The operating system kernel's single routines cannot be presented here in detail. Therefore, some statistics may suffice. The programs of the primary reaction layer are quite simple: 7 procedures with altogether less than 200 lines of high-level code. The programs of the secondary reaction level are a bit more complex. There are about 20 relatively simple procedures (less than 20 lines of code each) and two more complex ones (the procedures for task administration and to prepare the schedules of tasking operations). Together the programs consist of approximately 600 lines of code. Their typical complexity is of $O(n)$, with n being the number of tasks. Considering the limited sizes and complexities of the kernel functions, it may be possible to prove them correct with formal methods, which is quite important with regard to safety-related applications.

The primary reaction layer has the following basic functions.

Administrating the real-time clock: During power-on, all real-time counters throughout a system are reset. In the initialisation sequence the kernel co-processor acquires the current precise absolute time from a reliable source of Universal Time Co-ordinated (UTC) such as the Global Positioning System, adds the necessary (constant and known) overhead until the different counters in the system are started, and distributes it among all interested parties. Then, the system clock signal is enabled and all counters begin to count the same ticks. Hence, the relative times will be the same, and the constant offset to the absolute time known all over the system.

Administrating time events occurring in temporal schedules either for tasking operations or for continuation of their execution: SRL provides a vector of activities which are scheduled to be activated at certain times. PRL administers this vector, selects the closest time event and, upon its occurrence, provides information to SRL to take over the associated actions.

Receiving and handling signals from the process environment and monitoring occurrences of overruns: Events from the environment are received by a special external event recognition interface implemented in hardware and providing parallel digital I/O ports. Transitions on each of these ports set bits in a register. Upon periodic polling of the latter, set bits are cleared and registered in the operating system data structures together with time stamps. If an event appears more than once during the same polling cycle, an overrun bit is set indicating that at least one event was not serviced.

Enabling exact timing and/or synchronous operation: The exact timing feature offers the possibility to schedule *a part of a task* to be executed at an exactly defined instant. This can, in principle, not be accomplished by usual task-level scheduling on a time event. To achieve it, a task running in a task processor halts its own execution using an operating system call. The call associates a time schedule with this action, upon the fulfillment of which a continuation signal re-enables the program in the task processor by releasing the wait state. The continuation signals for all task processors can be triggered individually or simultaneously by disjunctive combination.

Notifying the actual events in the current system cycle to SRL by placing pertaining data into the common data structures, thus becoming available for actual scheduling of the associated tasks.

The secondary reaction layer communicates with the general processors, from which it receives calls for operating system services. These calls may require certain information about the states of the system or the tasks. Tasks may access the synchronisers and the common global variables residing in SRL. A change in status of these structures triggers an event to which a task activation may be associated. Important types of service calls are tasking requests. A task running on a general processor may request time-related and/or event-related scheduling of different tasking operations. The conditions are passed to PRL which triggers events upon their fulfillment. When such events occur, SRL invokes the tasks assigned to them, performs schedulability analysis, and actually places the ready tasks into the processor queue according to their deadlines.

6   Application Task Processors

The actual process control programs are executed on general processors. Only a small part of the operating system resides here performing communication with SRL and context-switching upon the latter's request. In a general processor's memory the program code of each task assigned to it is kept. Also, parts of these tasks' control blocks are residing there, holding the contexts of possibly pre-empted tasks. Basically, a general processor can be implemented using a wide variety of processing devices, such as microcontrollers, digital signal processors or automata based on programmable logic arrays. Important selection criteria are the envisaged purpose in the application domain, and determinism and predictability of the temporal program execution behaviour. Some features of the general processor are the following ones.

Intelligent process interfaces based on microcontroller- or programmable-logic-supported peripheral devices attach environments controlled to general processors via serial buses. Their services are available by calling pre-defined peripheral device drivers and providing parameters and data. By moving intelligence to peripheral devices, general processors are relieved from higher-level services, peripheral services become more flexible and fault-tolerant, and system safety is enhanced.

Peripheral devices must be designed carefully in a way rendering their timing behaviour deterministic and predictable. For instance, analogue-to-digital conversion can take different time in certain implementations depending on the input level. A consistent implementation of such a peripheral device is to permanently sample and convert the analogue value. Upon request always the value acquired last is returned without any delay. Assuming that the sampling interval is sufficiently small, the result is acceptable.

Exact timing of operations as already mentioned in the preceding section requires a counter-part in the general processors. After a task, reaching a point from where continuation at a certain time instant is requested, has issued the corresponding service call to the co-processor, it enters the wait state sending a wait signal to a simple circuit triggered by an I/O line. When the instant for resuming the task processor's operation and the execution of the task is reached, which is indicated by a time event, PRL generates the continuation signal which resets the wait signal and resumes operation.

While providing precise timing of process execution, e.g. for purposes of temporal synchronisation, this realisation seems to have the drawback of halting the processor, thus preventing other ready tasks from executing during the idle time until the instant of continuation. In practice, however, other tasks are not blocked, since the waiting times are kept short and are considered in the estimation of the corresponding tasks' run-times. As an alternative to this solution, and to prevent idle waiting, an exact timing feature can also be implemented on the level of intelligent peripheral interfaces having access to absolute time. Along with an I/O command, to such a peripheral the time is transmitted when the operation is to be performed. The calling task is suspended, waiting for the requested instant when the data are sent out or, respectively, latched into a buffer, ready to be read by the general processor. Which method is utilised depends on whether only peripheral operation or task execution as a whole is requested to be timed precisely.

Employing exact timing of input/output operations as introduced in [3], application designers can cope with the jitter problem: Just with a slight remaining jitter depending on the real-time clock, they can precisely prescribe when certain sensors are read or actuators set in closed regulatory loops.

Distributed processing: Process control and embedded applications are often implemented as distributed control systems in rather natural ways. The architecture proposed matches this approach on two levels, viz. on the one of task processors and on the level of intelligent peripheral interfaces.

7   Operating System Support and Tasking

Commensurating with their nature, scale, purpose, implementation etc., in embedded real-time control systems different options are realised with respect to system software functions. In some larger-scale and complex control applications complete operating systems can be employed. In smaller applications real-time executives are already sufficient, providing typical basic components of process control computer operating systems, such as interrupt handling, task management, communication and synchronisation, as well as time administration, input/output routines and operator interface. Often, these functions are custom-designed and directly incorporated into the application program code. A supervisor has a nucleus and a shell. Processes of an operating system nucleus are activated by interrupts, and handle events which require attention of the operating system. Shell processes, on the other hand, are handled in the same way as user tasks, i.e. under control of the task management.

The co-processor introduced here is dedicated to execute processes of the nucleus. Hence, it is home to event and time management, as well as to task management, communication and synchronisation. Since there is no intrinsic difference between user and shell processes in real-time environments, the functions of the supervisor shell, such as data exchange with peripherals and file management, can be provided in the form of tasks or subroutines running on the general processor(s). Thus, the presented approach constitutes a physical implementation of the layered model for real-time operating systems, involving a clear, physical separation between operating system nucleus on one side, and operating system shell and application software on the other.

To prevent unnecessary context-switches, the earliest-deadline-first policy is employed for task scheduling with a slight and simple modification: Even if a newly arrived task has an earlier deadline than the executing one, the running task is not pre-empted, unless the situation caused by the latest event requires immediate task re-scheduling. Apart from better performance due to considerably fewer pre-emptions, the problem of resource contention resulting from mutual exclusion of tasks using critical regions is thus minimised.

An application task, which resides on and is intended to be executed by a general processor, is in one of the following states:

Dormant: The task's code exists, and the task control block (TCB) holds its parameters. The TCB is split into two parts which hold (1) the system information about the tasks and (2) the tasks' current variable values. These parts reside in SRL and in the task processor, respectively.

Scheduled on event: The task is assigned to an event. As soon as the latter occurs, the task will be activated.

Ready: The task is moved into this state, when its condition to be run is fulfilled. Each time the task enters this state a schedulability analysis is dynamically performed to check whether its deadline is closer than the one of the executing task. If so, it is further checked whether the task's laxity allows the execution of the running task to be continued and, thus, a pre-emption to be prevented without violating any deadlines.

Buffered activation: Only one instance of the task may be active at the same time. If the task is already active and is to be activated anew due to fulfillment of some schedule, its activation is buffered, i.e. postponed until the already active instance is either completed or terminated.

Running: The task can only be put from the *ready* into the *running* state by the scheduler, which is part of the operating system being executed by SRL.

Suspended: Task activations may be suspended. In this state the task retains its internal logical state. As suspension is not temporally bounded, however, timing circumstances become invalid and must be restored upon continuation of task execution by defining a new deadline.

Waiting for synchronisation and critical regions: To synchronise with another one, the task may send, or wait for a signal. Also, to protect a part of a program, it may be enclosed into a critical region. If a certain signal is not present on "wait", or the task cannot enter an already occupied critical region, its state changes to *waiting for synchronisation*.

Tasks change their states upon operations such as *activate, terminate, end, suspend, continue* etc., which are included in the syntax of the programming language used to write application software. These operations can be scheduled to be executed upon fulfillment of a condition, called event, or a combination of several thereof. Events can be time-related and, then, of sporadic or periodic nature. They may occur at certain instants or after specified time intervals. Events not related to time are interrupts from the environment and value changes of shared variables. Schedules related or unrelated to time may be combined. This way, temporally bounded waiting for events from the environment is enabled. When a schedule is fulfilled, an associated task may be:

Activated: The task is put into the ready state and, consequently, actually run.

Terminated: The task is prematurely terminated and put into the dormant state. Also, all schedules related to the task are canceled.

Suspended: The task's activation is suspended, but its internal logical state is preserved, temporal circumstances are disregarded and, thus, become invalid.

Continued: After a suspension the task can be re-activated. A new deadline must be supplied.

Resumed: In general, "resume" is a combination of "suspend" and "continue", i.e. the task is immediately suspended and is resumed when the associated schedule is fulfilled. The actual execution of this function depends on the option "exactly": If not selected, the task changes its states from "running" to "suspended" and again to "ready", as it would if the functions "suspend" and "continue" were called explicitly. When "exact" timing is requested, however, the task does not leave the "running" state: Upon such a function call execution is halted, and continued immediately after occurrence of the scheduling event, which may be time-related or not, without any delays for scheduling, context switching and similar overhead. Waiting in the suspended state is temporally bounded by a "timeout" clause, being necessary to retain temporal predictability of task execution. When a timeout expires before the event has occurred, a given "ontimeout" sequence is executed. It is also possible to disregard temporal circumstances and set another deadline, which is reasonable when the "exactly" option is not chosen and the task must be re-scheduled for continuation.

Apart from the above, there are some other related actions, such as:

End: Normal task end when execution is completed.
Prevent: Cancellation of certain schedules.
Tstate, Sstate, Now: Monadic operators to acquire task or semaphore states, or absolute time.
Enable, Disable: Monadic operators to mask external signals.

For consistent inter-task synchronisation, send and wait functions are provided using signals. Further, mutual exclusion of tasks can be achieved using temporally bounded critical regions, which may be pre-emptable or not as indicated by an appropriate option. If any non-pre-emptable critical region exists in a task set, the longest one must be considered in schedulability analyses. Both features are implemented using semaphores and "lock" and "unlock" functions.

Waiting for a signal and to enter a critical region are both temporally bounded by "timeout" clauses. By providing corresponding "ontimeout" sequences, synchronisation delays become predictable and can be considered in task run-time estimation and in schedulability analysis. Similarly, it is possible to temporally bound any part of a program using a "during" construct. This has two functions: (1) to protect any temporally non-deterministic features (e.g. peripheral operations), and (2) to assert explicit estimation of a certain program part's run-time, whose automatically obtained estimate is expected to be imprecise and pessimistic. This assertion overrides automatic run-time estimations.

8   Conclusion

Conventional computers are still widely employed to run real-time and process control applications. With a minimum of additional features, viz. process peripherals, user-accessible interrupt lines and general multitasking operating systems, they are adapted to work in embedded systems. This primitive approach is insufficient and leads to a number of problems. Specifically, almost all hardware and software features of conventional computers, while improving traditional, *average* performance, do little for or even worsen the prospects for predictable real-time performance. These elements introduce unpredictable delays, unbounded contention and other plagues of predictable program execution and must, therefore, be considered harmful. Actually, contemporary real-time systems do not deserve to be called real time, since they do not use the notion of time. Rather, they are slightly modified multitasking systems allocating tasks on the basis of (often fixed) priorities, and handling real-time exceptions in a sudden, unpredictable manner. Thus, the state of affairs in using conventional von Neumann architectures in real-time computing is not acceptable.

In contrast, the architecture presented here supports the more appropriate, problem-oriented concept of time throughout. The scheduler makes sure that task deadlines are met under any circumstances. By utilising special-purpose hardware, event recognition times can be guaranteed, and the time behaviour of input/output operations can be planned precisely. The architecture incorporates parallelism in such a way that it does not lead to an increase in software complexity, because the architecture mirrors the parallelism inherent to the external real-time environments themselves. By allocating intrinsically independent functions to different hardware devices working in parallel, the architecture not only yields increased speed, but also and much more importantly, enhances predictability and dependability. Furthermore, the architecture enables the consequent development of a simple and small and, thus, dependable real-time operating system kernel. The semantic gap between hardware and application software is narrowed when incorporating the kernel as firmware into the architecture.

With its two dedicated and quite heterogeneous processors the proposed architecture resembles the human brain's distribution of immediate reactivity to midbrain, diencephalon, cerebellum and extended spinal cord, and of complex information processing to the cerebrum, in order to share with the human brain its property [1] "Man's evolutionary success is the capability of his prefrontal cortex to inhibit stimuli and to ponder before reacting."

References

1. Bauer, J.: Selbststeuerung – Die Wiederentdeckung des freien Willens. Karl Blessing Verlag, Munich (2015)
2. DIN 44 300 A2: Informationsverarbeitung. Beuth Verlag, Berlin-Cologne (1985)
3. Halang, W.A., Stoyenko, A.D.: Constructing Predictable Real Time Systems. Kluwer Academic Publishers, Boston-Dordrecht-London (1991)
4. Henn, R.K.J.: Deterministische Modelle für die Prozessorzuteilung in einer harten Realzeit-Umgebung. Ph.D. thesis, Technical University of Munich (1975)
5. Henn, R.K.J.: Feasible processor allocation in a hard real-time environment. Real-Time Syst. 1(1), 77–93 (1989)
6. Stankovic, J.A.: Misconceptions about real-time computing. IEEE Comput. 21(10), 10–19 (1988)

Towards the Ultimate Display for Neuroscientific Data Analysis

Torsten Wolfgang Kuhlen[1,2(✉)] and Bernd Hentschel[1,2]

[1] Virtual Reality and Immersive Visualization Group, Visual Computing Institute,
RWTH Aachen University, Kopernikusstraße 6, 52074 Aachen, Germany
kuhlen@vr.rwth-aachen.de
[2] JARA – High-Performance Computing, RWTH Aachen University,
Schinkelstraße 2, 52062 Aachen, Germany

Abstract. This article wants to give some impulses for a discussion about how an "ultimate" display should look like to support the Neuroscience community in an optimal way. In particular, we will have a look at immersive display technology. Since its hype in the early 90's, immersive Virtual Reality has undoubtedly been adopted as a useful tool in a variety of application domains and has indeed proven its potential to support the process of scientific data analysis. Yet, it is still an open question whether or not such non-standard displays make sense in the context of neuroscientific data analysis. We argue that the potential of immersive displays is neither about the raw pixel count only, nor about other hardware-centric characteristics. Instead, we advocate the design of intuitive and powerful user interfaces for a direct interaction with the data, which support the multi-view paradigm in an efficient and flexible way, and – finally – provide interactive response times even for huge amounts of data and when dealing multiple datasets simultaneously.

1 Introduction

Since the climax of its first hype-cycle in the early 90's, Virtual Reality (VR) technology has proven its value in a variety of application domains, e.g. product development, training, and psychology. Immersive visualization (IV) – defined as the interactive scientific visualization controlled by an immersive user interface – has been a particularly active field of research. First, IV promises faster, more comprehensive understanding of complex, spatiotemporal relationships owing to head-tracked, stereoscopic rendering and large field of regard. Second, it would provide a more natural user interface, specifically for spatial interaction tasks. In some domains of simulation science, like computational fluid dynamics, success stories of fully-fledged solutions as well as systematic studies have already proven the potential of IV to significantly enhance explorative analysis processes.

However, it is still an open question whether or not IV techniques make sense in the context of explorative analysis of neuroscientific data. In particular, the installation and sustained maintenance of high-end immersive VR systems, like CAVEs, is quite

© Springer International Publishing AG 2016
K. Amunts et al. (Eds.): BrainComp 2015, LNCS 10087, pp. 157–168, 2016.
DOI: 10.1007/978-3-319-50862-7_12

expensive. Operating immersive systems requires an expert team that provides both hardware management and user support. Finally, scientists must physically travel to the VR lab; it typically isn't "just next door." This creates an additional entry barrier for using such systems.

In order to become an integral part of scientific workflows in general – and those of neuroscientists in particular – immersive analysis tools will have to provide significant added value. In particular, they should feature intuitive user interfaces and concise visualization metaphors. Most importantly, a seamless integration into existing workflows will be a key to their wide-spread adoption.

In this article, we pick up arguments put forth in the last section of our 2014 article on "An explorative visual analysis of cortical neuronal network simulations" [Kuhlen2014a]. In particular, we would like to give some impulses for a discussion about how an "ultimate" display should look like to optimally support the neuroscience community. To this end, we will first provide a systematic overview of the various design aspects and options in terms of immersive displays. Then we will outline how immersive analysis platforms can be evaluated, followed by a discussion about the relevance of different display design parameters for high-fidelity platforms aiming at an analysis of neuroscientific data. Finally, we will give some conclusions and recommendations for the use of immersive displays in the context of explorative neuroscientific data analysis.

2   Brief Overview of Display Design Options

While resolution, size, contrast, and color depth are regular quality metrics for standard desktop monitors, high fidelity displays encompass additional design parameters like field of view or field of regard and, in particular, aspects of 3D visual perception, i.e. options to address stereo and motion parallax. These additional parameters should eventually contribute to an effect known as "immersion". In the context of Virtual Reality, (visual) immersion refers to perception of being physically present in an artificial, computer-generated environment. Contemporary VR systems create this illusion by covering large parts of the user's field of view with rendered images, created via computer graphic techniques. In contrast to a classical computer monitor display, the user does not only look at her data from the outside in, but can literally step into her data.

Available display technology achieves the effect of immersion by either a head-mounted or a room-mounted approach. Recently, solutions based on mobile devices have been proposed, particularly for use in a head-mounted setting. In their current form, however, they cannot provide a high degree of immersion. Yet, in combination with larger displays, mobile devices might contribute to a smooth interaction during a data analysis session though.

Head-mounted displays (HMDs) typically have one or two small LCD, LCOS, or OLED panels with lenses integrated in a helmet-like assembly. Since an HMD is worn by the user, its displays move along with the user's head motions. Besides resolution, field of view is a crucial quality metric for HMDs. The field of view (FOV) of a display, given as a solid angle, is the extent of the virtual scene that is seen at a specific moment in time. Ideally, the FOV provided by an HMD is identical or at least not significantly smaller than the human visual field of vision, which is nearly 180° in the horizontal plane. Since the built-in display panels are located in close distance to the user's eyes, it is a non-trivial task though to provide a large FOV in combination with a resolution that is high enough so that the user does not perceive single pixels.

In contrast, room-mounted displays are typically installed at a fixed place in a lab or an office environment. Classical room-mounted displays range from large desktop monitors, over combinations of several monitors up to large, tiled display walls, where multiple display panels are arranged in a matrix-style in order to provide ultra-high resolutions. Alternatively, display walls can be realized via rear projection technology. Again, by combining multiple projectors, high resolution walls can be implemented. Projection-based systems come at the cost of reduced contrast and a large spatial footprint, whereas panel-based systems currently available still suffer from bezels in-between individual panels.

Under the assumption that the user is looking straight at a display, large display walls offer a well-covered field of view. However, in room-mounted displays that aim at immersive VR, this assumption is invalidated: the user may freely move around and, in particular, rotate her head. This difference is captured by the term field of regard (FOR); in contrast to FOV, FOR does not exclude head rotations, i.e., it depicts the extent of the virtual scene that is seen when a user is allowed to move her head. Since in an HMD, screens move per definition with the user's head, they naturally provide full FOR. In room-mounted displays, FOR is influenced by the number of screens and their geometries, and the angles at which single screens face each other. High FOR has been shown to be intimately linked to high levels of immersion. In particular, FOR – and thus the level of immersion – can be enhanced by moving from a flat screen to a curved display surface, or by arranging multiple display walls around the user. Along these lines, a cube-like configuration led to the famous CAVE introduced by Cruz-Neira et al. [Cruz-Neira1992]. In their concept, a rear projection to all four walls, the floor, and the ceiling provides a fully-immersive room-mounted display with a 360° FOR.

In contrast to head-mounted displays, their room-mounted counterparts support collaborative data analysis in a more natural way. As a compromise between FOR on the one hand, and costs and footprint on the other hand, concrete implementations of CAVE-like systems omit up to two projection walls and/or the ceiling projection. Until recently, CAVE-like setups have exclusively relied on rear-projection. Diverging from that design, Reda et al. discuss the use of LCD-panel walls arranged in an almost cylindrical setup [Reda2013]. These systems provide significantly higher resolution and contrast. The level of immersion is considerably limited though, since the use of LCD panels currently precludes the realization of a floor projection. This leads to undesired clipping effects in the virtual scene. In particular, virtual objects in the user's immediate vicinity become problematic unless she stands extremely close to the horizontally aligned screens.

When designing a – yet hypothetical – optimal 3D display, aspects of visual perception in 3D space are key factors. These can be separated into psychological and physiological cues. Psychological cues like occlusion, perspective shortening, or light and shadows, can adequately be addressed by means of high-quality, high-performance rendering algorithms and lighting models. Stereo and motion parallax comprise the most important physiological cues. In head-mounted displays, stereoscopy can be achieved in a straight-forward manner via two different screens, one for each eye, or via splitting a single screen. Room-mounted displays rely on stereo technologies like polarization, INFITEC™, or the active shutter technique, just to mention the most prominent ones [see, e.g., Kuhlen2006]. While these technologies require the user to wear specific stereo glasses, autostereoscopic displays are – despite significant progress in the past decade – still lacking in terms of channel separation and thus not ready for wide-spread use. In order to implement motion parallax, the user's head motions need to be tracked in real-time. Whereas head tracking is optional for single display walls, it is obviously mandatory in HMD-based or CAVE-like VR systems. Traditionally, real-time motion tracking in 3D space has been challenging in terms of accuracy, precision, and latency. Fortunately, affordable and reliable tracking technologies, like opto-electronical systems based on infrared light reflecting markers, have become available in the last five to ten years, and even low cost systems developed for portable displays like smartphones are capable of doing a remarkably good job. In fact, smartphones have recently become popular as a key component of low cost HMDs, where they simultaneously serve as display as well as tracking device.

More than any other mode of visualization, data exploration is highly dependent of a high level of interactivity. In fact, we argue that a high level of both immersion and interactivity are the two driving factors behind immersive visualization. While the question how interactive an explorative visualization tool has to be is relevant in a desktop setting as well, an immersive setup opens possibilities for new interaction designs which critically depend on low latency, immediate feedback. Instead of just operating on images of the data, users can directly interact (work) with the data itself in 3D space.

To summarize, the question of preferring a high-fidelity display over a standard one is not a binary decision. Instead, it is a trade-off between several different factors, including display size, resolution, field of view, field of regard, aspects of 3D vision, and more. Even the question of a non-immersive versus an immersive display is not a binary one. Multiple levels of immersion for room-mounted displays exist, depending on the size and number of screens used. In fact, the level of immersion is mainly determined by the field of regard, ranging from a fully-fledged CAVE over single rear-projection or panel-based walls down to small VR-systems that fit into an office environment. Furthermore, a decision for immersive or at least semi-immersive opens the door for more design options with respect to user interfaces for data analysis. We can choose between 2D or 3D interfaces, between direct or indirect interaction metaphors, and even whether or not to include other modalities than just vision, e.g. audio and/or haptic feedback.

All display and interaction options come with specific pros and cons. In the remainder of this article we would like to start a discussion about the relevance of different design parameters for an adequate analysis specifically aiming at neuroscientific data.

3   How to Evaluate Immersive Analysis Platforms

It is a common observation that domain experts, e.g. from computational engineering science, require ever higher image resolutions for an adequate visual analysis of their data. For example, modern microscopy methods in neuroscience allow scientists to record brain tissue data at resolutions of about 100.000^2 pixels per slice [Axer2011, Reckfort2015]. This amounts to 10 billion pixels, only about 8 million (0.08%) of which can be captured at any given time on a high resolution UHD monitor. Hence, neuroscientific data analysis might decisively benefit from very high resolution and/or large display area beyond the capabilities of a single desktop monitor. But how much is a high-fidelity analysis platform really about screen real estate, i.e. raw pixel count and display size? Do immersive VR displays really have the potential to enhance the analysis process?

The fields of Virtual Reality and Immersive Visualization emerged in the late 80s and the 90s. From the very beginning, visual analysis of scientific data had been propagated as one of the "killer applications" for this technology. Steve Bryson from the NASA Ames Research Center undoubtedly pioneered the field with his introduction of the virtual wind tunnel, published at one of the first IEEE Visualization conferences [Bryson1991]. As soon as CAVEs became available, visual analysis was also ported to these systems. Above all, the inventors of the CAVE themselves have implemented scientific data analysis applications, e.g. molecular modeling and weather model analysis [Cruz-Neira1993]. Last but not least, oil and gas visualization developed by the Berkeley National Labs were among the most advanced VR applications in the 90's [Jacobsen1995].

For the subsequent decade, the seminal progress report by van Dam and his colleagues in [vanDam2000] formed an anchor point for an entire generation of IV research. The authors propose VR-enabled visualization as a mid-term solution to what they call the "accelerating data crisis", i.e. the fact that contemporary data sources (even then) produced data far faster than it could be analyzed, let alone turned into meaningful insights. With this growing size and complexity of data in mind, they claim that "IVR can provide powerful techniques for scientific visualization. The research agenda for the technology sketched here offers a progress report, a hope, and a call to action." Among other aspects, the report lists research and engineering challenges which – in the eyes of the authors – have to be solved before VR can become a useful tool. The discussion includes display technology, rendering performance, interaction metaphors, interoperability, and haptics as key factors.

Since then, quite several VR-based data analysis applications have been developed, which can be seen as success stories for the utility of immersive displays, in particular for the purpose of discussing and/or communicating complex scientific data with/to colleagues, stakeholders, and the broader public. Despite these successes, the actual "killer application" in which VR technology has proven its value as a necessary requirement for a significant scientific breakthrough is yet to come.

In order to provide evidence in favor of immersive VR for scientific data analysis, systematic user studies are necessary. Given the specific setting of explorative IV, meaningful studies with dependable results are extremely difficult to design, however. First, a large number of independent variables have to be taken into account. In particular, the utility of VR might depend on the characteristics of the specific data set that has to be explored, in combination with the concrete tasks that have to be performed on this data. This makes it difficult to derive general conclusions. Second, quite some side effects like the technical quality of the VR system in terms of resolution, stereo technology, brightness and brightness uniformity, tracking latency etc., must not be neglected. Finally, to come to relevant findings, sufficiently complex and realistic scientific data should be used in the studies. As a consequence, viable subjects for user studies have to be domain experts. This limits the number of adequate participants, which in turn reduces the expressiveness of statistic tests and hence of the overall study.

Despite these difficulties, a few studies have aimed at investigating the effects of VR-based visualizations in a systematic way. For example, Laha et al. recently provided more general, empirical evidence for the benefits of IV in the context of volume data exploration [Laha2012, Laha2014]. In particular, they separately examined the contribution of stereoscopy, head tracking, and field of regard on user performance. To keep the complexity of their studies within reasonable bounds, they limited their experiments to three different tasks and included three volume data sets with different characteristics. Indeed, their studies provide solid evidence that all investigated aspects of an immersive display make a positive contribution to the users' performance. Quite interestingly, they found the most significant, positive effect for field of regard, i.e. users performed far better in a CAVE scenario as compared to a single wall setup.

4   The Contribution of Immersion to Neuroscientific Data Analysis

Systematic studies about the utility of VR displays for the analysis of neuroscientific data do not exist, yet. In order to assess the contribution of VR technology to high-fidelity analysis platforms, we will therefore focus on two specific neuroscientific analysis applications which we have developed over the last few years. Analogously to other application fields, VR offers the promise of faster and more comprehensive understanding of complex, spatial relationships of neuroscientific data due to head-tracked, stereoscopic rendering and large field of regard. Second, VR provides a more natural user interface, specifically for spatial interaction tasks.

The first example called "InCytBrain" has resulted from our collaboration with the Institute of Neuroscience and Medicine INM-1 at the Forschungszentrum Juelich and targets the assessment of probabilistic tractography data [Rick2011]. Probabilistic tractography has become an established method to account for the inherent uncertainties of the actual course of fiber bundles in MRI data. InCytBrain relies on a VR-embedded, real-time direct volume rendering algorithm to display multiple volumetric data sets in a semi-transparent overlay. Besides the fiber tracts themselves, the depiction of brain areas gives an additional clue to the anatomical connection of fiber tracts. To facilitate intuitive exploration of the data, we not only emphasize spatial patterns but additionally allow users to interactively control the amount of visible anatomical information. A clipping cone called the "virtual flashlight" can be controlled by the user via a direct interaction metaphor in 3D space, which allows a precise inspection of anatomic structures in the direct vicinity of fiber pathways. The data analysis application is deployed on common desktop computers as well as on high-fidelity immersive displays up to CAVEs. In the former, its interaction is based on classical desktop hardware, i.e. mouse and – to a lesser extent – keyboard; in the latter, it relies on head-tracking and a 6DOF input device.

The second example "VisNEST" evolved from our collaboration with the Institute of Neuroscience and Medicine INM-6 at the Forschungszentrum Juelich and has been discussed in more detail in [Nowke2013, Kuhlen2014a]. VisNEST is an explorative analysis tool that visualizes simulation output of large neural networks. One of the driving challenges behind its development was the integration of macroscopic data with microscopic simulation results. As a consequence, unlike the first example, the focus is not exclusively on the rendering of volumetric data. Instead, a multi-view paradigm is used in order to combine structural and dynamic information via a selection of geometrical views and abstract data displays. The overarching design goal was to effectively and efficiently support neuroscientists in the exploration phase of a neuronal network model analysis [Nowke2015]. Again, the application scales from standard desktop workstations to large CAVE-like virtual environments. While the 3D interaction part in this example is not as pronounced as in the first one, the rather high resolution and the large amount of screen real-estate of modern high-fidelity displays enables the integration of a number of views in a single environment without sacrificing essential qualities, e.g. readability of individual plots or their legends. This feature is crucial to provide seamless integration of a number of different data modalities. Yet, because of the complexity of the depicted 3D data – both geometrical and graph-based – this application still benefits from a fully immersive display system [Kuhlen2014a, Kuhlen2014b].

After several months of experience with early prototypes of the two applications sketched above, it turns out that neuroscientists prefer to run them on small-scale, semi-immersive VR systems, allowing for stereoscopic, head-tracked rendering and direct interaction in 3D space, while fitting into the scientists' office environment. Occasionally, neuroscientists use RWTH Aachen University's aixCAVE, or the cylindrical stereo display wall installed at the Juelich Supercomputing Centre; yet they primarily call upon these systems to demonstrate research results to stakeholders and the broader public.

Typical statements resulting from informal interviews with neuroscientists are:

- "For my current neuroscientific research, semi-immersive displays became quite handy for visualizing complex 3D data. This is particularly true for data from different modalities such as in-vivo structural, functional and connectivity results and post-mortem high-resolution microstructural data. Visualizing these data across different scales in a common 3D framework helps to get a clear picture how they interact with each other."
- "The marketing aspect is unbeatable! Also, teaching could benefit from (semi-) immersive platforms. As a tool in neuroscientific research however, I am not satisfied yet. More functionality needs to be added to the prototypes to gain more benefit."
- "It is cumbersome to make people come to the lab".

We see these comments as a mixed blessing. On the one hand, they give early credit to IV techniques. On the other hand, they clearly point out where work has to be done. A few of the aspects raised here will be covered in the next section.

5   Conclusions and Recommendations

Based on the collaboration with neuroscientists from the Forschungszentrum Juelich within the EU's FET Flagship "The Human Brain Project", within the Helmholtz Portfolio Project "Supercomputing and Modeling of the Human Brain", and within JARA-HPC's Cross Sectional Group on Immersive Visualization, prototypical applications for neuroscientific data analysis, like "InCytBrain" and "VisNEST", have been developed. These applications, their continued development and in particular the strong focus on direct user collaboration provide valuable data points underpinning the design of a future high fidelity workplace for neuroscientific data analysis. In addition, the following considerations are based on almost two decades of experience with the operation of different high-fidelity, immersive displays on the one hand, and software development for scientific data analysis tools on the other hand.

Obviously, any non-standard display and interaction technology needs to provide a significant added-value for the data analysis process as compared to a standard, desktop session in order to become widely accepted by scientists. This added-value might not exclusively concern gaining scientific insight in terms of both, effectivity and efficiency, but might also include a communication or presentation of scientific results to stakeholders or a broader public in an intuitive and attractive way. In any case, the benefits offered by IV in a neuroscientific context have to outweigh its costs, namely in terms of hardware, software development, and process integration.

As a first conclusion, we argue that in the mid- to long-term, for an adequate analysis of neuroscientific data, ultra-high resolution displays will be needed. Beyond a more efficient analysis of high resolution microscopic brain data as already mentioned above, such high-fidelity displays allow for a convenient analysis of multiple views to neuroscientific data. As already demonstrated in [Kuhlen2014a], the multi-view paradigm is going to play an increasingly important role in neuroscientific data analysis. To approach a profound understanding of the human brain, the type of data integration facilitated by this paradigm will be a key: it will be necessary to establish correlations between structure and function, between simulation results and experimental data, and between data from different modalities and at the different scales. Such analyses not only need extremely high resolutions in terms of number of pixels to present these multiple views simultaneously to the users, but also require a much higher responsiveness as compared to standard analysis procedures.

In fact, neuroscientists state that their analysis processes are getting more and more explorative by their nature. In contrast to a confirmative analysis setting, which targets the verification of a pre-defined hypothesis, explorative analysis is characterized by a mostly undirected search in the data and by establishing links between different data modalities with the goal to identify hypotheses about the researched phenomena. It is this initial browsing that helps to establish initial hypotheses about the data at hand and its driving mechanisms. These hypotheses, in turn, might well form the basis for a new discovery. The resulting trial-and-error approach is significantly different from the much less interactive process of confirmative analysis. As a consequence, an adequate high-fidelity analysis workplace should enable short response times at interactive rates. This combination – a large number of pixels and high interactivity – already forms a research challenge in its own right. The system's latency, i.e. the time delay between a user's action, e.g. changing a visualization parameter, and the presentation of the result(s) on the display, should be short enough to support the explorative character of the analysis process. Most standard workplaces, and in particular WWW-based analysis tools, lack that performance, especially when multiple datasets, each of them potentially huge, get incorporated into an analysis session. As a second conclusion, we can thus derive that a high-fidelity analysis workplace needs to leverage high-performance computing resources and high-bandwidth data transmission to achieve the responsiveness needed. In particular, efficient parallel algorithms will have to be developed, which specifically target low latency feedback to the user. Note that this might not be identical to minimizing overall runtime [Wolter2006].

Whether an analysis of neuroscientific data will profit from immersive display features, like stereoscopic, viewer-centered projection and large field of regard, cannot be conclusively answered at this point. Interviews with neuroscientists (see above) indicate that these features are beneficial for communication and marketing purposes at least. Systematic user studies have demonstrated that immersive displays are beneficial for the analysis of volume data. The data sets in these studies are not about neuroscientific content, though. Our initial experiences lead to the assumption that, if scientific insight is the neuroscientist's goal, immersive displays probably don't provide significant added value for the analysis of standard-resolution volume data like, e.g., MRI or CT records. We are optimistic though, that immersive displays will become crucial once analysis tools will become available that allow for an analysis of extremely complex and inherently 3D data at interactive rates, such as 3D PLI records or 3D graphs representing the activities within huge, simulated neuronal networks. The techniques enabling such tools are part of the Human Brain Project's research agenda. Assuming immersive displays do improve the quality of the analysis process in principle, they must be integrated seamlessly into existing workflows in order to become a widely accepted part of a neuroscientist's daily work. For example, results and insights achieved during an immersive analysis session should be easily transferrable to other platforms for later re-use and dissemination at the scientists' desks.

Our third conclusion and recommendation is thus: beyond the design of a suitable output device, we advocate the design of natural 3D user interfaces, which go beyond contemporary device-based solutions and harness users' natural ability to navigate in and interact with 3D environments, and which still seamlessly integrate with the neuro-scientists' existing workflows. We anticipate that this aspect of natural 3D interaction will be a key to the adoption of IV techniques.

Also, practical issues like costs and footprint of immersive technology, as well as its accessibility are non-trivial factors. Today's high-end immersive systems, such as CAVEs, are expensive and have to be supported by qualified personnel. Contrasting this investment, the Oculus Rift [Oculus 2015] HMD recently provoked a new hype for VR; it promises to bring immersion into offices and homes around the world. It can be argued, however, in how far these consumer devices in their current form will be able to significantly contribute to scientific applications. Although the latest generation of HMDs features significant improvements in terms of resolution and tracking quality, both are not good enough just yet for an analysis of complex scientific data, not to mention principle issues like wearing comfort and motion sickness.

With today's technology at hand, tiled displays based on LCD panels might serve as a good compromise between resolution, costs, footprint, and level of immersion. Although they are still far from an ultimate display, they provide many pixels and at least some level of immersion. Also, first CAVE-like systems have become available which are based on LCD panel technology instead of rear projection. While it is not clear where the development of HW technology for displays will finally go, our final – and maybe most urgent – recommendation is to continuously advance the development of software tools for neuroscientific analysis. These next-generation tools should offer intuitive and powerful user interfaces for a direct interaction with the data, support the multi-view paradigm in an efficient and flexible way, and – finally – provide interactive response times even for huge amounts of data and when dealing multiple datasets simultaneously.

In this paper, we have argued that the key advantage of immersive visualization stems from natural, spatial interaction (see also [Kuhlen2014b]). This includes a range of techniques, e.g. head tracking and view dependent projection, which enable users to intuitively shift their viewpoint, and 3D interaction metaphors which allow them to control a variety of visualization parameters from "within their data". To be more specific, we believe that the potential of immersive visualization is neither about the raw pixel count, nor about other display-centric characteristics; it is about the users being immersed in their data.

This argument likely holds for data analysis tasks in general. With regard to neuroscience, we see several aspects that further complicate matters. Chief among these is the dire need to eventually fuse data from a vast variety of data sources differing in scale by several orders of magnitude. Moreover, this data is extremely diverse in nature: it covers classical 3D data modalities from medical imaging, derived atlases, simulated spike trains, experimental data, statistical properties, data derived from publications, etc. For all these data types, analysis tools and workflows have been developed for decades and the status quo represents the best effort in each separate field. So, realistically, no single data analysis tool will ever provide a solution for all analysis challenges in this exponentially large design space. However, a cleverly engineered framework that supports the integration of "the right tool for the job" wherever needed might be a step in the right direction. To this end, we argue that immersive user interfaces provide an even better tool for the job for a variety of tasks that arise regularly in neuroscientific workflows; and these tools will provide their ultimate value only when they are integrated in such a framework.

Acknowledgements. The research leading to this article has received funding from the European Union Seventh Framework Programme (FP7/2007-2013) under grant agreement 604102 (HBP) and from the Helmholtz Portfolio Theme "Supercomputing and Modeling for the Human Brain".

References

1. Axer, M., Amunts, K., Gräßel, D., Palm, C., Dammers, J., Axer, H., Pietrzyk, U., Zilles, K.: A novel approach to the human connectome: ultra-high resolution mapping of fiber tracts in the brain. NeuroImage **54**(2), 1091–1101 (2011)
2. Bryson, S., Levit, C.: The virtual windtunnel: an environment for the exploration of three-dimensional unsteady flows. In: Proceedings of IEEE Visualization 1991, pp. 17–24 (1991)
3. Cruz-Neira, C., Leigh, J., Papka, M., Barnes, C., Cohen, S.M., Das, S., Engelmann, R., Hudson, R., Roy, T., Siegel, L., Vasilakis, C., DeFanti, T.A., Sandin, D.J.: Scientists in wonderland: a report on visualization applications in the CAVE virtual environment. Commun. ACM **35**(6), 64–72 (1992)
4. Cruz-Neira, C., Sandin, D.J., DeFanti, T.A., Kenyon, R.V., Hart, J.C.: The CAVE: audio visual experience automatic virtual environment. In: Proceedings of the IEEE Virtual Reality Conference, pp. 59–66 (1993)
5. Gewaltig, M.-O., Diesmann, M.: NEST (NEural Simulation Tool). Scholarpedia **2**(4), 1430 (2007)
6. Hadwiger, M., Beyer, J., Jeong, W.-K., Pfister, H.: Interactive volume exploration of petascale microscopy data streams using a visualization-driven virtual memory approach. IEEE Trans. Vis. Comput. Graph. **18**(12), 2285–2294 (2012)
7. Hentschel, B., Tedjo, I., Probst, M., Wolter, M., Behr, M., Bischof, C., Kuhlen, T.W.: Interactive blood damage analysis for ventricular assist devices. IEEE Trans. Vis. Comput. Graph. **14**(6), 1515–1522 (2008)
8. Jacobsen, J.S., Bethel, E.W., Datta-Gupta, A., Holland, P.J.: Petroleum reservoir simulation in a virtual environment. In: Proceedings of the 13th SPE Symposium on Reservoir Simulation, pp. 233–247 (1995)
9. Kuhlen, T.W., Assenmacher, I., Jerabkova, L.: Interacting in virtual reality. In: Kraiss, K.-F. (ed.) Advanced Man-Machine Interfaces, pp. 263–314. Springer, Heidelberg (2006)
10. Kuhlen, T.W., Hentschel, B.: Towards an explorative visual analysis of cortical neuronal network simulations. In: Grandinetti, L., Lippert, T., Petkov, N. (eds.) BrainComp 2013. LNCS, vol. 8603, pp. 171–183. Springer, Heidelberg (2014)
11. Kuhlen, T.W., Hentschel, B.: Quo vadis CAVE – does immersive visualization still matter? IEEE Comput. Graph. Appl. J. **34**(5), 14–21 (2014)
12. Laha, B., Sensharma, K., Schiffbauer, J.D., Bowman, D.A.: Effects of immersion on visual analysis of volume data. IEEE Trans. Vis. Comput. Graph. **18**(4), 597–606 (2012)
13. Laha, B., Bowman, D.A., Socha, J.J.: Effects of VR system fidelity on analyzing isosurface visualization of volume datasets. IEEE Trans. Vis. Comput. Graph. **20**(4), 513–522 (2014)
14. Nowke, C., Schmidt, M., van Albada, S., Eppler, J., Bakker, R., Diesmann, M., Hentschel, B., Kuhlen, T.W.: VisNEST – interactive analysis of neural activity data. In: IEEE Symposium on Biological Data Visualization, pp. 65–72 (2013)
15. Nowke, C., Zielasko, D., Weyers, B., Peyser, A., Hentschel, B., Kuhlen, T.W.: Integrating visualizations into modeling NEST simulations. Front. Neuroinform. **9**(29) (2015)
16. Reckfort, J., Wiese, H., Pietrzyk, U., Zilles, K., Amunts, K., Axer, M.: A multiscale approach for the reconstruction of the fiber architecture of the human brain based on 3D-PLI. Front. Neuroanat. **9**, 118 (2015)
17. Reda, K., Febretti, A., Knoll, A., Aurisano, J., Leigh, J., Johnson, A., Papka, M.E., Hereld, M.: Visualizing large, heterogeneous data in hybrid-reality environments. IEEE Comput. Graph. Appl. **33**(4), 38–48 (2013)

18. Rick, T., von Kapri, A., Caspers, S., Amunts, K., Zilles, K., Kuhlen, T.W.: Visualization of probabilistic fiber tracts in virtual reality. In: Studies in Health Technology and Informatics, vol. 163, pp. 486–492. IOS Press (2011)
19. van Dam, A., Forsberg, A., Laidlaw, D.H., LaViola, J., Simpson, R.M.: Immersive virtual reality: a progress report. IEEE Comput. Graph. Appl. **20**(6), 26–52 (2000)
20. Wolter, M., Hentschel, B., Schirski, M., Gerndt, A., Kuhlen, T.W.: Time step prioritising in parallel feature extraction on unsteady simulation data. In: Proceedings of EG Symposium on Parallel Graphics and Visualization (EGPGV), pp. 91–98 (2006)

Sentiment Analysis and Affective Computing: Methods and Applications

Barbara Calabrese and Mario Cannataro$^{(\boxtimes)}$

University Magna Græcia of Catanzaro, Viale Europa, 88100 Catanzaro, Italy
{calabreseb,cannataro}@unicz.it

Abstract. New computing technologies, such as affective computing and sentiment analysis, are raising a strong interest in different fields, such as marketing, politics and, recently, life sciences. Examples of possible applications in the last field, regard the detection and monitoring of depressive states or mood disorders and anxiety conditions. This paper aims to provide an introductory overview of affective computing and sentiment analysis, through the discussion of the main processing techniques and applications. The paper concludes with a discussion relative to a new approach based on the integration of sentiment analysis and affective computing to obtain a more accurate and reliable detection of emotions and feelings for applications in the life sciences.

Keywords: Social network · Life sciences · Sentiment analysis · Affective computing

1 Introduction

Mood disorders, such as depression or bipolar disorders and anxiety have direct effects on emotions [1]. Psychologists reported changes in expressive facial and vocal cues for people affected by these disorders [2,3]. For example, in video recordings, avoiding eye contact and using short sentences with flat intonation are typical conditions of depressed people. Classification of facial expression and voice for detecting emotions concerns the affective computing discipline. This discipline involves multidisciplinary knowledge and describes computing that is connected to emotion. Affective computing technologies sense the emotional state of a user (via sensors, microphone, cameras, etc.) and respond by performing specific, predefined product/service features [4]. Recent works [5,6] focused on multimodal analysis of facial expression, voice and other variables relative to the movement or body posture. These approaches, that belong to affective computing field, could support clinicians in the diagnosis, monitoring and treatment of mood and anxiety disorders. Although affective computing provides several quantitative measurements, nevertheless, in the clinical and research context, specialists currently do not use quantitative and objective measures.

Today also sentiment analysis (i.e. sentiment analysis or opinion mining extracts, identifies and characterizes the sentiment content of a text, [7]), applied

© Springer International Publishing AG 2016
K. Amunts et al. (Eds.): BrainComp 2015, LNCS 10087, pp. 169–178, 2016.
DOI: 10.1007/978-3-319-50862-7_13

on textual data extracted from social networks, starts to receive attention for their usefulness at clinical and diagnostic level. The social networks represent a potentially infinite source of user data, usable both for scientific and commercial applications. Specifically, they store a lot of data regarding the single individual and behavior, as well as information related to individuals and their relationship with other individuals, i.e. a sort of collective behavior. Users are given opportunities to exhibit different behaviors such as sharing, posting, liking, commenting, and befriending conveniently [8]. Thus, analyzing social network data may be helpful to detect behaviour, sentiment, opinions, attitudes, emotions of individuals as well of communities. Some works have pointed out that the online depressed writers use more first person singular pronouns and more negative words [9]. Depressed users post generally in the night because they suffer from chronic insomnia. Moreover, social networks may be useful for self-monitoring, i.e. people's monitoring of and control over how they present themselves publicly [10]. In [11], the authors demonstrated that posts on Facebook could partially predict the users self-monitoring (SM), that is supposed to be linked with users expression behavior in the online environment.

However, the sentiment recognition and classification from text could be difficult and inaccurate due to some factors. For example, very short messages generally are quite noisy. Messages can be context-dependent and the analysis could become difficult.

Therefore, it is necessary to collect other data that convey information about user's context and integrate social data with other user data collected though external devices, such as voice, images and/or physiological signals correlated to person's emotions and feelings. The combination of behavior and sentiment analysis tools with methodologies of affective computing could allow the extraction of useful data that convey information for applications in several life sciences fields.

The goal of this paper is to present main methodologies of sentiment analysis and affective computing that may be used for life sciences applications. Moreover, a first architecture that integrates the two approaches is presented. The paper is organized as follows: Sects. 2 and 3 describe the main techniques and recent applications in affective computing and sentiment analysis; Sect. 4 present a new emergent methodology based on the integration of the affective computing and sentiment analysis, applied to social network data, and describes a software architecture to integrate such two approaches. Finally, Sect. 5 concludes the paper and outlines future works.

2   Affective Computing

Affective Computing is computing that relates to, arises from, or deliberately influences emotion or other affective phenomena [4]. Traditional emotion recognition systems are based on classification of facial expressions and voice analysis [12,13]. These approaches are limited because data acquisition is mainly based on the extraction of data from cultural and social environment of the subjects.

Therefore, to be more effective, the emotions recognition systems should include also the acquisition of other physiological signals, such as electroencephalogram (EEG), electromyogram (EMG), skin conductance, blood volume pulse, skin temperature [14]. Nevertheless, the last approaches are based on technologies that require special equipment or devices, e.g. skin conductance sensors, blood pressure monitors, ECG and/or EEG recording devices, whereas facial expressions and voice systems for emotion recognition, instead, use unobtrusive and low-cost devices that should be positioned in front of the face of the user or should always listen to the voice of user [15].

2.1   Methodologies for Affective Computing

Voice-Based Emotion Recognition. In the following sub-paragraphs, the focus is on some methodologies for data collection and processing for voice and electroencephalographic (EEG) signals in affective computing applications.

Typically, voice emotion recognition requires the following processing modules [16]:

- pre-processing: this module includes all processing operations that enable a more accurate and reliable features extraction and classification. Some examples regard signal sampling and quantization, pre-emphasis, framing and windowing [17];
- features extraction: main voices features for emotion recognition are prosody parameters, spectral parameters and sound quality;
- classification: some classifiers used for emotion recognition in voice processing are Hidden Markov Model, Adaptive Neural Networks, Rule-based classifiers. Generally, the emotions are classified as positive and negative and six classes have been studied and used: anger, disgust, fear, joy, sadness and surprise.

EEG-based Emotion Recognition. Several research works have studied emotion recognition from EEG signals in psychology [18,19]. The brain signals can be acquired through different electro-physiological methods, but the electroencephalography (EEG) is the most used non invasive method of signal acquisition for emotion recognition systems. EEG signals are acquired through scalp electrodes mounted on a cap to facilitate the positioning, according to the 10/20 International System [20]. However, the cost and the size of the acquisition setup should be minimal. Therefore, it is necessary to acquire EEG signals coming from a few electrodes in order to avoid high costs and obtrusive equipment that influences signal acquisition.

The processing of EEG signals requires specific pre-processing techniques to improve the poor EEG spatial resolution and to increase Signal to Noise Ratio (SNR). Generally, the features studied for emotions recognition include EEG power parameters in specific bands. Specifically, EEG signals are analyzed in frequency domain by using Fast Fourier Transform in order to obtain power spectrum of the collected signals. Alternative approaches are based on autoregressive (AR) model and successive power spectrum calculation starting from AR model.

The vector of features extracted in the previous stage is given as input to the classifier, which assigns this to a particular class associated with a specific emotion. Regarding the EEG-based emotion recognition problems, many classification approaches have been investigated, such as Support Vector Machine (SVM), Hidden Markov Model (HMM), Neural Network, Naive Bayes classifier. Among them, the best accuracy and overall performances is obtained by SVM [21,22].

2.2 Applications of Affective Computing

In the following some specific studies on emotion recognition are presented and discussed.

Nie et al. [23] presented an EEG-based emotion recognition method to classify two kinds of emotions, positive and negative with movie clip stimuli. Six subjects were involved in their experiments, and log band powers with 62 channels were used for the features. An average test accuracy of 87.53% was obtained by using all of the features together with a support vector machine.

In [24], Fast Fourier Transform analysis is used to extract features and the feature selection based on Pearson correlation coefficient is applied. The paper proposes a probabilistic classifier based on Bayes' theorem and a supervised learning using a perceptron convergence algorithm. To verify the proposed methodology, they use an open database.

C. Peter et al. proposed a wearable system architecture for collecting emotion-related physiological signals such as heart rate, skin conductivity, and skin temperature of users [25]. They developed a prototype system, consisting of a glove with a sensor unit, and a base unit for receiving the data transmitted from the sensor unit.

S.V. Ioannou et al. realized an emotion recognition system based on the evaluation of facial expressions [26]. They implemented a neuro-fuzzy network based on rules which have been defined via analysis of facial animation parameters (FAPs) variations of users. With experimental real data, they also showed an acceptable recognition accuracy higher than 70%.

In [15], the authors present a machine learning approach to recognize emotional states through the acquisition of some features related to user behavioral patterns (e.g. typing speed) and the user context (e.g. location) in the social network services. They developed an Android application that acquires and analyzes these features whenever the user sends a text message to Twitter. They built a Bayesian classifier that recognizes seven classes: one neutral and six relative to basic emotions with an accuracy of 67,52%.

The paper [27] describes an intelligent and affective tutoring system designed and implemented within a social network. The tutoring system evaluates cognitive and affective aspects and applies fuzzy logic to formulate the exercises that are presented to the student. The authors use Kohonen neural networks to recognize emotions through faces and voices and multi-attribute utility theory to encourage positive affective states.

3   Sentiment Analysis

Sentiment analysis is a computational study of opinions, sentiments, emotions, and attitude expressed in texts about a specific topic [28,29]. Most of works in this research area focus on classifying texts according to their sentiment polarity, which can be positive, negative or neutral. Therefore, it can be considered a text classification problem, since its goal consists of categorizing texts within classes by means of algorithmic methods.

3.1   Methodologies for Sentiment Analysis

As pointed out in [30], the input of a sentiment analysis system is a corpus of documents available in different formats such as PDF, HTML, XML, Word. The documents are converted in text and pre-processed by using different techniques such as stemming, tokenization, part of speech tagging, entity extraction and relation extraction. The core of the system is the analysis module that utilizes a set of linguistic and lexicon resources to annotate the pre-processed documents with sentiment annotations. The document analysis can be performed at different level, the output is positive negative or neutral:

– document-based sentiment analysis: aims to classify the whole document;
– sentence-based sentiment analysis: aims to classify specific sentences;
– aspect-based sentiment analysis: aims to classify the sentiment with respect to the specific aspects of entities.

Sentiment analysis methods can be also grouped in lexicon-based approaches and machine learning approaches [28]. Lexicon-based methods include:

– dictionary-based approaches;
– corpus-based approaches, that include statistical and semantic methods.

Machine learning techniques could be based on supervised approaches (that require labeled data to train classifier) or unsupervised ones.

The paper [31] offers a comprehensive review about this topic and compares some free access web services, analyzing their capabilities to classify and score different pieces of text with respect to the sentiments contained therein. An other interesting review of methodologies and techniques applied in sentiment analysis is [32].

3.2   Applications of Sentiment Analysis to Social Networks Data

In the last years, thanks to the increasing amount of information delivered through social networks, many researches have been focused on applying sentiment analysis to social networks data [33,34]. Sentiment analysis aims at mining users opinion and sentiment polarity from the posted text on the social network.

In [9], the authors apply data mining techniques to social network data for psicological applications, specifically to the field of depression, to detect depressed users in social network services. They create an accurate model based on sentiment analysis. In fact, the main symptom of the depression is severe negative emotions and lack of positive emotions. Specifically, they firstly design a method for sentence polarity detection (positive, negative or neutral). Secondly, they train classifiers (J48, Naive Bayes, Decision Rules) to classify (optimistic - pessimistic) micro-blogs collected in a week.

Rodrigues et al. [35] proposed a Sentiment Analysis tool, named SentiHealth-Cancer, that improves the detection of emotional state of patients in Brazilian online cancer communities, by inspecting their posts written in Portuguese language. The posts were analyzed by sentiment analysis tools that support the Portuguese language and by their proposed method called SentiHealth.

In [36], a new method for sentiment analysis in Facebook has been presented aiming: (i) to extract information about the users sentiment polarity (positive, neutral or negative), as transmitted in the messages they write; and (ii) to model the users usual sentiment polarity and to detect significant emotional changes. The authors have implemented this method in SentBuk, a Facebook application [37]. SentBuk retrieves messages written by users in Facebook and classifies them according to their polarity, showing the results to the users through an interactive interface. It also supports emotional change detection, friends emotion finding, user classification according to their messages, and statistics, among others. The classification method implemented in SentBuk follows a hybrid approach: it combines lexical-based and machine-learning techniques. The results obtained through this approach show that it is feasible to perform sentiment analysis in Facebook with high accuracy (83.27%).

Finally, a comparison between popular sentiment analysis methods applied to social network information is presented in [38]. The analyzed tools include: PANAS-t, Emoticons, SASA, SenticNet, SentiWordNet, Happiness Index, SentiStrength, LIWC. The authors propose a free web services called iFeel for accessing and comparing results across different sentiment methods for a given text [39].

4   Integration of Sentiment Analysis and Affective Computing

Recently, some attempts to integrate sentiment analysis and affective computing methodologies have been performed [40,41]. Acquisition and analysis of data coming from multimodal sources could guarantee different advantages in terms of robustness and accuracy, expecially in a particular context such as life sciences applications. However, this integration poses some challenges, such as the classification and analysis of heterogenous data coming from multiple sources. Generally, the features extracted through specific methods for multimodal data should be concatenated in a unique vector and give in input to classifier (features fusion) or they should be classified separately and the classifiers results should be combined to obtain a final result.

Poria et al. [42] have proposed a novel multimodal information extraction system, which infers and aggregates the semantic and affective information associated with user-generated multimodal data in contexts such as e-learning, e-health, automatic video content tagging and human-computer interaction. In particular, the developed intelligent agent adopts an ensemble feature extraction approach by exploiting the joint use of tri-modal (text, audio and video) features to enhance the multimodal information extraction process. In preliminary experiments using the eNTERFACE dataset, their proposed multi-modal system is shown to achieve an accuracy of 87.95%.

An other example of approach based on the combination of affective computing and sentiment analysis has been presented in [41]. In this paper a preliminary design of a software system's architecture for emotions and feelings detection has been proposed. Figure 1 presents a more detailed architecture, according to the discussion of the previous paragraphs.

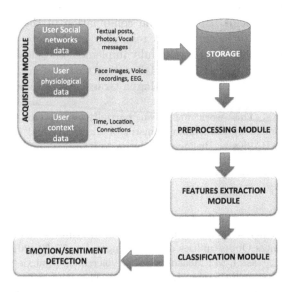

Fig. 1. Block diagram of an integrated system for sentiment and behavior analysis from social networks and sensors devices.

Specifically, the architecture of the proposed software system provides the following modules:

- acquisition module: this module includes all the functions needed to manage and synchronize the acquisition of data coming from (i) external devices (i.e. EEG signals), (ii) from microphone and camera on computer (i.e. voice and facial expressions), and (iii) social networks (i.e. textual posts, voice recordings and images extracted by using specific APIs, Application Programming Interfaces);

- storage module: this module is responsible of data storage through, for example, the emerging NoSQL databases well suited to store graph-based data, such as those extracted from social networks;
- processing modules: these include pre-processing, features extraction and classification modules. According to the specific data characteristics and features of interest, appropriate techniques should be implemented.

5   Conclusions

The applications of computing methodologies, such as affective computing and sentiment analysis, in life sciences could open new scenarios in research and clinical practice. Specifically they could support the diagnosis, monitoring and treatment of some mood disorders or anxiety conditions. As described in this paper, both affective computing and sentiment analysis rely on accurate methodologies of analyis and classification. Different applications have been proposed, even in life sciences fields. However, the combination of these methodologies could guarantee a better accuracy and reliability in the detection of emotions and feelings. As future work we plan to fully implement the software architecture described in Fig. 1 and to test it in collaboration with the medical units of the University Hospital of the University Magna Graecia of Catanzaro.

Acknowledgments. This work has been partially supported by the following research project funded by the Italian Ministry of University and Research (MIUR): PON03PE_00001_1 BA2Know-Business Analytics to Know.

References

1. Valstar, M.: Automatic behaviour understanding in medicine. In: Proceedings of the Workshop on Roadmapping the Future of Multimodal Interaction Research including Business Opportunities and Challenges, pp. 57–60 (2014)
2. Martinez, C.C., Cassol, M.: Measurement of voice quality, anxiety and depression symptoms after speech therapy. J. Voice **29**(4), 446–449 (2015)
3. Schaefer, K.L., Baumann, J., Rich, B.A., Luckenbaugh, D.A., Zarate, C.A.: Perception of facial emotion in adults with bipolar or unipolar depression and controls. J. Psychiatr. Res. **44**, 1229–1235 (2010)
4. Picard, R.W.: Affective Computing. MIT Press, Cambridge (1997)
5. Koelstra, S., Patras, I.: Fusion of facial expressions and EEG for implicit affective tagging. Image Vis. Comput. **31**, 164–174 (2013)
6. Poria, S., Cambria, E., Howard, N., Huang, G., Hussain, A.: Fusing audio, visual and textual clues for sentiment analysis from multimodal content. Neurocomputing **174**, 50–59 (2016)
7. Pang, B., Lee, L.: Opinion mining and sentiment analysis. J. Found. Trends Inf. Retrieval **2**(1–2), 1–135 (2008)
8. Zafarani, R., Liu, H.: Behavior analysis in social media. IEEE Intell. Syst. **29**(4), 9–11 (2014)

9. Wang, X., Zhang, C., Ji, Y., Sun, L., Wu, L., Bao, Z.: A depression detection model based on sentiment analysis in micro-blog social network. In: Li, J., Cao, L., Wang, C., Tan, K.C., Liu, B., Pei, J., Tseng, V.S. (eds.) PAKDD 2013. LNCS (LNAI), vol. 7867, pp. 201–213. Springer, Heidelberg (2013). doi:10.1007/978-3-642-40319-4_18

10. Snyder, M.: Self-monitoring of expressive behavior. J. Pers. Soc. Psychol. **30**(4), 526–537 (1974)

11. He, Q., Glas, C.A.W., Kosinski, M., Stillwell, D.J., Veldkamp, B.P.: Predicting self-monitoring skills using textual posts on Facebook. Comput. Hum. Behav. **33**, 69–78 (2014)

12. Armony, J.L.: Affective computing. Trends Cogn. Sci. **2**(7), 270 (1998)

13. Calvo, R.A., D'Mello, S.: Affect detection: an interdisciplinary review of models, methods, and their applications. IEEE Trans. Affect. Comput. **1**(1), 18–37 (2010)

14. Zeng, Z., Pantic, M., Roisman, G.I., Huang, T.S.: A survey of affect recognition methods: audio, visual, and spontaneous expressions. IEEE Trans. Pattern Anal. Mach. Intell. **31**(1), 39–58 (2009)

15. Lee, H., Choi, Y.S., Lee, S., Park, I.P.: Towards unobtrusive emotion recognition for affective social communication. In: 9th Annual IEEE Consumer Communications and Networking Conference, pp. 260–264. IEEE (2012)

16. Batliner, A., Schuller, B., Seppi, D., Steidl, S., Devillers, L., Vidrascu, L., Vogt, T., Aharonson, V., Amir, N.: The automatic recognition of emotions in speech. Emotion-Oriented Syst. **2**, 71–99 (2011)

17. Dai, W., Han, D., Dai, Y., Xu, D.: Emotion recognition and affective computing on vocal social media. Inform. Manage. **52**, 777–788 (2015)

18. Lee, Y.Y., Hsieh, S.: Classifying different emotional states by means of EEG-based functional connectivity patterns. PLoS ONE **9**, 1–13 (2014)

19. Delle-Vignea, D., Wangb, W., Kornreicha, C., Verbancka, P., Campanellaa, S.: Emotional facial expression processing in depression: Data from behavioral and event-related potential studies. Neurophysiol. Clin. Clin. Neurophysiol. **44**, 169–187 (2014)

20. Klem, G.H., Luders, H.O., Jasper, H.H., Elger, C.: The ten - twenty electrode system of the International Federation. Electroencephalogr. Clin. Neurophysiol. **52**, 3–6 (1999)

21. Wang, X.-W., Nie, D., Lu, B.-L.: EEG-based emotion recognition using frequency domain features and support vector machines. In: Lu, B.-L., Zhang, L., Kwok, J. (eds.) ICONIP 2011. LNCS, vol. 7062, pp. 734–743. Springer, Heidelberg (2011). doi:10.1007/978-3-642-24955-6_87

22. Bhuvaneswari, P., Kumar, J.S.: Support vector machine technique for EEG signals. Int. J. Comput. Appl. **63**(13), 1–5 (2013)

23. Nie, D., Wang, X.W., Shi, L.C., Lu, B.L.:EEG-based emotion recognition during watching movies. In: 2011 5th International IEEE/EMBS Conference on Neural Engineering (NER), pp. 667–670 (2011)

24. Yoon, H.J., Chung, S.Y.: EEG-based emotion estimation using Bayesian weighted-log-posterior function and perceptron convergence algorithm. Comput. Biol. Med. **43**(12), 2230–2237 (2013)

25. Peter, C., Ebert, E., Beikirch, H.: A wearable multi-sensor system for mobile acquisition of emotion-related physiological data. Affect. Comput. Intell. Interac. **3784**, 691–698 (2005)

26. Ioannou, S.V., Raouzaiou, A.T., Tzouvaras, V.A., Mailis, T.P., Karpouzis, K.C., Kollias, S.D.: Emotion recognition through facial expression analysis based on a neurofuzzy network. Neural Netw. **18**(4), 423–435 (2005)

27. Barrón-Estrada, M.L., Zatarain-Cabada, R., Beltrán V., J.A., Cibrian R., F.L., Pérez, Y.H.: An intelligent and affective tutoring system within a social network for learning mathematics. In: Pavón, J., Duque-Méndez, N.D., Fuentes-Fernández, R. (eds.) IBERAMIA 2012. LNCS (LNAI), vol. 7637, pp. 651–661. Springer, Heidelberg (2012). doi:10.1007/978-3-642-34654-5_66
28. Medhat, W., Hassan, A., Korashy, H.: Sentiment analysis algorithms and applications: a survey. Ain Shams Eng. J. **5**(4), 1093–1113 (2014)
29. Ravi, K., Ravi, V.: A survey on opinion mining and sentiment analysis: tasks, approaches and applications. Knowl.-Based Syst. **89**, 14–46 (2015)
30. Feldman, R.: Techniques and applications for sentiment analysis. Mag. Commun. ACM **56**(4), 82–89 (2013)
31. Serrano-Guerrero, J., Olivas, J.A., Romero, F.P., Herrera-Viedma, E.: Sentiment analysis: a review and comparative analysis of web services. Inform. Sci. **311**, 18–38 (2015)
32. Batrinca, B., Treleaven, P.: C.,: Social media analytics: a survey of techniques, tools and platforms. AI Soc. **30**, 89–116 (2015)
33. Go, A., Bhayani, R., Huang, L.: Twitter sentiment classification using distant supervision. Technical report. Stanford University, Stanford Digital Library Technologies Project (2009)
34. Pak, A., Paroubek, P.: Twitter as a corpus for sentiment analysis and opinion mining. In: Proceedings of the Seventh Conference on International Language Resources and Evaluation, pp. 1320–1326 (2010)
35. Rodrigues, R.G., das Dores, R.M., Camilo-Junior, C.G., Rosa, T.C.: SentiHealth-Cancer: a sentiment analysis tool to help detecting mood of patients in online social networks. Int. J. Med. Inform. **85**, 80–95 (2016)
36. Ortigosa, A., Carro, R.M., Quiroga, J.I.: Predicting user personality by mining social interactions in Facebook. J. Comput. Syst. Sci. **80**, 57–71 (2014)
37. Martin, J.M., Ortigosa, A., Carro, R.M.: SentBuk: sentiment analysis for e-learning environments. In: 2012 International Symposium on Computers in Education (SIIE), pp. 1–6. IEEE (2012)
38. Gonçalves, P., Araújo, M., Benevenuto, F., Cha, M.: Comparing and combining sentiment analysis methods. In: Proceedings of the First ACM Conference on Online Social Networks (2013)
39. Araújo, M., Gonçalves, P., Cha, M., Benevenuto, F.: iFeel: a web system that compares and combines sentiment analysis methods. In: Proceedings of the Companion Publication of the 23rd International Conference on World Wide Web Companion (2014)
40. Poria, S., Gelbukh, A., Cambria, E., Hussain, A., Huang, G.: EmoSenticSpace: a novel framework for affective common-sense reasoning. Knowl.-Based Syst. **69**, 108–123 (2014)
41. Calabrese, B., Cannataro, M., Ielpo, N.: Using social networks data for behavior and sentiment analysis. In: Fatta, G., Fortino, G., Li, W., Pathan, M., Stahl, F., Guerrieri, A. (eds.) IDCS 2015. LNCS, vol. 9258, pp. 285–293. Springer, Heidelberg (2015). doi:10.1007/978-3-319-23237-9_25
42. Poria, S., Cambria, E., Hussain, A., Huang, G.: Towards an intelligent framework for multimodal affective data analysis. Neural Netw. **63**, 104–116 (2015)

Deep Representations for Collaborative Robotics

Luis J. Manso[1], Pablo Bustos[1], Juan P. Bandera[2], Adrián Romero-Garcés[2],
Luis V. Calderita[1,2], Rebeca Marfil[2], and Antonio Bandera[2(✉)]

[1] RoboLab Group, University of Extremadura, Cáceres, Spain
{lmanso,pbustos,lvcalderita}@unex.es
[2] Dept. Tecnología Electrónica, University of Malaga, Málaga, Spain
{jpbandera,adrigtl,rebeca,ajbandera}@uma.es
https://robolab.unex.es/
http://www.grupoisis.uma.es/

Abstract. Collaboration is an essential feature of human social interaction. Briefly, when two or more people agree on a common goal and a
joint intention to reach that goal, they have to coordinate their actions
to engage in joint actions, planning their courses of actions according to
the actions of the other partners. The same holds for teams where the
partners are people and robots, resulting on a collection of technical questions difficult to answer. Human-robot collaboration requires the robot to
coordinate its behavior to the behaviors of the humans at different levels,
e.g., the semantic level, the level of the content and behavior selection
in the interaction, and low-level aspects such as the temporal dynamics of the interaction. This forces the robot to internalize information
about the motions, actions and intentions of the rest of partners, and
about the state of the environment. Furthermore, collaborative robots
should select their actions taking into account additional human-aware
factors such as safety, reliability and comfort. Current cognitive systems
are usually limited in this respect as they lack the rich dynamic representations and the flexible human-aware planning capabilities needed
to succeed in tomorrow human-robot collaboration tasks. Within this
paper, we provide a tool for addressing this problem by using the notion
of deep hybrid representations and the facilities that this common state
representation offers for the tight coupling of planners on different layers
of abstraction. Deep hybrid representations encode the robot and environment state, but also a robot-centric perspective of the partners taking
part in the joint activity.

Keywords: Deep representations · Cognitive robots · Agent-based
robotic architecture

1 Introduction

In order to engage humans in interactions, the new generation of robots should
be able to emanate responses at human interaction rates and exhibit a proactive behaviour. This proactive behaviour implies that the internal architecture

© Springer International Publishing AG 2016
K. Amunts et al. (Eds.): BrainComp 2015, LNCS 10087, pp. 179–193, 2016.
DOI: 10.1007/978-3-319-50862-7_14

of these robots should not only be able to perceive and act, but also to perform off-line reasoning. Cognition is the ability that allows us to internally deal with information about the external world and, hence, this ability is subject to the existence of an internal representation of this information. Classical cognitive systems posit an inner realm richly populated with internal tokens that stand for external objects and states of affair [27]. These internal representations, however, are not valid to generate predictions or reasoning. Recent works suggest that cognitive architectures cannot work on a passive, bottom-up fashion, simply waiting to be activated by external stimuli. Instead, these architectures must continuously use memory to interpret sensory information and predict the immediate future. These predictions about the outer world can be used to actively drive the resources to relevant data in top-down modes of behaviour, allowing an efficient and accurate interpretation of the environment [27,37].

The concept of deep representations was clearly described by Beetz et al. [33]: *representations that combine various levels of abstraction, ranging, for example, from the continuous limb motions required to perform an activity to atomic high-level actions, subactivities, and activities.* This definition is however provided in a paper where the robot performs its activities alone. If a collaborative robot has to cooperate with a human partner as a work companion, it should be endowed with the abilities to consider its environmental context and assess how external factors could affect its action, including the role and activity of the human interaction partner in the joint activity. Efficient collaboration not only implies a common plan for all involved partners, but also the coordination of the behavior of each agent with those of the other ones, i.e. to gain a joint intention. This coordination should be simultaneously addressed at different levels of abstraction, and to correctly satisfy it, the robot has to internalize a coherent representation about the motions, actions and intentions of the rest of partners. Additionally, a major difficulty in human-robot collaboration (HRC) scenarios is that people cannot only exhibit a rather non-deterministic and unstable behavior, but they also tend to perceive current robots as slow and unintelligent. These factors difficult HRC. To overcome them, the robot should continuously try to guess their partners' goals and intentions, triggering appropriate reactions -i.e. being socially proactive.

Symbolic and metric representations have been separately proposed in many different forms and uses. Symbolic knowledge representation have been at the core of AI since its beginnings [21,23] and cover all forms of relational formalizations such as production rules, frames, schemes, cases, first order logic or situational calculus. At a high level of abstraction, the Robot Learning Language (RoLL) [32] could be used for learning models about human behaviour and reactions, joint plan performance or recognizing human activity. Also, human models have been employed by the Human-Aware Task Planner (HATP) [34]. A symbolic graph structure was proposed in [14] as part of our previous architecture RoboCog [6]. On the other hand, metric and kinematic representations are commonly used as part of 3D simulators and graphics engines [39,40]. However, the concept of deep representations [33] implies an unified, hierarchical organization of the knowledge that ranges from the symbolic layer to the motor one, mapping abstract concepts to, or from, geometric environment models and sensor data structures of the robot. The inclusion of a detailed physical layer on the representation will allow the robot to solve naive physics problems, which cannot be performed based on abstractions, using temporal projection [26]. The presence of a detailed representation of the spatial state of the problem is also required in the work of Wintermute: ... *actions can be simulated (imagined) in terms of this concrete representation, and the agent can derive abstract information by applying perceptual processes to the resulting concrete state* [35]. The use of a situational representation of the outer world to endow the robot with the ability to understand physical consequences of their actions can be extended, in a collaborative scenario, to support proactive robot behaviors. This possibility has been addressed in the LAAS Architecture for Autonomous Systems proposed by Ali et al. [36].

The rest of the paper is organized as follows: First, Sects. 2 and 3 present arguments that support the former claims. Section 4 describes the functioning of our proposed architecture as a set of agents interacting through the deep state representation. Section 5 briefly presents several application scenarios where the world model is currently been tested. Conclusions and future work are drawn at Sect. 6.

2 Agency

The concept of agent in Computer Science and Artificial Intelligence is rather broad and their varied meanings cover most of what a program can do. Franklin [10], after a through review of many proposals, synthesizes an autonomous agent as *a system situated within and a part of an environment that senses that environment and acts on it, over time, in pursuit of its own agenda and so as to effect what it senses in the future.* We propose here a similar definition of the term,

A computational entity in charge of a well defined functionality, whether it be reactive, deliberative of hybrid, that interacts with other agents inside a well-defined framework, to enact a larger system.

When several of these agents are somehow interconnected to enact a higher-level function, they are called Agent-based Architectures. In robotics and AI, they have been used for a long time [13,22] being Minsky's Society of Mind [17], probably the most famous one.

From the point of view of the implementation, we map agents to software components in a one-to-many or one-to-one policy. To complete the definition, a software component is a program that communicates with other programs inside a well defined framework. Components are usually created as an instance of a formal component model [4,5,25]. Note that there is not much difference between agents and components and in many contexts both are interchangeable. However, we use component here in the more restricted sense of being a program, rather than a more general functional abstraction, like agents.

The CORTEX architecture is implemented using the component-oriented robotics framework RoboComp [15]. The choice of a agent-based architecture responds to computational simplicity and elegance. Agents are functional units that can be easily combined to form in a given structure. They can be defined recursively as made up of other simple agents, and there is always a rather simple connection to the underlying software components. This is the first reason why CORTEX is an agent-based architecture.

In CORTEX, higher-level agents define the classic functionalities of cognitive robotics architectures, such as navigation, manipulation, person perception, object perception, dialoguing, reasoning, planning, symbolic learning or executing. These agents operate in a goal-oriented regime [23] and their goals can come from outside through the agent interface, and can also be part of the agent normal operation. For our needs, we want agents to be autonomous and obedient, at the same time. Autonomous to provide opportunistic behavior so non-planned events in the environment can be detected, and obedient so when new goals arrive to the system, all task-oriented agents start working to achieve the current sub goal. Thus, regarding the kind of function they perform, agents can be anything in the reactive-deliberative spectrum, although in this paper and to simplify the exposition we will refer to them whether as deliberative or reactive. This flexibility in the internal organization of the agents, as the building blocks on CORTEX, is the second reason why we have chosen an agent-based architecture.

Communication among agents define the structural part of the architectures. In cognitive robotics architectures, instead of a search for a correct model of human intelligence, what is explored is the design space of embodied intelligence [24]. We adopt here the broad view that these systems encompass two main flows of information. First, a deliberative one, in which agents must provide a symbolic description of the robot and the world to the deliberative agents, so they can reason about facts and plan a course of actions to achieve the current goal. These actions are sent back to the non-deliberative agents as local goals. Second, a reactive one, in which non deliberative agents interact to perform a sort of multi-modal behavior. These behaviors can be triggered by external goals or by a recognizable situation ahead. Note that other horizontal functions of the architecture such as memory and learning are left here to the internal functioning of the agents and the representational mechanisms that they share.

An important requirement for the architecture is to facilitate the transition between deliberatively controlled behaviors and autonomous behaviors, so there can be an overall improvement of task achieving performance. Either by hand coding or by automatic learning, the way the architecture interconnects agents must facilitate the incremental creation of autonomous, efficient and reliable skills. Let's examine now a simple situation in which two agents have to interact to complete a task. The agents are a *Manipulation* agent and an *Object-Perception* agent. Within the deliberative flow, to locate and grasp an object both agents must be coordinated by an *Executive* agent following a previously computed plan. The basic steps could be,

1. DetectTarget(t)
2. MoveHand(t)
3. Grab(t)

A plan like this, when executed by the action and perceptual agents, although it might succeed, will perform poorly. The reason is that there are many assumptions being made about the robot and the world that will result in a slow, failure prone and rigid behavior. It would be similar to someone following low-level orders to do some new manipulation task. The solution is assuming that the target is static, the position of the target obtained by the camera and the position to where the hand will arrive are the same, i.e. perfect calibration, that the arm movement is very precise, that there is not uncertainty in the target position as detected by the camera, among others. In real scenarios with uncertainty in the measurement process, low cost mechanics and errors in the kinematic calibration of the body-arm-head ensemble, a much more reliable method would be to use a two-fold sequence. First, a sort saccadic arm movement takes the hand to a zone close to the target, then, a visual servo loop re-positions the hand in the reference system of the camera, thus canceling all calibration errors between the camera and the hand [11,12]. This is a clear example of a skill that requires a fluid interchange of information between *Object-Perception* and *Manipulation*. Note that the visual perception of the hand would also correspond to *Object-Perception*. Adapting the former sequence of steps,

1. DetectTarget(t)
2. MoveHand(t)
3. InitiateVisualServo()
4. Grab()

MoveHand() is now an autonomous skill that involves both agents and requires and intense interchange of information between them. The robotics cognitive architecture must be prepared to incorporate these kind of changes. The communication channels among agents must be flexible enough to allow for these kind of reorganizations. Note that even if the agents would have been chosen differently, so there were no need to transfer information externally, there will be always other situations in which different agents would need to communicate[1]. So the claim here is that a smart decision for an architecture would be to think of some mechanism that could communicate information among agents without much restrictions and still, be flexible enough to allow modifications, whether by the programmer, or automatically through learning algorithms. This is the third reason why CORTEX is built as a set of loosely coupled agents whose communication channels can be chosen in many different ways. We want to anticipate the possibility of future improvements that will come in the near future, and the design space provided by an agent-based architecture with regard to how agents communicate is large. In particular, and as a solution seeking flexibility, we propose here that they communicate through a shared data structure, as explained in Sect. 3.

---

[1] Obviously we are discarding here the one big agent-doing-everything case.

3   The Deep State Representation

The Deep State Representation (DSR) is a graph structure that, within COR-TEX, holds the representation of the robot and its environment. It is not the first time that a graph structure is used for this purpose. However, to our knowledge, the first works that proposed a graph as an internal representation for a robotics architecture focused only in geometric data. ROS' transform library, *tf* [9], BRICS Robot Scene Graph [3] and RoboCog's InnerModel [20] all appeared in 2013 as a response to the need for such a structure: a centralized representation of robot and world kinematics. Even tough those constructions are important advances towards better robotic architectures, a richer, and deeper representation was needed to hold the complete set of beliefs of the robot. In CORTEX, the graph structure of the DSR holds symbolic and geometric data, and is accessed by all agents during their operations. In fact, the DSR is the only means for the agents to communicate. Figure 1 shows a small DSR graph with multiple labeled edges representing heterogeneous attributes.

Fig. 1. Full graph of the DSR.

The idea of a shared representation among agents has its roots in several classical papers [8,18,19] that developed the concept of the blackboard architecture. Later, Hayes-Roth [2] extended this idea into a complete control architecture. As A, Newell himself put it,

> Metaphorically we can think of a set of workers, all looking at the same blackboard: each is able to read everything that is on it, and to judge when he has something worthwhile to add to it. This conception is just that of Selfridge's Pandemonium [19]: a set of daemons, each independently looking at the total situation and shrieking in proportion to what they see that fits their natures...

In the original blackboard systems, agents where conceived more as problem solvers, heterogeneous experts that contribute to the overall problem in a hybrid planned-opportunistic way. They communicate through a shared structure where goals, sub goals and problems state were incrementally updated. In CORTEX, agents solve not only deliberative tasks but also perceptual, motor and behavioral, so their communication needs are somewhat different. Nevertheless, we gather some ideas from these architectures [7,16] and also others from graph theory and distributed databases.

3.1   Why Is the DSR a Graph?

The first reason to use a graph in CORTEX is because all internal information defining the state of the robot and its beliefs about the environment, can be stored according to a predefined structure. That structure is a model of how sensor data can be interpreted and organized. As general data structures, can hold any relational knowledge composed of discrete elements and relations among them. In this broad category fall almost all symbolic knowledge representation methods including frames, schemes, production rules and cases, and also the geometric knowledge that the robot has to maintain about itself and the environment. This geometric knowledge includes instances of the types of objects recognizable in the world like i.e. chairs, tables, cups or generic obstacles of undefined form. Also human bodies and its parts like arms, heads, legs, etc. All these parts are kinematically related through 3D transformations forming a scene-tree.

A second reason is that the graph can be made to evolve under some generative rules. Assuming that the type of nodes and edges are predefined, the graph can evolve by inclusions or deletions of parts, causing structural changes. Also it can evolve by changing the value of the attributes stored in nodes and edges. The structural changes can be regulated by a generative grammar that defines how the initial model can change. A typical example would be that of the robot entering a new room and, after exploring it, it would add a new node to the graph. The grammar would impede the new node to be connected to something else but the corresponding door, and maybe it would be oriented parallel to one of the walls of the proceeding room. So graphs gives us the capacity needed

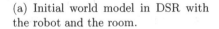

(a) Initial world model in DSR with the robot and the room.

(b) A person enters the room, and when detected by the *Person* agent, inserted in the DSR.

Fig. 2. Illustration of various worldModel State. The symbol robot has been constrained to one symbol for explanatory reasons.

to store objects and their relations, and combined with a grammar to control its evolution, gives us a coherent growing model. Figure 2 shows how the graph changes when a person enters the scene. In the left side only the robot and the rooms are represented. In the right side, a person enters the room and the graph incorporates her as sub graph correctly related to the existing structure and with symbolic attributes denoting what is known about her.

A third reason to use a graph structure is the possibility of translating it into a PDDL instance. Depending on what is stored in the graph and the PDDL version this procedure has certain restrictions but it allows a direct use of start of the art planning algorithms that otherwise would have required an important additional effort. Further details on how this translation is done can be found in [14].

A fourth reason to support the choice of graphs is the facility to visualize its contents. Graph's contents can be displayed in multiple ways using available 3D technology and that is a crucial feature to debug the code of the agents, specially when interacting among them. In CORTEX, visualization of DSR is done using the open source 3D scene-graph OpenSceneGraph, OSG [1] and a class implementing the observer pattern that keeps DSR and OSG synchronized. The DSR graph can be drawn in different ways. The geometric nodes and edges are drawn as a normal 3D scene, using the meshes and 3D primitives that can be stored as attributes in DSR. The symbolic relations can be drawn as an independent graph or as a superimposed structure on its geometric counterpart.

3.2   DSR Formalization

DSR is a multi-label directed graph which holds symbolic information as logic attributes related by predicates. These are stored in nodes and edges respectively. Also, DSR holds geometric information as predefined object types linked by 4×4 homogeneous matrices. Again, these are stored in nodes and edges respectively. With DSR, the hand of the robot can be at a 3D pose and, at the same time, it can be *close_to_the_door knob*, being this a predicate computed by measuring the distance between the hand and the knob, in the graph representation. Note that this distance could also had been measured with more precision by direct observation of both the knob and the hand once they are inside the frustum of the robot's camera but, at the end, that information would be stored in the graph and propagated to the other agents.

As a hybrid representation that stores information at both metric and symbolic level. The nodes store concepts that can be symbolic, geometric or a mix of them. Metric concepts describe numeric quantities of objects in the world that can be structures like a three-dimensional mesh, scalars like the mass of a link, or lists like revision dates. Edges represent relationships among symbols. Two symbols may have several kinds of relationships but only one of them can be geometric. The geometric relationship is expressed with a fixed label called "RT". This label stores the transformation matrix between them. A formal definition of DSR can be given as a multi-label directed graph $G = (N, E)$ where N represents the set of nodes $\{n_1, ... n_k\}$ and E the set of edges $\{e_1 .... e_r\}$.

$$G = (V, E) \text{ where } E \subseteq N \times N, uv \neq vu (\text{without loops } vv) \qquad (1)$$

According to its symbolic nature, edges properties are:

1. For each pair $e = uv$ the inverse does not exist $e = uv \neq e^{-1} = vu$
2. For each pair $e = uv$, e can store multiple values
3. The set of e is defined as $L = \{e_1, ... e_r, (l_1, l_2, ... l_s)\}$ where $l_i \neq l_j$

According to its geometric nature and the properties of the transformation matrix RT, the characteristics of geometric edges are:

1. For each pair $e = uv = RT$, e is unique
2. For each pair $e = uv = RT$, define the inverse of e as $e^{-1} = vu = RT^{-1}$

Therefore the kinematic chain $C(u, v)$ is defined as the path between the nodes u, v and an equivalent transformation $RT*$ can be computed by multiplying the equivalent transformations corresponding to the sub paths from each node to their closest common ancestor. Note that sub path from the common ancestor to v will be obtained multiplying the inverse transformations.

This geometrical relations are showed in Fig. 3.

4   CORTEX Internal Organization

The functioning of the architecture as a set of agents interacting through the DSR can be easily explained if we picture it as a large dynamical system. Starting in a quasi-stationary state, the perceptual modules try to keep the internal representation synchronized with the world, updating parts of it as things change. But when a new mission is requested, a plan is generated and injected into the symbolic graph. This alteration creates a disequilibrium to which the whole system reacts trying to restore the initial balance. In the process of going back to normality the system extends its internal model, capturing more details of

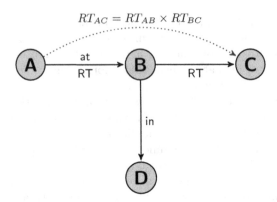

Fig. 3. Unified representation as a multi-labeled directed graph. Edges are labeled "at" and "in" denoting logic predicates between nodes. Also, edges between A,B and B,C have a geometric type of label, "RT" that codes a rigid transformation between them. Geometric transformations can be chained or inverted to compute changes in coordinate systems.

the external world. The new knowledge is used in the next perturbation. Furthermore, the idea of opportunistic control by which agents can write in the blackboard is driven not only as a result of solving a local goal but triggered by internal events. A typical situation for a visual perceptive agent would be to configure, search and track types of objects specified in the current plan, but these agents are also in charge of other secondary *unconscious* tasks like obstacle detection for navigation or simply, novelty detection if in a well known environment. In this cases the agent would inject the percepts into the shared graph so the information can be used somewhere else.

To complete the picture of how CORTEX is organized, Fig. 4 shows a very schematic sketch of the main agents and their connection through the DSR.

- The central part of the figure represents the DSR. It is enclosing all the Executive, a module in charge of managing the inclusion of new changes on the DSR or publishing the new DSR to the agents.
- In the figure, the squared boxes that surround the inner representation represent networks of software components -agents. They encode complete robotics functionalities -e.g. navigation, conversation, planning, etc- and share information about the state through the representation. The current picture shows the instantiation of CORTEX within Gualzru.
- Finally, the boxes on the top part of the figure enclose action modules (e.g., for moving the robot or speech a phrase). The boxes on the down part enclose perception modules (e.g. for capturing a laser scan or the battery level). The WinKinectComp module is a specific component that provides information taken from the Kinect sensor from Microsoft (skeletons, joins, faces...) and speech transcriptions. All these modules encode the Hardware Abstraction Layer (HAL).

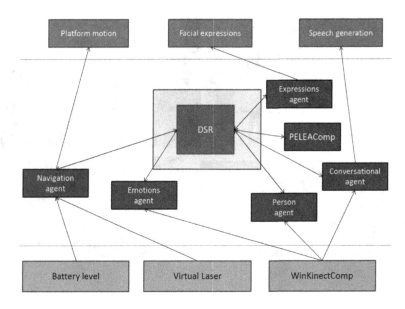

Fig. 4. Overview of the shared world model and its location within the cognitive architecture. The picture shows the proposed framework within the Gualzru scenario described at Sect. 5 (see text for details).

5   Experimental Results

As an initial validation of CORTEX and DSR in a real robot interacting with humans we tested the ideas on Gualzru [30]. Gualzru is a salesman robot that works autonomously in crowded scenarios and has to step out when a potential client passes by. Gualzru will approach the customer and start a conversation trying to convince her to go to an interactive sales panel. If the robot succeeds, it will walk the person to the panel and then will start a new search.

In previous versions of the robot, we found that some synchronization problems were caused by having a fragmented internal representation. The robot used two separate graphs, one for the kinematic state and one for symbolic attributes and predicates. There several architectures that keep these representations separated [6] and it is a reasonable choice since both hold different contents and require different types of processes. However, in complex interaction scenarios, an integrated representations simplifies synchronization making all data available to all agents at the same time. The introduction of DSR in Gualzru solved those problems and agent communications worked flawlessly.

Other important drawback was related to its limited conversational abilities. These limitations greatly affects its performance. Speech recognition is hard to solve in noisy, crowded scenarios in which even people find difficulties in understanding each other (see Fig. 5). It is also difficult to understand what the robot is saying. To improve the ability of the robot to communicate within this scenario, we have added a tactile screen on the robot. This screen displays what

Fig. 5. The Gualzru robot interacting with people at the University of Malaga.

Fig. 6. Shelly is closing one mission.

the robot is saying. It allows the person to answer to the robot by touching the desired response on the screen. All this information is shared among agents using the symbolic annotations added to DSR. It is important to note that these concepts can be updated by the agents at interaction rates. The ADAPTA project started on 2012, and different representations were evaluated. The last trials on September 2015 allowed to deeply test that the new representation is able to engine the whole architecture at human interaction rates.

The CORTEX architecture was also endowed within Shelly, an autonomous mobile robot that, contrary to the Gualzru robot, has two arms, with 7 DoFs and a final end-effector. The initial aim is to locate and grasp objects. Figure 6 shows how Shelly is bringing one cup to the user. All the robot's activity (room and table perception, speech recognition and command identification, cup localisation and grasping, etc.) is performed without human supervision. The total number of software components is now greater than 20, all of them organised on agents that are connected to the DSR. This remains as the only way for interchanging information among agents. The robot is able to correctly analyse the context and solves the commanded missions.

6   Conclusions and Future Work

This paper has presented our proposal for internalizing a deep state representation of the outer world. After testing the previous approaches in very demanding scenarios, the unified representation arises as our final approach for endowing the full kinematic tree with symbolic information; and providing the geometric information to the high-level planner. The unified representation is currently interfaced by a set of task-related networks of agents, which will provide broad functionalities such as navigation, dialog or multi-modal person monitoring. The current implementation guarantees that the agents are able to feed the unified representation with new geometric models or symbolic concepts, and that the data stored in the representation is kept synchronized with the real world by updating actions performed by different agents.

Future work will focus on exploiting the hierarchical structure encoded within the DSR. This will allow the agents to subscribe to specific parts of the representation (e.g. the person or the robot arm). It is also needed to evaluate the computational times associated to the management of our graphs. Although it is clear that the number of nodes/arcs is relatively small, it must be noted that this graph is currently shared with all the agents on the architecture.

Acknowledgments. This paper has been partially supported by the Spanish Ministerio de Economía y Competitividad TIN2015-65686-C5 and FEDER funds, and by the Innterconecta Programme 2011 project ITC-20111030 ADAPTA.

References

1. http://www.openscenegraph.com
2. Hayes-Roth, B.: A blackboard architecture for control. Artif. Intell. **26**(3), 251–321 (1985)
3. Blumenthal, S., Bruyninckx, H., Nowak, W., Prassler, E.: A scene graph based shared 3D world model for robotic applications. In: 2013 IEEE International Conference on Robotics and Automation, pp. 453–460, May 2013. http://ieeexplore. ieee.org/lpdocs/epic03/wrapper.htm?arnumber=6630614
4. Brugali, D., Scandurra, P.: Component-based robotic engineering (Part I). IEEE Robot. Autom. Mag. **16**, 84–96 (2009)

5. Brugali, D., Shakhimardanov, A.: Component-based robotic engineering (Part II): systems and models. IEEE Robot. Autom. Mag. **17**(1), 100–112 (2010)
6. Calderita, L.V., Bustos, P., Suárez Mejías, C., Fernández, F., Bandera, A.: THER-APIST: towards an autonomous socially interactive robot for motor and neurorehabilitation therapies for children. In: 7th International Conference on Pervasive Computing Technologies for Healthcare and Workshops, vol. 1, pp. 374–377 (2013). http://ieeexplore.ieee.org/xpls/abs_all.jsp?arnumber=6563970&tag=1
7. Corkill, D.D.: Blackboard systems. AI Expert **6**(9), 40–47 (1991)
8. Erman, L.D., Hayes-Roth, F., Lesser, V.R., Reddy, D.R.: The Hearsay-II speech-understanding system: integrating knowledge to resolve uncertainty. ACM Comput. Surv. **12**(2), 213–253 (1980)
9. Foote, T.: tf: The transform library. In: 2013 IEEE International Conference on Technologies for Practical Robot Applications (TePRA), pp. 1–6. Open-Source Software workshop (2013)
10. Franklin, S., Graesser, A.: Is It an agent, or just a program?: A taxonomy for autonomous agents. In: Müller, J.P., Wooldridge, M.J., Jennings, N.R. (eds.) ATAL 1996. LNCS, vol. 1193, pp. 21–35. Springer, Heidelberg (1997). doi:10.1007/BFb0013570
11. Gratal, X., Romero, J., Bohg, J., Kragic, D.: Visual servoing on unknown objects. Mechatronics **22**(4), 423–435 (2012). http://dx.doi.org/10.1016/j.mechatronics.2011.09.009
12. Hutchinson, S., Hager, G., Corke, P.: A tutorial on visual servo control. IEEE Trans. Robot. Autom. **12**(5), 651–670 (1996). http://ieeexplore.ieee.org/lpdocs/epic03/wrapper.htm?arnumber=538972
13. Maes, P.: The agent network architecture (ANA). SIGART Bull. **2**(4), 115–120 (1991)
14. Manso, L.J.: Perception as stochastic sampling on dynamic graph spaces. Ph.D. thesis, Universidad de Extremadura (2013)
15. Manso, L., Bachiller, P., Bustos, P., Calderita, L.: RoboComp: a tool-based robotics framework. In: SIMPAR, Second International COnference on Simulation, Modelling and programming for Autonomous Robots (2010)
16. McManus, J.W.: Design and analysis of concurrent blackboard systems. Ph.D. thesis, College of William and Mary, Virginia (1992)
17. Minsky, M.: The Society of Mind. Simon & Schuster, New York (1988)
18. Newell, A.: Some problems of basic organization in problem-solving programs. Technical report, RAND Corporation (1962)
19. Oliver, G.S.: Pandamonium: a paradigm for learning. In: Proceedings of the Symposium on the Mechanization of Thought Processes, pp. 511–529 (1959)
20. Bustos, P., Martnez-Gomez, J., Garca-Varea, I., Rodrguez-Ruiz, L., Bachiller, P., Calderita, L., Manso, L.J., Sanchez, A., Bandera, A., Bandera, J.: Multimodal interaction with loki. In: Workshop of Physical Agents, Leon, Spain, pp. 1–8 (2013). http://ljmanso.com/files/Multimodal_interaction_with_Loki.pdf
21. Poole, D., Mackworth, A.: Artificial Intelligence: Foundations of Computational Agents. Cambridge University Press, Cambridge (2010). http://artint.info/index.html
22. Rao, A.S., Georgeff, M.P.: BDI agents: from theory to practice. In: ICMAS, pp. 312–319 (1995)
23. Rusell, S., Norvig, P.: Artificial Intelligence: A Modern Approach, 3rd edn. Pearson, Upper Saddle River (2009)

24. Sloman, A., Wyatt, J., Hawes, N., Chappell, J., Kruijff, G.J.: Long term requirements for cognitive robotics. In: Cognitive Robotics Papers from the 2006 AAAI Workshop Technical Report WS0603, pp. 143–150. No. McCarthy (2006). http://www.aaai.org/Papers/Workshops/2006/WS-06-03/WS06-03-022.pdf
25. Wang, A.J.A., Qian, K.: Component-Oriented Programming. Wiley, Hoboken (2005)
26. Kunze, L., Dolha, M.E., Guzman, E., Beetz, M.: Simulation-based temporal projection of everyday robot object manipulation. In: Proceedings of the 10th International Conference on Autonomous Agents and Multiagent Systems (AAMAS 2011) (2011)
27. Clark, A.: An embodied cognitive science? Trends Cogn. Sci. **3**(9), 345–351 (1999)
28. Jelinek, F.: Statistical Methods for Speech Recognition. MIT Press, Cambridge (1997)
29. Calderita, L.V., Manso, L.J., Bustos, P., Suárez-Mejías, C., Fernández, F., Bandera, A.: THERAPIST: towards an autonomous socially interactive robot for motor and neurorehabilitation therapies for children. In: JMIR Rehabil Assist Technol (2014)
30. Romero-Garcés, A., Calderita, L.V., González, J., Bandera, J.P., Marfil, R., Manso, L.J., Bandera, A., Bustos, P.: Testing a fully autonomous robotic salesman in real scenarios. In: Conference: IEEE International Conference on Autonomous Robot Systems and Competitions (2015)
31. Manso, L.J.: Perception as stochastic sampling on dynamic graph spaces. Ph.D. dissertation, University of Extremadura, Spain (2013)
32. Kirsch, A., Kruse, T., Msenlechner, L.: An integrated planning and learning framework for human-robot interaction. In: 4th Workshop on Planning and Plan Execution for Real-World Systems (held in conjunction with ICApPS 09) (2009)
33. Beetz, M., Jain, D., Msenlechner, L., Tenorth, M.: Towards performing everyday manipulation activities. Robot. Autonom. Syst. **58**, 1085–1095 (2010)
34. Alami, R., Chatila, R., Clodic, A., Fleury, S., Herrb, M., Montreuil, V., Sisbot, E.A.: Towards human-aware cognitive robots. In: AAAI-06, Stanford Spring Symposium (2006)
35. Wintermute, S.: Imagery in cognitive architecture: representation and control at multiple levels of abstraction. Cogn. Syst. Res. **1920**, 129 (2012)
36. Ali, M.: Contribution to decisional human-robot interaction: towards collaborative robot companions, Ph.D. thesis, Institut National de Sciences Appliquées de Toulouse, France (2012)
37. Holland, O.: The future of embodied artificial intelligence: machine consciousness? In: Iida, F., Pfeifer, R., Steels, L., Kuniyoshi, Y. (eds.) Embodied Artificial Intelligence. LNCS (LNAI), vol. 3139, pp. 37–53. Springer, Heidelberg (2004). doi:10.1007/978-3-540-27833-7_3
38. Manso, L.J.: Perception as stochastic sampling on dynamic graph spaces. Ph.D. thesis, University of Extremadura, Spain (2013)
39. http://wiki.ros.org/urdf
40. https://www.khronos.org/collada/

Author Index

Printed in the United States
By Bookmasters